NFL Football

A History of America's
New National Pastime

Richard C. Crepeau

University of Illinois Press
Urbana, Chicago, and Springfield

Library of Congress Cataloging-in-Publication Data
Crepeau, Richard C., 1941–
NFL football : a history of America's new national pastime /
Richard C. Crepeau.
pages cm — (Sport and society)
Includes bibliographical references and index.
ISBN 978–0–252–03289–9 (hardback) —
ISBN 978–0–252–08020–3 (paperback) —
ISBN 978–0–252–09653–2 (e-book)
1. National Football League—History. 2. Football—
United States—History. I. Title.
GV955.5.N35c74   2014
796.332'6406—dc23   2014007470

publication completed with a pass from
Figure Foundation

Contents

Acknowledgments

I want to thank several people who have been indispensable in the completion of this project. Michael Oriard offered both guidance and encouragement in the early stages of research. Holly Pinheiro, my research assistant at the University of Central Florida, located sources and took notes on several important biographies and other works. Mel Adelman deserves special thanks, as he read the manuscript twice and offered important corrections and advice. Bill Regier, the director of the University of Illinois Press, offered important guidance throughout the course of the project. His patience through many delays was above and beyond anything one could reasonably expect and is greatly appreciated. Finally, to Pat Crepeau, special thanks for your patience and love throughout the research and writing process, as well as the nearly fifty years of having to deal with me.

Introduction

The history of the National Football League unfolds across time, in many dimensions, carried along by those forces that have shaped modern American history. It was the product of forces transforming twentieth-century America into a consumer society pursuing leisure. It was a product of changing technologies: the automobile, radio, television, and the Internet. It was the product of the willingness of government at all levels to subsidize sport. It benefited from an increasing concern over issues of masculinity in a sedentary world, and from expressions of masculinity through vicarious violence. Above all it was the product of any number of individuals who understood how to manipulate and exploit these forces.

The NFL has had its ups and downs, its champions and its critics, and a great deal of internal turmoil. Through it all the league survived and prospered to become both an obsession and the new national pastime. NFL commissioner Pete Rozelle is at the center of this history, a force in his own right who took the NFL to its position of prominence. In many ways he was simply the right man in the right place at the right time. All of the NFL's achievements and problems seem to pass through Pete Rozelle. Those who came before him set the stage, and those who followed him rearranged the scenery. This is the story of a struggle to build a successful sports business by entrepreneurs with large egos who grasped for power and markets. It is the story of success and failure and the creation of a national obsession. This history seeks to place the history of the NFL within the larger context of American social, economic, and technological history.

There have been a number of written histories of the National Football League. They have varied in purpose and quality, but all have offered something to fans and to others who might be interested in professional football.

These histories record the memories of participants in the league, draw on the vast amount of periodical literature on the NFL, and build on a combination of sources both primary and secondary: court records, congressional testimony, legislation, and many other public documents. What I hope to offer is a synthesis of this work and a general history of the league.

There are two other important pools of information from which I have drawn. Recent years have brought a growing treasure trove of academic scholarship on sports, ranging from a focus on economics, to government policy, to social and labor history. In addition there is a growing body of biographies, some with an interpretive edge, pertinent to the history of the NFL.

Amateur and professional analysis, widely varying in quality, is available on the Internet. ESPN, HBO, and the NFL Network have made the materials of NFL Films available to the average fan and researcher. NFL.com, NFLPA.com, and Superbowl.com offer massive amounts of information. Despite the self-serving character of some, the official histories and autobiographical publications in both print and electronic form are valuable in clarifying events.

Although at times it may not seem so, I have the highest regard for the skills and talents of those who built the NFL. I do not share the awe with which the NFL is held by a sometimes fawning public and media. Nonetheless I retain a sense of wonder at the incredible success of the NFL, now clearly the most powerful organization in American sport. It is important to remember that the National Football League is a *football* league. Professional football is a game of beauty and violence played by highly talented athletes who provide the public with an extremely popular form of entertainment. When human activities of any kind are performed at a very high skill level, at times approaching perfection, these actions inspire us. That is true on the football field as it is true elsewhere.

This history is divided into three large sections containing several chapters each: The Formative Years, the Rozelle Era, and the New NFL. It initially follows the traditional chronological form of organization. In the Formative Years the three chapters correspond roughly to four time frames: from the late nineteenth century through World War I and the decade of the 1920s, the period of the Great Depression and World War II, and the postwar period and decade of the fifties.

The largest section of the book, and the defining decades for the NFL, are in the age of Commissioner Pete Rozelle that spans nearly three decades. The six chapters, 4 through 9, devoted to the Rozelle Era are divided both topically and chronologically. Chapter 4 focuses on the struggle between the NFL and the American Football League (AFL). Chapter 5 examines the decade of the sixties from a number of perspectives, both substantive and symbolic. Chapter 6 is devoted to the emergence of television as an integral part of the growth, development, and success of the NFL. Chapter 7 has as its centerpiece the struggle between the NFL and Al Davis, or between Rozelle and Davis, over franchise movement, the outcome of which transformed the NFL. Chapter 8 delineates the decline of Rozelle's power following the court victory by Davis, and also looks in depth at the drug issue. Chapter 9 is thematic, dealing with the monumental struggle between the owners and the players. Despite the league's many victories over the NFLPA, this chapter covers part of the story of Rozelle's waning influence over the NFL, and it ends with his resignation as commissioner.

The third section of the book consists of three chapters. Chapter 10 is primarily devoted to Commissioner Paul Tagliabue's years and touches on a wide array of issues, including the achievement of labor peace, television, and the branding of the NFL. Chapter 11 examines the issues that have occupied Roger Goodell in the short time he has been commissioner, some of which remain active. The final chapter is devoted to the Super Bowl. I have chosen to deal with the Super Bowl separately because it has become such a huge phenomenon in popular culture and has taken on the identity of a national holiday. The focus is primarily off the field and it is intentionally excessive, matching the chapter's themes. It is a tribute to the cultural dominance the NFL has achieved in both the sporting culture and the wider national culture.

Certain dominant personalities, such as Vince Lombardi, became significant symbols of the league and eras of American culture, and their influence reached well beyond the stadium. These symbolic figures will receive particular attention.

The attribution of sources is not conventional. Although endnotes are used, they do not follow the strict conventional rules of documentation. For the most part, these annotations identify the multiple works used in summarizing a topic. This results at times in no citations over several paragraphs, and then when one does appear it references multiple works and pages. This means that at times quotations will appear that are not followed immediately by a citation. However all material is properly attributed. This is a work of synthesis and owes everything to those who have preceded me, and from whom I have learned a great deal. The endnotes clearly indicate such.

I

The Formative Years

1

The First Pros

Super Bowl XLV between the Green Bay Packers and the Pittsburgh Steelers took place at Cowboys Stadium in Arlington, Texas, on February 6, 2011, to determine the champion of the National Football League. Attendance was 103,219, just a few hundred shy of the Super Bowl record. Another 111 million saw the game on television. It was the biggest television audience in U.S. history.

In 1920, the first season of the American Professional Football Association (renamed the National Football League in 1922), average attendance at games reached just over four thousand, with the largest crowds estimated at between ten thousand and twenty thousand. Because of uneven scheduling, the League Championship was not decided on the field, but rather at the winter meetings in Akron, Ohio, in April 1921. A vote resulted in the awarding of a loving cup as league champion to Akron, who "defeated" the claims of both Canton and Buffalo.[1]

The journey from Akron to Arlington has been a long and convoluted one. Its roots are found primarily in the late nineteenth century among the professional and semiprofessional teams and leagues spread across the Ohio Valley and westward. These teams constituted the core of those entrepreneurs who formed the NFL after World War I, driven by growing optimism and prosperity and building upon the intense interest in high school and college football.

In the 1890s in western Pennsylvania and eastern Ohio, football at the semipro and professional level was easy to recognize as the game in its modern form. The field was a bit smaller and narrower; there were no hash marks and no end zone. Goal posts were on the goal line, 18½ feet apart, as they are now, but only ten feet high. Passing was not allowed. The players were small by current standards, as the average lineman weighed 171 pounds, while backs averaged 151. Equipment was limited, the game was rough, and there was no substitution except for injury.[2]

Throughout these early years, football rules continued to evolve, with colleges taking the lead. Following the college football crisis of 1905 precipitated by eleven deaths on the field of play, the schools adopted rule changes designed to make the game safer and more attractive to spectators. The professionals accepted those changes, which included allowing the forward pass.[3]

The first documented case of pay for play occurred on November 12, 1892, when the Allegheny Athletic Association paid William "Pudge" Heffelfinger a reported $500 plus $25 in expense money to play for their club against the Pittsburgh Athletic Club. Three other players were also paid for this game, and by the late nineties there were at least five professional teams in Pennsylvania. Denial of professionalism was so much a part of the sporting culture that Heffelfinger spent the remainder of his years denouncing professionalism in football.[4]

The transition from amateur to professional football was driven by the desire to win, and nowhere was that more apparent than in central Ohio, where the rivalry between Massillon and Canton led both teams to pay players as they pursued Ohio supremacy. Massillon was the first to cross the line, with a $1,000 payroll for the 1904 season. This opened the professional era in Ohio football. It also led to the signing of the first African American to a professional football contract when Charles Follis was inked by Shelby in 1904.[5] Professional football in Ohio stabilized by 1910. Driven by boosterism and a willingness to spend a bit of money on ringers, and fueled by gate receipts and betting profits, a few teams were able to win championships and turn a small profit in the process.[6]

By the end of the 1890s, professional football had spread across America. It was a reality in Butte, Montana, where a wealthy copper mining entrepreneur decided to become a professional football owner. There were athletic clubs in California, Oregon, and Washington sponsoring professional football teams. Coleman Brown of the Santa Barbara AC and the Los Angeles Stars was one of the first African American stars on the West Coast. Many considered him the best back of the decade.[7]

The success of pro football depended on management, community support, and newspaper coverage. Managers handled all arrangements: they hired players, built schedules, arranged playing venues, negotiated guarantees, made travel arrangements, hired officials, sold tickets, and created advertising, plus handling all other details and problems that arose in the process of staging a game.[8]

Following World War 1 and the influenza epidemic, professionalism was increasing as organization and structure grew: "Most importantly, the best independent football teams took on an all-star character that was reflected in the number of All-Conference and All-American college players recruited to play on their teams. These conditions marked a transition from independent, semi-professional football to professional football."[9]

Professional teams had a variety of sponsors: railroad companies, commercial enterprises, church groups. They were invariably connected to local boosterism. The games drew fans primarily from the factories and mills of towns and small cities. With the factories running on six and six and a half-day work weeks, Sunday became the day for recreation. The football entrepreneurs moved to fill that need, offering tickets at prices below those for the college game. Blue-collar fans enjoyed the toughness and violence of the pro game and it gave them local heroes with whom they could identify. For entrepreneurs, pro football was a high-risk venture. The uncontrollable variables included weather, the volatility of the cost/revenue ratio, and the sustained appeal of the team. Keith McCellan argues that these risk takers had "the heart of a pirate and the mentality of a con man."

Sportswriters and the college crowd looked down on the professional game or simply ignored it. The upper classes and middle classes objected to the concept itself. Casper Whitney, a self-proclaimed guardian of the moral code of sportsmanship who wrote for *Outing* magazine, condemned the intrusion of professionalism into the amateur world of gentlemen. He was appalled by the notion that one could sell loyalty for personal gain. Whitney and his colleagues were caught up in that ludicrous professional-amateur distinction imported from British upper-class sport, which was, ironically, both inappropriate for and simultaneously appealing to Americans. Even though Americans accepted this distinction, it was never rigidly enforced, as it was more convenient to allow winning to trump amateurism. So, the best players were paid under the table, allowing them to maintain the fiction of amateur standing and enhancing the possibilities of victory. College players who dabbled in the professional game played under assumed names, or did so only when they lost their eligibility for the college game. At times, anonymity was maintained in deference to objections to playing games on Sunday.

"However, if you were a working stiff—a mill worker, railroad worker, or factory worker—you saw it differently. You were not worried about developing manly virtues, you had them by the nature of your work." You were not concerned about being a gentleman or about your alma mater. You simply enjoyed the opportunity to cheer for the home team on that one day a week available for rest and relaxation. "Scorned and ridiculed by the college crowd, loved only by factory workers and a few fanatics, professional football was taking root in America's midwestern factory towns."[10]

Professional football remained on shaky ground throughout the 1910s and into the 1920s. Many teams existed Sunday to Sunday. Sponsors helped, with railroad companies providing transportation or breweries providing cash for jerseys. Survival was a struggle. In Catholic communities, local priests organized teams and fans loved watching Catholic players, particularly those from Notre Dame, even if they were playing under assumed names.[11]

The game itself continued to evolve. By 1912 the field was altered to one hundred yards, with ten-yard end zones. A rule change moved the kickoff from midfield back to the forty yard line. Another change required seven offensive players on the line of scrimmage. There were four downs to move the ball ten yards for a first down. All restrictions on the quarterback were eliminated. Equipment remained minimal, with some players using a mouthpiece and a few pads, and some wearing nose guards.[12]

In 1919 Massillon, Akron, Cleveland, and Youngstown fielded teams that constituted an Ohio League of sorts. When the managers met they agreed on officials' salaries, as well as on a nontampering rule, but they could not reach agreement on player salary limits. This failure led inevitably to overspending. Looking ahead, those close to the professional game called for the creation of a strong league along the lines of professional baseball that could control salaries and contracts and end the use of college players.[13]

Laying the Foundation at Canton

These developments set the stage for bold entrepreneurs, men of vision who loved football, to move the professional game onto a new stage with the creation of the National Football League. This was the central story of the 1920s. It was not a story of instant success and glory. Franchises came and went. It was a decade of progress, glory, growth, and development, in which the foundation of the NFL was laid. The decade brought struggle and success that centered on George Halas and Red Grange, and it ended in the economic uncertainty of the Great Depression.

On August 20, 1920, seven men representing four teams met in Canton, Ohio, at Ralph Hay's Hupmobile Agency, hoping to establish a professional football league. All four teams were from Ohio: Canton, Akron, Dayton, and Cleveland. The result was the creation of the American Professional Football Conference. Less than a month later, on September 17, a second meeting convened at the Hupmobile Agency, and the American Professional Football Association (APFA) was officially born.

This second meeting included representatives of seven additional teams. Among them was George Halas, who recalled sitting with others on the fenders and running boards of Hupmobiles, "drinking beer from buckets while we tried to plan the future of professional football." The work at hand included an attempt to bring some regularity to scheduling, establish control of bidding for players, control salaries, and prevent the raiding of rival rosters by league members. Jim Thorpe, the most prominent football name present, was elected league president.[14]

In addition to the four Ohio franchises, the APFA brought aboard Rochester, Buffalo, and Hammond at the August meeting. The next month brought teams from Decatur, Rock Island, Columbus, Detroit, Muncie, and Massillon, plus the Chicago (Racine) Cardinals and the Chicago Tigers.[15]

So began the first season of the APFA. There was little press interest and virtually no fan interest outside league cities. Such simple matters as who won, including who won the league championship, remained in doubt. Even the identity of the first game in league history was a matter of at least minor dispute. Given the inability to answer these basic questions, one could argue that the APFA was a league in name only, a reality only in the world of public relations and perhaps not even there.[16] The small crowds of the 1920s paled in comparison to the growing popularity of the college game. There, crowds for the biggest games exceeded 100,000 in a decade of stadium building and expansion.[17]

At the end of its first season, APFA representatives from each team reported on finances. The news was less than encouraging. Nonetheless, the league made a decision to move forward into a second season. Owners approved a constitution and bylaws and decreased the cost of association membership from $100 to $50. The goal of the APFA was to sign up every significant pro team in America. It was agreed that college players would not be used, and any team violating the rule would be expelled. No player, unless first declared a free agent, could be signed away from another team in the APFA.

Joe Carr replaced Jim Thorpe as president of the APFA, as Thorpe lacked business skills, seemed more interested in playing than administering, and was having problems with alcohol. Carr was a sportswriter, promoter, and manager of the Columbus Panhandles football team, and founded the Columbus baseball team in the American Association. He was content to administer, leaving the major decisions to George Halas. Twenty-one teams contested the 1921 league championship, with ten new franchises joining. Only thirteen teams survived to the end of this second season.

Team owner A. E. Staley decided to get out of the football business. He wrote a check for $5,000 to George Halas to help the team get through the 1921 season. Halas took on Dutch Sternaman as a partner and chose the "Bears" as the new nickname for the team, a bow to Halas's beloved Chicago Cubs.[18] It was a modest beginning for the long and storied professional football career of George Halas, a Chicago native who had played college football and graduated from the University of Illinois. Starting with a $50 investment and the bankroll of $5,000, Halas became principal owner of the Chicago Bears, a team valued at no less than seventy million dollars when the grand-old-man of the NFL died in 1983.[19]

A New Name with Much the Same

In the June 1922 league meetings held in Cleveland, owners renamed the association the National Football League. Issues surrounding schedules and salaries were discussed, and new franchises were awarded. The league grew to eighteen members, including the all–Native American Oorang Indians, based in Ohio.

In 1921 the Green Bay Packers had been expelled from the league for using college players. The 1922 Packers struggled financially. Facing disaster, the team arranged for a $2,500 loan from a local newspaper. Then, the Packers sold shares in the team for five dollars. Each shareholder received a season ticket. By the end of the 1923 season, the Packers had $5,000 in the bank and a unique arrangement with its fans.[20]

The Packer resurrection was one of several remarkable developments in the volatile early history of the NFL. Nearly forty franchises populated the NFL in the 1920s. Many came and went in the course of one or two seasons. By the middle of the decade, many of the smaller towns that had been founding members were gone, and many individuals, including Joe Carr, who envisioned the future of the NFL in the bigger cities across America, were happy to see them go. As NFL president, Carr did his best to standardize and reorganize league procedures and regulations. Uneven scheduling, teams that played entirely on the road, weak and failing franchises, and the determination of the league champion occupied his energies. He responded with plans for reorganization and rationalization of NFL operations, and by the late twenties he was confident in the league's progress.

Credibility increased for the NFL as it attracted more attention when star college players, a number of them African Americans, entered the league. Such stars as "Fritz" Pollard, Ernie Nevers, Johnny Blood, and Red Grange created considerable buzz for the league. In the case of Grange it also created considerable friction with college football authorities and set off a national debate over the legitimacy of professional football.

Getting the Attention of the Football Nation

The biggest story of the 1925 season and postseason was in Illinois, where the Bears made massive headlines with the signing of Harold "Red" Grange, the "Galloping Ghost," a record-setting running back from the University of Illinois. It was one of the biggest stories of the decade, as Grange was much more than just a college football player. He was a character of mythic proportions spoken of in similar tones as the other members of the sports trinity of the decade, Babe Ruth and Jack Dempsey.

The 1920s was America's first age of celebrity and sports heroes, and this trinity was at the top of the heap. All three came from poor and obscure backgrounds, rose to the top of their sport, and had the charisma to capture the imagination of the public. It was a decade in which the public focus turned away from Europe and the world and inward in search of what President Harding had identified as normalcy. America entered a consumer culture spurred on by the booming advertising industry, as Americans sought pleasure and instant gratification from the world of materialism and celebrities.

consumer

Grange came from Wheaton, Illinois, where he was raised on the simple values of America's heartland. In four years of high school football, he scored seventy-five touchdowns, converted eighty-two extra points, and earned sixteen varsity letters in four sports. In twenty college games at Illinois Grange scored thirty-one touchdowns and gained 3,362 yards, while becoming the idol of the

Red Grange—Superstar Leaves College for NFL. Photo courtesy of the Library of Congress.

sports pages and newsreels where football fans across the country could watch his magic unfold. Grange spent his summers delivering ice in his hometown as a means to stay in shape. Photos of Grange with a block of ice on his shoulder led to a second nickname, "The Wheaton Ice Man." Robert Zuppke, the University of Illinois football coach, recognized the potential talent of the boy from Wheaton, recruited him, and built his Illini team around Grange.

One of the many highlights of Grange's college career came during the 1924 season against the University of Michigan. "Hurry-up" Yost, the highly regarded Michigan coach, announced that his game plan against Illinois was simple: Stop Grange. Every time Grange carried the ball, Yost promised, there would be eleven Michigan tacklers bearing down on him. The opening kickoff went to Grange at the five yard line, and he weaved his way through the entire Michigan team for a touchdown. The next time he touched the ball, he went sixty-seven yards for a touchdown. His third carry went for fifty-six yards and another touchdown. On the next Illinois possession, Grange ran forty-five yards for his fourth touchdown of the game. He added one more touchdown in the fourth quarter.[21] It was the stuff of legend.

As Grange's final season progressed, rumors circulated that he had signed a contract with the promoter C. C. Pyle and was therefore a professional. The Big Ten Conference had no desire to find that Grange had turned pro. The interest in Grange's future was massive, and the press descended on Columbus to witness the final college game by the national icon. A crowd of eighty-five thousand packed the Ohio State stadium, and another twenty thousand were turned away at the gates.

Five minutes after the game ended, Grange announced to a crush of reporters that he was leaving the University of Illinois and turning pro. Coach Zuppke was described as "visibly shaken" and accompanied Grange back to the team hotel trying to dissuade him. Grange added that he was heading home to Wheaton, failing to mention he would stop in Chicago to sign the paperwork with C. C. Pyle and the Chicago Bears.

Grange left the hotel by fire escape to avoid the press and took the next train to Chicago. The following day he signed one contract making Pyle his manager and another with George Halas and the Bears. It is not clear that Grange anticipated the controversy he had created by leaving college before graduation, nor the demands that would be placed upon him over the next several months. Fame and fortune, he learned, had its price.

Following the signing, Grange attended the Bears/Packers game at Cubs Park, where the fans roared when they saw him on the bench. The police had to restrain the crowd from mobbing their idol. Grange stayed in the clubhouse during the second half, and three thousand people gathered in front of the door refusing to return to their seats until their idol appeared. When he did, "it required a squad of police to get him through the frenzied mob and safely back to the bench."[22]

The signing of Grange set off a barrage of hypercritical and hypocritical attacks from the defenders of "pure amateur college sport." Grange was accused of being a professional while still playing college football, of being ungrateful and disloyal to his college and his coach, and of being corrupted by the "professionals" in the form of C. C. Pyle and representatives of the Chicago Bears. Within months the Big Ten passed a rule forbidding anyone who played football for pay from coaching at Big Ten schools. The American Football Coaches Association banned membership in its organization to anyone who was connected in any way to professional football.[23]

University administrators, coaches, and sportswriters joined the chorus, as did Grange's college coach, whose relationship with Grange was permanently damaged. As for the public, there seemed to be little concern for the purity of college sport or the academic issues attendant on Grange's departure from the halls of academe. For the public the real story was money, be it the football money, endorsement money, or movie deals. For the press, other than those attached to college football, the money was seen as a just reward for the talents of "Red" Grange. Few resented the Wheaton Ice Man on this count.[24]

As for Grange, he was quite clear that it was all about the money. He was hoping to pay back his father for the cost of his college education, provide for his family's security, and return to a normal life as quickly as possible. The first two objectives were more easily achieved than the last. While it was clear that Grange could have made considerable sums of money by cashing in on his celebrity in other areas, he chose pro football because it was an area in which he had obvious talent. And Grange chose football because that is where C. C. Pyle led him.

The Red Tour of Football America

Red Grange began his professional career on Thanksgiving Day at Cubs Park, where the Bears played their local rivals, the Chicago Cardinals. The initial run of twenty thousand tickets was sold out in three hours, and more were printed. The game attracted a standing-room-only crowd of thirty-six thousand, with another twenty thousand turned away. George Halas reportedly cried when he counted the gate receipts, and later said, "I knew then and there that professional football was destined to be a big-time sport." Three days later another twenty-eight thousand ventured out to Cubs Park to see the Bears take on the Columbus Tigers.

It was a good beginning to a highly lucrative tour that took Grange and the Bears across the country. This proved, however, to be a brutal schedule that left both Grange and the Bears battered. The Bears had five games remaining on their schedule and C.C. Pyle, looking to maximize cash flow, added three more games with non-NFL opponents. The Bears played eight games in twelve days, during which Grange was under contract to play a minimum of thirty minutes each game.[25]

After stops in St. Louis and Philadelphia, the tour rolled into New York City, where Grange, if not Pyle, was welcomed as a savior of the Giants franchise. Tim Mara's team had rolled up considerable debt and Grange's drawing power made it disappear. New York Mayor Jimmy Walker had 250 police on crowd-control duty at the Polo Grounds, while another fifty of New York's finest escorted Grange to the locker room. A crowd of more than seventy thousand, the largest to ever see a football game in the city as well as the largest crowd in pro football history, produced gate receipts of $142,000.

The New York stop was about much more than football. Endorsement contracts were signed and Pyle flashed a phony $300,000 check in front of reporters intimating that it was for a movie contract. The actual endorsement take for the day was close to $40,000. Grange endorsed a sweater, a football doll, shoes, ginger ale, a cap, meat loaf, and "Red Grange Chocolates," which Pyle claimed sold six million bars in the first month in New York. He turned down a cigarette endorsement that required him to say he smoked that brand, but accepted a cigarette endorsement that only required that his name be used, with no claim that he actually smoked the brand, thus displaying a kind of "fudged" integrity. Another dozen endorsements followed over the course of the next year.[26]

On December 6 in New York Grange had his best game, as he led the Bears to a 19–7 win, but he took a physical beating in the process. It was the second game in as many days. Two days later on December 8 a series of five games in six days in five cities opened in Washington. Before it was over, Grange was diagnosed with a torn ligament and broken blood vessel in his arm. The doctor recommended rest, but Grange continued playing. By the time the tour closed back in Chicago, Grange and his teammates were exhausted.

The second phase of the tour, covering more than seven thousand miles, began in Florida on Christmas Day and proceeded through the month of January in the Pacific Northwest. Better planning by Pyle made this leg of the tour a much less grueling ordeal. Dressed in matching sweaters embossed with *BEARS,* knickers, and new socks, the players traveled by Pullman car with porters handling their luggage. There were few back-to-back game days.

The Florida crowds were disappointing, as local promoters charged prices at four and five times the going rate for NFL games. In Tampa, Grange was seen on the social circuit and by traffic police speeding at seventy-five miles per hour through the city. Like so many others, Grange and Pyle were attracted by the Florida land boom, and together they invested $17,000 in real estate. Their money was literally blown away by the hurricane that hit the state later in the year. The highlight of the Florida phase of the tour featured an all-star team led by the Stanford star Ernie Nevers in a game in Jacksonville.

When the tour arrived in New Orleans, Grange was the guest at the racetrack for the running of the Red Grange Handicap, won by Prickly Heat. The horse was awarded a pink floral football by Grange. As to the football game, sixty-seven hundred fans were in attendance. Los Angeles was the next stop. Damon Runyon described the stir caused by Grange's anticipated arrival as "astonishing." Movie stars were much in evidence with Grange and his teammates as they posed together for photos. Seventy-five thousand fans attended the game in Los Angeles. Including endorsements, Pyle and Grange took away a quarter of a million dollars each from the tour. As for the Bears, they took in approximately $100,000, and each Bears player made about $3,000 for the seventeen-game spectacle.

While it would be inaccurate to say that Red Grange "saved" pro football, or that pro football gained a national following because of Grange and the tour, it is accurate to say that Grange and Pyle put a lot of money into the pockets of a lot of people besides themselves. Among the greatest beneficiaries were Tim Mara of the Giants, George Halas and Ed Sternaman, co-owners of the Bears, some of the promoters of the games, Bears players, and those who opposed the Bears on the field. Sellers of the merchandise surrounding the tour and whose products Grange endorsed also turned a profit.[27]

The American Football League

As it turned out, the past was only prologue. Grange's contract with the Bears ran through the two phases of the tour, which posed the question, "What next?" Pyle met with Halas and Sternaman on the return trip to Chicago. The Bears were willing to continue the existing arrangements, while Pyle wanted a one-third ownership share in the Bears for the Pyle-Grange partnership. The Bears rejected that arrangement.

Pyle announced that he and Grange would form a new team built around Grange. The businessman signed a five-year lease for the use of Yankee Stadium and took his proposal to the NFL meetings in February in Detroit. Tim Mara was there wielding his territorial rights to veto another franchise in the city, and Joe Carr supported Mara's veto. All attempts at compromise failed, as Mara had developed a strong dislike for Pyle's arrogance. At one point during a meeting between the two, Mara was reported to be ready to punch "C.C.'s lights out."

Tim Mara knew the Giants could not survive financially if they had to compete for fans with a team featuring Grange. Carr's support for Mara no doubt stemmed from the fact that Carr had encouraged Mara to buy the New York franchise, and that Mara had spent large sums of his own money to keep the Giants afloat in difficult times. Loyalty could sometimes be a powerful force.

The next move belonged to Pyle and Grange. A new league was their answer. The American Football League would have franchises in New York, Boston, Philadelphia, Cleveland, Chicago, Brooklyn, and Newark. There were two road teams: Rock Island, a team that defected from the NFL, and the Los Angeles or Wilson Wildcats. Pyle owned a controlling interest in the AFL and he and Grange each held a half-interest in the Los Angeles and New York franchises. The two men also poured money into the league for support of the weaker franchises. The AFL was able to sign a number of NFL veterans and big-name players.[28]

The NFL response to the AFL was quick and aggressive, if not entirely wise. Seeking to challenge the new league for players and locations, the NFL expanded. Technically there were now twenty-six teams in the league, although four of them suspended operations for the year. Three new cities—Los Angeles, Brooklyn, and Hartford—fielded teams. Racine, Wisconsin, resumed operations after a year's absence and Pottsville returned. Two franchises made significant signings, as the Bears picked up Patty Driscoll when the Cardinals could no longer afford to keep him. The Duluth Eskimos, a road team, signed Ernie Nevers, the former Stanford star and the second most famous player in professional football. This helped to compensate the NFL for the loss of Grange.

Even under the best of circumstances, the AFL and many of the NFL franchises would have had difficulty surviving. Unfortunately football that year was plagued by nearly constant rain along the East Coast. Tim Mara and the Giants lost a reported $40,000 trying to compete with the AFL football Yankees, who drew 220,000 fans for their fourteen games. Indeed the AFL drew better than the NFL for their big games, but only Grange could consistently put fans in the stands. With the exception of Philadelphia, the AFL franchises were swimming in red ink and soon were drowning in it.

Only four AFL teams survived to the end of the season: the Yankees, the Wildcats, the Philadelphia Quakers, and the Chicago Bulls. The Philadelphia Quakers were likely saved by Pyle's financial assistance. Cleveland and Newark did not make it through October, Brooklyn merged with the NFL franchise in early November, and by mid-November Boston was gone. A week later the Rock Island team was broke and stranded in Chicago.

As is so often the case in the early days of new sports leagues, a number of franchises in the AFL were undercapitalized, couldn't make payroll, and couldn't create a viable fan base. The AFL's problems were compounded by dull football, as teams averaged only one touchdown per game. In an attempt to salvage something, Red Grange led a postseason tour of the South and California, which he said softened his personal financial blow.[29]

At the July 1927 meetings, the NFL granted permission for twelve franchises to suspend operations for one year. They took this option rather than simply leave the league, which was their other alternative. Franchises would be given a year to reactivate or withdraw from the league. No new franchises would be added until the disposition of all suspended franchises was settled. The disposition of the Brooklyn franchise awaited the settlement of the NFL and AFL relationship. All of this was part of Carr's plan to eliminate the small and weak franchises in the NFL and center the league in larger markets.

Pyle had planned for a merger of equals between his AFL and the NFL. In August Joe Carr announced that the AFL would be merged into the NFL, but on the NFL's terms. Historian Don Smith commented that this was a merger only in the sense that a minnow is merged with a bass. The Yankee franchise would lease the Brooklyn franchise from Tim Mara, and the Yankees would be allowed to play only four games in Yankee Stadium, one of those against Mara's Giants, while their remaining twelve games were on the road. There would only be one date on which both New York teams played in the city, the first Yankee home game of the season. Mara disliked Pyle intensely and didn't want him in the league, but Mara recognized the value of "Red" Grange to the NFL. In Chicago the Bulls merged into the two Chicago NFL teams.

New Faces, Old Places, and Red's Legacy

The NFL came out of this struggle with twelve teams and more and bigger stars than at any time in its history. At the head of the list were Grange, Nevers, "Wildcat" Wilson in Providence, and Benny Friedman in Cleveland. The NFL looked forward to what many predicted would be the best year in its history. The merger also meant that there was a surplus of three hundred available players, with the result of better play on the field and a cut in salaries, something always welcomed by owners.[30]

The 1927 season was successful at several levels. President Carr reported record league attendance, although Buffalo did not get through the 1927 season before suspending operations, and Cleveland and Duluth did not come back for the 1928 season. In addition, those teams that suspended operations for the 1927 season never returned, leaving the overall strength of the league improved.

All the news in 1927 was not good. The New York Yankees visited Chicago for a game with the Bears, during which Red Grange caught his cleats in the turf and was simultaneously hit on the side of the leg. Grange's right knee took the brunt of the blow and he missed the remainder of 1927 and the entire 1928 season. Knowledge of the knee and treatments of knee injuries were primitive and Grange received all sorts of contradictory advice on what to do. Surgery was risky and success rates were low. After a few months he was finally able to walk, and after another year he was able to return to football, not as a great runner but simply a good one.

The legacy of Red Grange is a matter of some dispute. George Halas regarded Grange as someone who contributed to the growth, development, and ultimate success of the NFL. Certainly he had an impact on the immediate coverage of the NFL in both Chicago and New York. Others with a bit more historical perspective view him as contributing to the growth of professional football. On the other hand, the signing out of college and the tour further damaged the relationship between college and professional football, affirming for many that the professional game was unworthy of gentlemen. Historian Craig Coenen believes that the Grange signing actually hurt the league more than it helped, as the brief burst of publicity and selective prosperity led others to emulate Halas's strategy of pursuing and selling heroes, rather than implementing the necessary reforms for NFL success.[31] There is much to be said for this assessment.

For the New York Giants and Tim Mara, 1927 was a very good year. Not only had Mara succeeded in marginalizing the New York Yankees and C. C. Pyle, he also watched his powerful football team win their first NFL championship. The final two games of the season were Giant-Yankee games, and the Giants blanked the Yankees twice, giving them ten shutouts in a thirteen-game season. Canton had shutout nine opponents in twelve games in 1922 and allowed fifteen fewer points than the Giants, but many observers felt that the Giant defense of 1927 was more impressive, as the level of competition that year far exceeded that of 1922.[32]

The 1928 season was a disastrous one for C. C. Pyle, as Grange was out with injury and had completed and terminated his contract with him. Pyle decided to go forward but had difficulty raising the $2,500 for the required guarantee. It would be the last year for him in the NFL, as his franchise was turned over to Tim Mara and operated in Brooklyn in 1929.

Steam Rollers, Eskimos, and the Twilight of an Era

The NFL was still a precarious operation, especially in the smaller cities where stability was elusive. The Providence Steam Roller had a very good year in 1928. In only their third year in the NFL they won the championship with an 8-1-2 record. In 1929 after several players retired, the Steam Roller had a reversal of fortune, with a record of 4-6-2. The big crowds of the championship season vanished, and with the arrival of the Great Depression never returned. In the money in 1928, the Providence ownership turned their franchise over to the league at the end of the 1931 season.

Success was both fleeting and fragile in the still-fledgling National Football League. In many medium and large cities in the 1920s and 1930s, NFL teams found survival difficult. Local boosterism and civic pride were not potent enough to carry a franchise. "From 1920 to 1932, twenty-three medium-sized and large cities fielded more than fifty pro football franchises" but only a handful survived.[33]

One of the oddities of the early NFL was the so-called "Road Team." Perhaps the most successful, and certainly the most colorful of these homeless home teams, was the Duluth Eskimos, the Eskies, or as Grantland Rice dubbed them, the "Iron Men of the North." Football in Duluth began in 1910 with teams composed of former high school players. The First World War proved to be a boon as the Duluth shipyards attracted workers, many of whom played on semipro teams, and eventually in the NFL. The teams also attracted college players, who played under assumed names.[34]

Despite on-field success in 1924 the Duluth Kelley's were in debt and could not survive. At the end of the season Ole Haugsrud and his partner Dewey Scanlon bought the team for $1 and the assumption of the team debt. Haugs-rud had big plans. Ernie Nevers had been a star at Stanford, with nearly as high a national profile as Red Grange. Nevers had grown up in Willow River,

Minnesota, and moved to Superior to play basketball, leading Central High to state titles in both basketball and football. Haugsrud had met him there.

Reports were that Nevers had signed for $15,000 with the AFL, but Haugsrud traveled to St. Louis, met with Nevers, and found that Nevers had signed nothing. Haugsrud offered Nevers $15,000 and 10 percent of the gate receipts to come home to Duluth.[35] When Haugsrud announced his coup at the 1926 NFL league meetings, he was immediately overwhelmed with scheduling opportunities, although no one wanted to play in Duluth. He turned that into another opportunity, demanding a $4,000 guarantee for each game, plus a percentage of the gate over $8,000. No objections were heard, and Haugsrud quickly put together a schedule of fourteen league games and fifteen exhibitions.

Haugsrud also decided the team needed a new name, a new logo, and new uniforms. They were now the Ernie Nevers' Eskimos, with colors of midnight blue and white. The white jersey had midnight blue trim, with an Igloo set against a seven-sided polygon of midnight blue. The players were provided with "custom-tailored, oversize, double-breasted, thigh-length mackinaw coats to wear when they were on the sidelines and while traveling." On the back of each of the coats were "ERNIE NEVERS' ESKIMOS" and "DULUTH" along with the igloo.[36]

It was a long and difficult season for the homeless home team. Each player had off-field assignments and was required to pack his own bags. Injuries led to playing with shortened rosters. The Eskies finished with a record of 6-5-3, good for eighth place in the twenty-two-team NFL. At the end of the NFL season Duluth was between six and seven thousand dollars in the red, but following their postseason California tour, where Nevers was highly marketable, they ended with $4,000 in the bank. Nevers picked up $65,000 from gate receipts along with his $15,000 base pay. He missed only twenty-seven of the 1,700 minutes played by the team in twenty-nine games over 117 days. These were indeed iron men. Three "Eskies" became members of the NFL Hall of Fame: Nevers, Johnny Blood, and lineman Walt Kiesling. Nevers and Blood were in the first class inducted at Canton.[37]

Two days after signing Nevers, Duluth inked one of the most colorful characters in professional football in the 1920s, Johnny McNally, better known as Johnny "Blood." McNally pulled his alias off a theater marquee where Rudolph Valentino was starring in *Blood and Sand*. He needed a fictitious name at a tryout for a team offering six dollars a game. McNally did not want to lose his remaining year of college eligibility. Once asked if he knew what a great name it would be, he said, "No, not consciously. . . . But I can't speak for my subconscious. The idea was probably lurking around in there somewhere. You never really know what your subconscious is doing, and it's always up to something." Johnny Blood was a drinker, gambler, brawler, thinker, and a reader and writer of poetry.[38]

After a difficult 1927 season, Ernie Nevers announced that he was returning to the West Coast, and without Nevers the Duluth Eskimos had to suspend operations. In 1929 Ole Haugsrud was forced out as owner. In his settlement with the NFL he accepted $2,000 and a provision that if the NFL ever put another franchise into the state of Minnesota, he would have the right to make the first bid. This eventually brought him 10 percent interest in the Minnesota Vikings.[39]

The 1929 season was punctuated by the stock market crash in October. As the decade came to a close, the National Football League had managed to persevere and prosper but was struggling, as was the country, with the fallout of the Great Depression. Out of this adversity the league was reshaped, losing its weaker franchises and positioning itself for recovery and continued growth during the 1930s.

2

Depression and War

Great in depth and duration, the Great Depression left an imprint on the psyche of a generation of Americans. For the middle class it shattered the basic rules of achievement: work hard, live the frugal and moral life, and success will be your reward. Suddenly hard-working, morally upright Americans found themselves "failures" under the old rules. Out of work and struggling day to day, many Americans felt as if the rules of the American capitalist system had been turned on their head.

Dreams were shattered as few American institutions or businesses came through the economic crisis unscathed. Some did not survive, and those that did were affected in fundamental ways, as was the American system itself. Late in the decade it seemed that survival was assured. Then World War II arrived to alter lives and institutions yet again. Survival returned as an issue, albeit in somewhat different terms. Though the war brought hardship in the United States, most historians would argue that the stimulus it provided is what truly brought the country out of economic depression. Life was altered significantly and fundamentally, and when the country emerged victorious, it was a different world.

Sport in America was not exempt from any of these forces. The NFL survived but not without some basic changes. Trauma required change in the way in which business was conducted, and these changes, both within the NFL and the world around it, resulted in a stronger and ultimately more successful league. By the end of the 1930s the NFL had a new look and new leadership poised to move forward. At least one sports historian, but by no means all, saw these years as transformative, as the NFL went from a "barnstorming league to a major sports entity."

The economic crisis seemed less severe for the NFL than for Major League Baseball. The NFL was operating at a much lower economic level and therefore did not have so far to fall. The Depression pushed the league toward the model that Joe Carr and others envisioned. The loss of the small and weak franchises positioned the NFL to focus on building its strengths in the larger markets. There were changes in league structure, competition, and ownership. On the technological front the NFL embraced radio, initiating a significant and profitable relationship with the emerging broadcast media. On a more sobering note, the NFL adopted an unwritten rule of racial segregation similar to that practiced in baseball.

Negatives Can Be Positives

Green Bay was the only small-market team to survive the Depression, while larger-market teams struggled. Between 1930 and 1934, franchises failed in Dayton, Buffalo, Boston, Cleveland, Minneapolis, Newark, Providence, and Frankford, Pennsylvania. Franchises were added in Boston in 1932, Pittsburgh and Philadelphia in 1933, and Cleveland in 1937, the same year that the Boston team moved to Washington, D.C. The Portsmouth, Ohio, team moved to Detroit in 1934. The result was more stability in a ten-team league.[1]

Another sign of prosperity for the NFL can be found in the fact that in both 1935 and 1940 new leagues were inaugurated. Both were named the "American Football League." Although neither survived, the second AFL offered one other tidbit to the lore of pro football when they instituted a league draft of the top fifty college players of 1940, and allowed them to sign with whichever team they chose.[2] The two AFL efforts indicated that there were people out there, whatever their motives and wisdom, who believed that professional football was a viable product that could find a fan base. The example of the NFL was attractive enough to encourage others to take a financial plunge into the new and growing world of pro football.

The Depression decade began with the Green Bay Packers concluding a three-peat with league championships in 1929, 1930, and 1931. Over those three seasons the Packers posted a record of 34-5-2 and were undefeated in 1929. Curly Lambeau was the coach, and the Pack was led by Johnny "Blood" McNally, who was an excellent pass receiver and runner. The Packers added another league championship in 1936 and a Western Division title in 1938. Clarke Hinkle, the great Packer fullback, recalled that when they went on the road the Packers drew big crowds. "We were the Notre Dame of pro football. We used their shift, and we were the small town team that won."[3]

The Packers survival of the Depression seems remarkable, but in fact there were rational explanations for it. First, the Green Bay economy did not suffer the devastating effects of the Depression. The production of toilet tissue and paper towels experienced significant growth starting in the midthirties, and these were manufactured in paper plants in the Green Bay area. Second, Green Bay civic pride continued to offer strong support to the team. Facing a $10,000 debt at mid-decade, the Packers decided to issue "nonprofit voting stock" for public sale. It took only ten days to sell all the stock, and another $13,000 in contributions from local boosters followed. Stockholders were given the right to vote on any team relocation, which was an issue. League officials pushed Green Bay to move to Milwaukee, and as a result some home games were moved to the larger city. Some two thousand Green Bay fans traveled to Milwaukee for those games, using the occasion to promote their city.[4]

For the Chicago Bears, 1930 was also a memorable year, as Bronko Nagurski came to town to establish himself as a great star. His name still evokes feelings of strength and power in Bears fans and Minnesotans, as well as images of the "frozen tundra" along the Canadian border in International Falls. Born in Ontario in 1908 the son of Ukrainian parents, his family moved to International Falls when Bronko was four. Nagurski became a legend, first at the University of Minnesota and then with the Bears. He was a bruising runner and a deft short passer. Nagurski signed for $5,000 in 1930, making him one of the highest-paid players in the NFL.

Kevin Britz, in "The Meaning of Bronko Nagurski," described him as a man of great strength, virility, and purity. Nagurski was compared to the great Minnesota hero of the 1920s, Charles Lindbergh, a modest, quiet man who did not seek fame or fortune. As with many of the heroes of the interwar period, Lindburgh affirmed traditional American values, even as the world that had nurtured those values was fading. For Britz, Nagurski too "represented the virtues of a frontier age nourished by the wilderness: family, faith, loyalty, and appreciation of the land, and love of sport for its own sake." Nagurski appealed to sports fans, "both rural and urban, through his reaffirmation of America's uncomplicated beginnings; a product not of the city but of the farm, not of schools or technical training but of individual freedom and talent borne of nature." The legends and myths were legion. One of the best was a tale of Nagurski having been found in the woods living on his own, where he was captured and brought to the University of Minnesota. There he was fed raw red meat just before game time. Several immigrant communities claimed Bronko as their own. He was known as both the "Durable Dane" and the "Pulverizing Pole." There were stories that he once tackled a horse and it later died, and another that he tackled a Model

T (1af (11ee Ild) (o lie luwed away, evuking (lie folk legend uf Paul Bunyan. He became extremely popular as a professional wrestler, drawing sellout crowds to Midwest arenas.[5]

The Chicago franchises, both the Cardinals and Bears, struggled through the Depression. Charles Bidwell was a key to the survival of both, as he took ownership of the financial disaster that was the Chicago Cardinals in 1932. For Bidwell it was the purchase of a toy, and he was willing to keep the team afloat over the next decade and a half. As for the Bears, the debts mounted. Bidwell, a lifelong Bears fan, was willing to save the team from extinction. Similarly in New York, the Giants were sustained by Tim Mara's money.

It seemed as if one answer to the NFL's problems was owners with deep pockets. Indeed men of considerable wealth became NFL owners in the Depression decade. Five were added between 1932 and '34: George Preston Marshall with the Boston Redskins, Bert Bell with the Philadelphia Eagles, Dan Topping with the Brooklyn Dodgers, Art Rooney with the Pittsburgh Steelers, and George Richards with the Detroit Lions. Three more came into the league in the early forties: Dan Reeves, Alexis Thompson, and Fred Mandel. Of this new breed of owner, four had inherited their wealth, one married into money, two made money in gambling, one was a lawyer with ties to Al Capone, and one was a laundromat entrepreneur. The deep pockets brought considerable stability to the NFL, as only one franchise failed between 1933 and 1945: the 1933 Cincinnati Reds, who moved to St. Louis in 1934 and lasted one year there.[6]

The 1932 championship was postponed for a week and forced indoors by snow and bitterly cold weather. Portsmouth and Chicago tied for the league lead, so arrangements were made for a championship playoff. Chicago Stadium was not suited to football and led to several innovations, including the first use of hash marks by the NFL. Several rule changes came out of the "indoor circus," as some called the 1932 championship game. Essentially the changes were designed to increase scoring and open up offenses. The goal posts were moved up to the goal line. Hash marks were put ten yards from the sidelines, with no ball spotted outside the hash mark. The forward pass was allowed from anywhere behind the line of scrimmage. The idea was to make this a much more attractive game than that played by the collegians by producing more offense, which it did. Taking up an idea that had been proposed for several years by the smaller franchises, the NFL split itself into two divisions, further promoting local rivalries such as the Bears and Packers in the west and the Giants and Redskins in the east.

The African American Players

The other significant development of the early thirties was the unannounced coming of segregation to the NFL after more than a decade of African American participation, a policy that lasted until after World War II. Unlike professional baseball, there was no unofficial color line in the NFL. Unlike American society generally, there was no segregation on the professional football field. This is not to say that all was cordial, or that African Americans were welcomed with open arms. Certainly that was not the case. African American players found life in the NFL difficult but tolerable, and there might well have been more African Americans in the league if circumstances surrounding the game of football and the NFL were different. One inhibiting factor to African American participation in professional football was the relative dearth of black players in the college football ranks. In addition, those industries that operated or sponsored football teams had few employment opportunities for black players.

The first African American to play professional football was Charles W. Follis, who played for pay for the Shelby Athletic Club on September 15, 1904. Follis had been a baseball catcher at Wooster College in Ohio and played football for the Wooster Athletic Club. When Wooster played the Shelby Athletic Club, Shelby fans were impressed. As a result, Follis was hired to work at a local hardware store, where his hours were arranged so he could practice and play football for the Shelby Athletic Club. As with those who came after him, Follis had to contend with hostile words, knees, and fists on the field, and hostile words off the field.

One of the best known of all the African American players, and the first to play in the NFL, was Fritz Pollard. In 1916 Pollard had earned a national reputation among football fans when he led Brown University over the major powers of Harvard, Yale, and Rutgers and on to the Rose Bowl. The best known African American player was Paul Leroy Robeson at Rutgers, who transcended racial identity by being referred to as "the greatest living football player."[7]

After his college career ended, Pollard took up duties as football coach at Lincoln University, a historically black institution. He played professional football games to keep in shape. In November 1919 Pollard received a call from Ralph "Fat" Waldsmith, the coach and owner of the Akron Indians, asking him to come and play a game for Akron against Massillon. This was the beginning of Pollard's career in what soon became the National Football League.

In Akron Pollard got a "chilly reception" from his teammates. Despite star status, Pollard was never fully accepted off the field. He was not allowed to use the team's locker room, even when he was the coach; also, he was unable to stay in city hotels and get service in local restaurants. Pollard was subjected to racial taunts from fans and players alike.[8]

There were thirteen African Americans playing in the NFL between 1920 and 1933, and their treatment was often harsh. Football is a violent game and the line between incidental and intentional violence is often difficult to discern. Pollard handled the racially motivated violence well. After being tackled he would get up, smile at those who taunted him, and redouble his effort. He also developed a habit of rolling over on his back with cleats in the air to discourage anyone inclined to pile on with a late hit.[9]

In 1921 Pollard recruited Paul Robeson, the All-American from Princeton, to join him in Akron. At the time, Robeson was studying law at Columbia University and pursuing his music and acting careers. It was another successful season in the making for Akron until injuries hit both Pollard and Robeson while playing on an icy field in Buffalo.

The following year, Pollard and Robeson went on to Milwaukee, where Pollard had accepted an offer to organize a new team. Here Pollard signed another African American player, Frederick "Duke" Slater, from the University of Iowa. At the end of the season, Pollard organized an all-star team of African American players and they defeated a white all-star team in a game that did not attract much notice.

In 1923 Alva Young of Hammond, Indiana, an NFL road team, signed Pollard to play and coach. Hammond had two other African American players: John Shelbourne, who played at Dartmouth, and Jay Mayo "Inky" Williams, a former teammate of Pollard at Brown. Pollard played sparingly at Hammond. In a little-noticed event, Paul Robeson became the first black quarterback in NFL history in a game against Dayton that same year.

Pollard's career path cut a wide swath in 1925 when he played and coached for three different NFL teams. In 1926 there were five African American players in the league, matching the 1922 and 1923 totals. In that 1926 season Sol Butler suited up for Canton when the New York Giants, led by their southern players, refused to play the team because they objected to competing against a black man. The Giants management backed the players and claimed that their fans opposed any competition against African American players. Butler withdrew from the game.

Over the next few seasons, the number of NFL and other professional teams was shrinking as the AFL merged into the NFL after the 1926 season. The number of teams dropped to twelve in 1927. Only "Duke" Slater survived in the league that year. Harold Bradley joined Slater in 1928, but by the following year, Slater was again alone. For many years after 1926, there were never more than two African American players in the league. Three more African Americans played in the NFL before the league adopted a policy of segregation. The number of black players dropped under the old rule in the American marketplace, "Last hired, first fired." Pollard believed that the increased popularity of the NFL meant that African American stars were no longer needed to draw crowds. There were few black fans, as the African American press chose not to cover the NFL, which in turn made it easier for the NFL to exclude African American players.[10]

In 1933 there were two remaining African American players in the NFL. Ray Kemp played five games for Pittsburgh but was dropped from the team when the NFL cut rosters to twenty-two. Kemp played his last game in New York City in December, where he was denied a hotel room with his teammates. Joe Lillard played for the Chicago Cardinals from 1931 through 1933. He had been a star at Oregon, where he was victim of racist policies by the Pacific Coast Conference that kept him out of the Rose Bowl. His Cardinal years were disrupted by poor relations with his coach, Jack Chevigny, who was accused of racial prejudice by the African American *Chicago Defender* newspaper. Lillard was subjected to a great deal of on-field violence.

At the end of the 1933 season NFL owners met and instituted the color line. There is little existing evidence of what occurred in that meeting. NFL owners subsequently suffered from amnesia and/or denial as George Halas, Art Rooney, Tim Mara, and Tex Schramm all denied that any policy of segregation existed. It is now generally accepted that the policy was adopted at the insistence of George Preston Marshall, owner of the Boston, later Washington, Redskins.[11]

Stability and Visibility

Ironically, while closing off the talent pool, the NFL looked for ways to even the competition on the field. In 1935 Bert Bell suggested that the NFL implement a college player draft, which it did the following year. Unfortunately the draft alone could not ensure parity. The four dominant franchises of the league—the Bears, Giants, Packers, and Redskins—continued to dominate because they had effective management that realized the importance of scouting, and therefore were better prepared at each draft. In each season from 1933 through 1945, the championship was won by the Giants, Packers, Bears, and Redskins, with only two exceptions. In each of those championship games, the winner was opposed by one of those four teams.[12]

Two events involving the NFL and college football helped increase the prestige of the pro game. After the 1930 season the Giants agreed to play a charity game for the New York Unemployment Fund. The Giants faced a group of Notre Dame all-stars led by Coach Knute Rockne and his famous Four Horsemen. Most observers felt the Irish would easily handle the pros. When the Giants won 22-0 and allowed the Irish only one first down, many eyes were opened to the quality of the professional game. In 1933 the Bears played a similar game against Notre Dame all-stars and defeated them.

In 1934 another encounter between the pros and the collegians was arranged by Arch Ward in Chicago. Ward was a sports editor for the *Chicago Tribune* and had organized the first baseball All-Star Game in 1933. The Bears played the College All-Stars to a tie before nearly eighty thousand fans at Soldier Field on August 31. The next year brought a rematch, after which NFL owners insisted that the NFL champion be matched against the collegians. Between 1934 and 1945 the College All-Star Game was the single largest revenue producer for the NFL, as crowds ranged up to one hundred thousand.[13]

In the mid-1930s the NFL created a publicity department run by Ned Irish. The year 1935 brought the first *Official Guide of the National Football League,* published by Spalding. One year later, when its publication seemed endangered by costs, the NFL stepped forward to subsidize half and guarantee that the guide would continue. By 1940 the NFL had assumed total control of the publication.[14]

A willingness to exploit new technologies was important for developing public awareness of the professional game. Films of the All-Star Games were produced, and by 1940 highlights were shown as part of movie newsreels. The NFL was quick to embrace radio, and in the twenties several teams broadcast their games. In 1934 the first Thanksgiving game from Detroit was broadcast on a national radio network of ninety-four stations. This was the start of an NFL tradition. The first experiment with television came in 1939, then the NFL Championship aired nationally on radio the following year, but the war postponed any further development.

There was a steady increase in attendance in the decade, going from an average of 11,063 with 6,997 paid in 1932 to 23,343 with 19,328 paid in 1940. Additionally, there was a corresponding increase in attention given to the NFL by newspapers and national periodicals. For the first time, national football publications gave some space to the NFL.

Michael Oriard regards a 1939 *Time* magazine story by Robert Kelley as something of a landmark. Kelley reported that the reputation of the pro game was changing. It was a new kind of game for a new kind of audience. Kelley found the pro game more open, with "more spectacular offenses." The pros were more experienced, and played with more technical expertise, polish, and "better football judgment." Among the national periodicals, increasing numbers of positive articles were appearing, many written by NFL people, including Red Grange, George Halas, and George Preston Marshall. Celebrity profiles of players such as Byron "Whizzer" White and Sammy Baugh appeared.[15]

The product on the field remained the most important element in the league's success, and that product depended heavily on the quality of its players. The Depression made professional football an attractive employment choice for those coming out of college. Increasing numbers of graduates chose to join the league, with 85 percent of the players having earned college degrees in the 1930s. Fifty-eight percent of NFL players came from white-collar backgrounds, while only 25 percent of the U.S. population fit that category. What this meant was that better athletes were entering the league, and more married men with families were playing in the NFL, increasing its respectability in mainstream America. As the public profile of the NFL expanded, opportunities for product endorsement for the best players increased, although salaries did not. Bronko Nagurski appeared on a Wheaties box in 1937, the first NFL player to do so.[16]

It is often claimed that for maximum success, professional sports leagues must have a strong team in New York City. A strong team could crack into the New York press and get the kind of attention the NFL needed in the communications center of the country. In the 1930s the New York Giants were such a team. They advanced to the title game in 1933, '34, '35, '38, and '40, winning the league championship in 1934 and 1938. In the 1934 game the Giants beat the undefeated Bears on an icy field, a victory often attributed to the Giants wearing sneakers.[17]

For all of the changes and positive developments during the Depression, the most important one may have been George Preston Marshall's decision to move the Redskins franchise from Boston to Washington, D.C. From the beginning it was apparent that this franchise would be different. Local media and city officials welcomed the team, and it was clear that the Redskins were regarded as a civic asset. They signed their first draft choice, Sammy Baugh of Texas Christian University, in the summer of 1937 for $8,000. He held a major press conference attended by all the local media. Interest in the team was growing, and four thousand fans turned up for practice sessions. The first three home dates drew a total of 63,042, or more than all seven home games had drawn the previous year in Boston.

Marshall was a showman and developed elaborate halftime performances, started a Redskins band that became the heart of the fan base, and changed the team colors to burgundy and gold. Sammy Baugh had a very good rookie season, and in late November the Redskins played a game in New York that would determine the divisional championship. Eight thousand Redskin fans, including the owner, boarded the "Redskin Special" train for New York, with some wearing full Redskins regalia. After the victory Skins fans stormed the field and tore down the goal posts. A large crowd welcomed the team back home, and during the week there was an active market in D.C. for pieces of goal post from the Polo Grounds.[18] The trips to New York on the "Redskin Special" became a major event and a highlight of the season, as ten to fifteen thousand fans conspicuously marched up Eighth Avenue. In 1941 the Redskins sold 14,500 season tickets, leading the league in that category.[19]

The 1940 championship game between the Bears and the Redskins before a crowd of 36,024 at Griffith Stadium in Washington was remarkable, memorable, and trend setting for many things beyond the 73-0 final score, in favor of the Bears. First, Chicago had redesigned their offense and made Sid Luckman the first star of the new "T" formation. The new offense had been developed over several years by George Halas, line coach Hunk Anderson, and former University of Chicago coach Clark Shaughnessy.

The dominance of the Bears on that day was total. Ten different players scored touchdowns, and three of the eight pass interceptions were run back for touchdowns. The Redskins rushed for a total of five yards and got inside the Bears twenty yard line only three times. Touchdowns came so fast at one stage that Red Barber, doing the radio broadcast, said he felt like a cashier at a grocery store. Seven of the eleven touchdowns came on the ground, as the Bears rushed for 381 yards. This was the first national broadcast of the championship game, and Mutual Broadcasting System paid $2,500 for the radio rights. The winner's share for each Bear player was $873.99 and the loser's share was $606.25. It was also the beginning of Bear dominance, with three titles over the next four years.[20]

Two other changes in the NFL were significant. After the death of NFL President Joe Carr in May 1939, the owners decided they wanted a high-profile figure to replace him. They settled on Elmer Layden, the athletic director and head football coach at Notre Dame. Layden was given the title "commissioner."[21] The same day that the Bears set their championship records, Art Rooney sold his Pittsburgh team, bought into the Philadelphia franchise, and then was back to Pittsburgh again in a matter of months. In the end Rooney traded the Philadelphia franchise for the Pittsburgh franchise with Alexis Thompson, heir to a steel industry fortune, who had bought the Pittsburgh franchise from Rooney in the first place.[22]

As the 1940s began, the National Football League was in the best condition in its history. Ownership was relatively stable, attendance and press attention was up, the game was clearly more exciting, and an array of new stars had emerged. The league had a new leader and league offices were now centered in Chicago, a more central media hub than Columbus, Ohio, but things were about to change again.

The Shadow of War

There were three games scheduled on December 7, 1941. In Chicago the Bears and Cardinals were playing at Wrigley Field. In Washington the Redskins and Eagles were winding down the season. In New York at the Polo Grounds the fierce rivalry between the Giants and the Dodgers was renewed. The first word of the attack at Pearl Harbor came over the wire services into the press box, although the public address announcer did not choose to pass the announcement to the fans. At the Polo Grounds an announcement was made asking Col. William J. Donovan to call Operator 19 in Washington immediately. At Griffith Stadium in Washington, newspaper reporters were told to report to work immediately. Fans knew something was happening but many were not sure exactly what until they returned home.[23]

What the consequences would be for them and for the NFL was not immediately clear. In the short term the season ran its course. The Bears and Packers tied for the Western Division title, and so the first divisional playoff in league history took place the next Sunday. More than forty-three thousand fans braved a sixteen-degree day to see their Bears handle the Packers 33-14 and move on to the championship game, where the Monsters of the Midway beat the Giants 37-9 before a sparse crowd at the same venue.

These same Bears came back in 1942 and finished the season 11-0. Bears Head Coach George Halas left for service in the Navy at midseason. In 1943 the Bears roared again, finishing 8-1-1 and beating the Giants in the championship game 56-7 as Sid Luckman threw for a record seven touchdowns. This team also featured Bronko Nagurski, who had come out of retirement to help the undermanned Bears.[24]

The NFL tried its best to put on a "game face" for the war. Although there was some consideration given to suspending league operations during the war, it was never a serious possibility. Commissioner Layden talked of the necessity to maintain quality in the face of the military draft and of the need for sport and relaxation on the home front during the war. Curley Lambeau talked of the NFL providing inspiration and guidance for youth as it carried on regardless of the sacrifice involved. By May 1942, 112 of the league's 346 players, or 32 percent, were in military service. In addition, each year as players left college they too were drafted, making the NFL's own draft much more difficult. Player shortages plagued a number of teams, and the lending of players from one franchise to another was not uncommon. In total, 638 active NFL players entered the armed forces, sixty-nine earned decorations, and twenty-three were killed.[25]

The most difficult years were 1943 and 1944, when manpower shortages caught up to a number of franchises. The Department of War Transportation also placed travel restrictions on the NFL, ordering a 27 percent cut. The league responded by revising schedules. Some teams suspended operations temporarily or merged with other franchises for survival. The Cleveland Rams shut down entirely for the 1943 season, but returned to action in 1944. In 1943 the Philadelphia Eagles merged with the Pittsburgh Steelers to become the Phil-Pitt Combine (unofficially the Steagles), and the following year the Steelers were combined with the Chicago Cardinals to become the Card-Pitts, and some shortened that to Carpets as others in the league ran over them. Not surprisingly, league attendance suffered during the war years.

The Steelers-Eagles merger was necessitated by a severe shortage of players on both teams. The two head coaches became co-coaches, Greasy Neale from Philadelphia and Walt Kiesling from Pittsburgh. Because the two men came to hate one another, they divided duties between the offense and defense (Neal taking over the offense and Kiesling the defense), which some say produced the precedent for the use of offensive and defensive coordinators. Players worked forty-hour weeks in defense plants to show their patriotism and to survive economically. They practiced three hours a night, six days a week.

The NFL demonstrated its patriotism during the war by the regular playing of the national anthem prior to each game, a practice that continued after the war. More substantive was the $680,000 raised by the NFL from fifteen exhibition games for war relief charities. This was the highest amount raised by any single athletic organization. The NFL and its players also assumed a major role in the selling of war bonds, amounting to $4 million in 1942. Easily the most impressive endeavor in this connection was the reported $2.1 million raised by Curly Lambeau, Cecil Isbell, and Don Hutson of the Green Bay Packers in a single night at a rally in Milwaukee.[26]

Another important development that emerged from World War II was a significant increase in the regard for football as a training and morale vehicle for the young men of the nation. The longer-term results on both college and professional football could be seen in the military-style training camps for football, and the number of coaches and players who came out of these programs into the NFL. The most prominent example was Paul Brown, who was the head coach at Great Lakes Naval Training Center. It is not an exaggeration to say that one of the war's unintended consequences was a growth in the popularity and quality of professional football in the postwar era.

As World War II came to an end and players began to return to their teams, rosters were expanded to thirty-three players, a rule change moved the hash marks to twenty yards from the sidelines, and the number of people seeking NFL franchises jumped. Sportswriter John Lardner predicted that professional football was the game of the future. Colleges would continue to play big-time football, but Lardner believed that the pros would become the number-one choice of the fans, and that the colleges would become a minor league development system for the professionals. Young men who attended college to play football would leave for the pros as soon as possible.[27]

The war produced changes, some momentous and others of a lesser significance, across the entire spectrum of American society. Professional football proved no exception.

The NFL Comes of Age

The first decade and a half after the war brought tremendous change in American life. As the United States came to grips with its new status as the world's preeminent economic and military power, the American public entered an age of consumption on a scale never before seen in human history. By the end of the 1950s disposable income was rising, along with the average standard of living. For entertainment and sport, this resulted in a corresponding rate of growth. When coupled with the rapid expansion of the television industry, the first fifteen years of the postwar period produced a perfect storm for professional football.

On the front lines of race in America, it was clear that the status quo of segregation would be challenged, and all areas of public life in America were impacted. The world of sport, including professional football, was no exception. The uneven advance in race relations was an important part of the NFL story in the postwar world.

As people calculated the impact of the war, there were those who positioned themselves to take advantage of the new prosperity. Entrepreneurs across America looked to sport, and often to professional sport, where they saw room for the expansion and the development of markets. Individuals envisioned opportunities to capitalize on the anticipated demand for sport and entertainment.

The changes in professional football involved not just the National Football League but also the All-America Football Conference, which was organized in 1944 and began on-field operations in 1946. This prosperous decade and a half ended with a second challenge to the NFL in the form of the American Football League. Both the AAFC and the AFL were led by men who thought that the market for professional football was not yet satiated, and by men frustrated by the unwillingness of the NFL to expand. Both leagues mounted a considerable and successful challenge to the NFL.

The economics of pro football was impacted, negatively in the short run, but positively in the long run. In both cases the status of the African American football player was a factor. In the AAFC the result was desegregation, which ironically came first in the NFL when the Rams left Cleveland and moved to Los Angeles. In the second instance it was not until the emergence of the American Football League that desegregation accelerated and African Americans had something approaching equality of opportunity in professional football.[1]

The AAFC

On June 4, 1944, two days before D-Day, a group described by one writer as "men of millionaire incomes," met in St. Louis.[2] The meeting was called by the sports editor of the *Chicago Tribune,* Arch Ward, who had made a name for himself as a sports entrepreneur when he created both the baseball and football all-star games. The meeting's purpose was to organize a new professional football league. Ward calculated that there would be a surplus of football talent coming out of the war, from which new teams and a new league of quality could be formed. Representatives of Buffalo, Los Angeles, New York, San Francisco, Chicago, and Cleveland attended.

A second meeting in Chicago on September 3, 1944, attracted additional talent and money. Gene Tunney was there to represent Baltimore, contractor Sam Cordovano and oilman James Breuil represented Buffalo, and actor Don Ameche represented a Los Angeles group. Lumber magnate Tony Moribito was seeking a franchise for San Francisco, as was Yellow Cabs owner Arthur McBride for Cleveland, and Eleanor Gehrig and oilman Ray Ryan for New York. A number of these owners had deep pockets and were ready to spend heavily to challenge the NFL.[3]

The AAFC chose James Crowley as their new commissioner, setting up a battle between two of Notre Dame's four horsemen, as Elmer Layden was the head man at the NFL. The AAFC pledged to sign no college players with eligibility remaining and no NFL player who was under contract. In April 1945 before play began, the AAFC suggested a merger with the NFL to avoid a war that would drive up salaries. Layden rejected the overture and was quoted as saying that the AAFC might want to "first get a football, then make a schedule, and then play a game." This was not an insult that any AAFC member would soon forget.[4]

Before play began the competition off the field heated up. Chicago Bears tackle Lee Artos was the first player from the NFL signed by the AAFC. Nearly one hundred such signings followed, driving up salaries that cost both leagues an estimated $5 million. The AAFC aggressively pursued the best college players and signed forty-four of the sixty who played in the 1946 College All-Star Game.

Bad news came for the NFL in January 1946 when Dan Topping, Yankee baseball and football owner, announced he was taking his Brooklyn franchise out of the NFL and joining the AAFC. This meant direct competition with Tim Mara's Giants, and it meant that the AAFC had just acquired another owner with extremely deep pockets.

Discontent with Elmer Layden's leadership boiled over at this development. On the night before the January NFL meetings, a group of four owners agreed that Layden must go. When he arrived in New York for the meetings, George Preston Marshall announced that Layden would be reelected "over my dead body." Marshall lived through the meetings and Layden resigned. The owners turned to one of their own, Bert Bell, as the new commissioner.

Bert Bell was born to great wealth and lived a wild life as a young man, but totally reformed when he met his future wife, Francis Upton, a Ziegfeld dancer and a great beauty who told him she would never marry a drinking man. In 1933 Bell purchased the bankrupt Frankford Yellow Jackets, moved them to Philadelphia, and with co-owner Lud Wray renamed them the Eagles after the Blue Eagle, the symbol of FDR's National Recovery Administration. Bell consistently lost money, and facing a crisis in 1940 sold the Eagles and bought a share of the Steelers. When Bell was named commissioner he divested himself of his stake in the Steelers.[5]

The bad news for the NFL (or was it good news?) did not end there. Once Bell was chosen commissioner, Dan Reeves took the floor to once again seek approval to move his Rams from Cleveland to Los Angeles. Once again, his fellow owners rejected his request. Reeves, despite the fact that the Rams were NFL champions in 1945, lost money and had accumulated major debt in the war years. He was in dire financial straits. Following the vote against him, Reeves calmly announced to his fellow owners that the Cleveland franchise was no more, and he walked out. After considerable discussion among the owners, a delegation headed by George Halas pleaded with Reeves to reconsider. He remained firm, and it was the NFL that reconsidered, but at a price. The league granted Reeves's wish to relocate the team, but with a stipulation: visiting teams in Los Angeles received an additional $5,000 guarantee over the normal guarantee of $10,000. The NFL owners voted to approve the move, followed by another vote to have no further contact with the AAFC.

The first season of competition seemed like a good one for both leagues, as attendance was strong. In 1946 NFL attendance was up about 20 percent over the previous season, with a reported average attendance at thirty-three thousand. The AAFC averaged a reported twenty-five thousand. In total some three million fans attended games in 1946, up 100 percent over the previous year. This did not necessarily translate into profits. The AAFC charged lower ticket prices than the NFL and distributed a significant number of free tickets in their communities, as did the NFL. Only the Giants and Redskins of the NFL and Cleveland of the AAFC showed a profit. Cleveland drew nearly four hundred thousand fans to their games. Other AAFC franchises lost an average of $100,000 for the season.

The AAFC tried to create more competitive balance in the league and continued to spend heavily on players. In the 1947 season AAFC attendance exceeded that of the NFL, but free tickets were still distributed and financial losses mounted. The NFL too was beginning to feel the economic pinch. The AAFC owners remained confident they could win the war, a feeling that may have been encouraged by favorable coverage in the sports media.

The big winners in all this were the players. There were reports that stars in the NFL were offered as much as $35,000 to jump to the new league, at a time when NFL top salaries were $15,000. This forced the NFL to increase salaries. Steve Van Buren re-signed with the Eagles for as much as $50,000. From 1945 to 1946 Bob Waterfield, the Rams' quarterback, enjoyed an increase in salary from $9,000 to $20,000. Average compensation on the Rams grew by 32 percent, and Philadelphia Eagles' salaries doubled. Needless to say, revenues did not keep pace and nearly everyone lost money.[6]

Free spending continued driving everyone deeper into debt. In addition, both leagues suffered from championship dominance. In the NFL four franchises—the Giants, Redskins, Bears, and Packers—dominated from 1936 to 1946. The NFL broke that cycle in 1947, but in the AAFC the Browns were the only champion that league ever had. That year proved the high point for both the AAFC and the Browns. Cleveland averaged more than fifty-six thousand fans per game in 1947, and then in 1948 it dropped to forty-five thousand, and in 1949 to thirty-one thousand.

In December 1947 the NFL showed its first cracks when Alexis Thompson of the Eagles became the first owner to publicly recognize the AAFC as an equal and urge an end to the war. In Detroit, Lions owner Fred Mandel had lost a reported $600,000. In Los Angeles Dan Reeves sold one-third of the Rams in order to stay afloat. A year later, as the bleeding continued, the NFL began exploratory talks with the AAFC. The NFL wanted unconditional surrender, which the AAFC rejected.

Talks continued. The NFL was willing to take the Browns and the San Francisco 49ers, but the disposition of the AAFC franchise in Baltimore was a major issue. The Redskins owner agreed to accept the Baltimore franchise but demanded $200,000 for territorial rights. There would be no settlement. Franchises across both leagues were pushed to the wall during the 1949 season. In the off-season Marshall lowered his compensation demands to $150,000, and a Baltimore millionaire stepped forward to save that franchise.[7]

As the merger was agreed upon, Cleveland collected another AAFC championship and Philadelphia was crowned NFL champion. Bert Bell understood the appeal of a game between champions. In making the schedule for the new league, he set the season opener as the Eagles versus the Browns in Philadelphia on a Saturday night.

George Preston Marshall had famously said that the worst team in the NFL could beat the best team in the AAFC. Others in the NFL, including Eagles coach Greasy Neale, believed that the AAFC was but a minor league and would not be competitive in the new NFL. As the Cleveland Browns prepared for the season opener, they won five straight exhibition games, including one against the Bears in Cleveland that drew more than fifty thousand fans.

The opening game in Philadelphia drew the largest crowd in the history of professional football, 71,237. The media called it the World Series of football, and Bert Bell presented a special trophy to the winning team. The much-anticipated game turned out to be not much of a contest. The final score was 35-10 in favor of the Browns, and the Eagles didn't reach the end zone until the fourth quarter. The Browns had two touchdowns called back on what Cleveland coach Paul Brown described as phantom penalties. NFL commissioner Bert Bell called the Browns the best-coached team he had ever seen, and Otto Graham was named MVP of the game. Graham was 21 of 38 passing for 346 yards and three touchdowns. Brown announced that this was the best football team he had ever seen.

Coach Neale was also complimentary, but added that the Browns looked like a basketball team because all they ever did was pass the ball. Brown took note of the comment, and Neale would receive another humiliation in the rematch at Cleveland later in the season. In that game Brown told his team they would not pass as long as the game was tied or they were leading. They did not pass and won the game 13-7, gaining only sixty-eight yards of offense. The fact that the game was played in rain and mud may have been

Paul Brown (left), Bert Bell (center), and Los Angeles Rams head coach Joe Stydahar at NFL Annual Meeting, January 18, 1952. AP Photo/Matty Zimmerman.

more significant than any revenge motive. Whatever the case, Neale was not only humiliated but fired following the game. Years later Neale recalled the game as one in which Philadelphia did not allow Cleveland to complete a single pass. His glass apparently remained more than half full.

The leagues' merger resulted in three AAFC teams entering the NFL: the Browns, Colts, and 49ers. There were two divisions, the American and National, later changed to Eastern and Western, with Cleveland, the New York Giants, Philadelphia, Pittsburgh, Washington, and the Chicago Cardinals in the American Conference, and Los Angeles, the Chicago Bears, the New York Yankees, Detroit, Green Bay, and San Francisco in the National Conference. With thirteen teams in the League, the Baltimore Colts were designated the swing team, playing each club in the league once per season.[8]

Paul's Browns

For all the problems of the AAFC, one franchise and one man stood out as an exceptional force building his team and an innovator who transformed coaching. Football was the focal point of Paul Brown's early life in Massillon, Ohio. He played football in high school and then at Miami University in Ohio. After graduation he decided against law school and took a job coaching football at a Maryland prep school. In 1932 Brown was hired as head coach at Massillon Washington High. Massillon could only be described as a fanatical football town, and Paul Brown jumped at the chance to coach there. The Massillon High and Ohio State University coaching positions were his two dream jobs, and he ultimately held each.

At Massillon Brown amassed a record of 80-8-2. He developed a booster club with twenty-five hundred members, and in 1940 that translated into 182,000 fans attending the ten home games. He was in total control of his program and his players, and probably the school and the town. In 1941 Brown moved on to Ohio State, where in 1942 he won a national championship.

After the 1943 season, in which he lost many of his players to the military and had a losing season, Paul Brown joined the Navy. He was assigned football coach and athletic director at Great Lakes Naval Training Center, where the base commander was building powerhouses in baseball and football. While at the center, Arch Ward and Mickey McBride approached Brown about a job coaching the Cleveland entry in the AAFC. It was a generous offer, including 5 percent ownership in the team and total control over football decisions.

Brown moved quickly in building a coaching staff. He began with Blanton Collier, whom Brown met at Great Lakes when he began hanging out at football practices. Collier turned out to be a brilliant football mind, developing innovative pass defenses as the backfield coach. Brown quickly recognized Collier's talents and expanded his role. Fritz Heisler was hired as guard coach and then offensive line coach. He developed pass-blocking techniques to protect the quarterback, creating "the pocket" from which the quarterback operated.

Brown sent his coaches out looking for talent among those individuals who had played both for and against Brown's teams. The first major acquisition was Otto Graham, the Hall of Fame quarterback out of Northwestern University. Graham was an excellent all-around athlete, a brilliant student, and talented in the musical arts. Brown offered Graham a salary in line with the NFL standards at $7,500, and gave him a signing bonus of $1,000 and a monthly stipend of $250 for as long as he remained in the military. Graham signed without hesitation, leaving the Detroit Lions holding his draft rights. Other players were signed from the NFL, and also a number who were in the military and still had college eligibility. Such great players as Lou Groza, Dante Lavelli, Edgar "Special Delivery" Jones, and Lou Saban all signed with the Browns.[9]

Paul Brown set the standards and drew the blueprint for the modern professional football coach. His techniques and innovations transformed professional football and coaching. His firsts were many, as he:

- called plays for his quarterbacks
- gave his players IQ and personality tests
- was the first to time his players in the forty-yard dash
- hired his coaching staff on a year-round basis

- used game film to scout his opponents
- gave exams on the playbook
- kept his team together in a hotel the night before a home game
- organized and systematized drills at practice in advance
- did not hold practices that exceeded ninety minutes because the learning curve declines after that amount of time
- allowed the least physical contact in practice of any team
- scouted for and systematized his draft strategy
- designed a passing offense to attack specific weak points in opposing defenses
- devised defenses to counter the offenses he created
- invented the "taxi squad"
- developed the draw play[10]

Brown began training camp each year with the same two-hour speech in which he told his players what was expected of them both on and off the field. He was a strict disciplinarian, and violations of team rules meant swift and stern punishment. Many have described Brown as a severe man with a cold personality, at times distant, but always conscious of where the spotlight was shining. He knew more about football than anyone else, and he knew that he did, and was proud of that fact. Brown was offended when anyone suggested otherwise. His basic objective was to build a pro football dynasty and become the New York Yankees of football.

Brown believed in preparation, both physical and mental. He employed a large number of part-time scouts across the country. Brown and Collier spent the entire off-season watching film and breaking down every play, cataloging what each of the twenty-two players did on every play. On a weekly basis Brown developed a grading system for his players based on a breakdown of the game film. Coaches prepared specific lesson plans for each practice. Each coach and player had a notebook that contained the plays and the terminology, and they were expected to take notes at each team meeting. Players were told everything they needed to know, and were expected to record that in their playbooks, and ultimately in their heads.

There were rules of conduct covering public smoking, drinking, and a dress code. Brown even tried to control the sex lives of his players with the "Tuesday Night Rule." Like many coaches of his time, he believed that sexual activity could sap the energy of players. The rule mandated that his players not have sex with their wives after Tuesday night during game weeks. According to Otto Graham, when players asked about the single guys, the coach simply ignored the question, much to the amusement of the team.[11]

Desegregating the Professional Game

Beyond all of these innovations and the great success of Paul Brown, the Cleveland Browns were known as one of the teams that moved professional football out of the era of segregation. The AAFC announced at the outset that race would not be a factor in the league. For Paul Brown, race was not an issue; only finding the best players to win football games mattered. He had coached African American players at Ohio State and at Great Lakes, and had a memory for great African Americans he saw play elsewhere.

Brown signed Bill Willis, who played for him at Ohio State, where Willis was an All-American tackle. The coach also signed Marion Motley, who played for him at Great Lakes. This was not a social statement, but rather signings that made the Cleveland Browns a better football team. Nonetheless, Brown is often praised as a pioneer, signing two of the four African Americans who played professional football in 1946.

Indeed Paul Brown's actions and motives were not simple. When the Browns were organizing, Marion Motley wrote to Brown asking for a tryout. Brown replied that he had enough running backs. Willis too had written to Brown, and he was told that the coach would get back to him. When the Browns went into training camp there were no African American players present. Willis waited a year to hear back from Brown, and then, as Willis was leaving to play for Montreal in the CFL, he got a call from a Columbus sportswriter and friend of Paul Brown. Willis was asked to come to Columbus for a tryout. After one day of practice, the team signed Willis. Then, a few weeks later, Motley was contacted by the Browns to come for a tryout. The result was the same.

Why this circuitous route was followed is not clearly understood. Brown claimed that he wanted the two men on his team all along but that things were done in this way to keep pressure off them. Perhaps it was to keep pressure off Paul Brown. Years later Brown told sportswriter Mickey Herskowitz that it was Collier who had pressed for the signing of Motley. Dan Daley and Paul O'Donnell offer another explanation. According to them, during training camp, the Browns lost two fullbacks, and that led to Motley's signing. Also during camp, Brown concluded that the team was weak at guard, and this led to Willis's signing.[12]

The initial desegregation of the NFL was a matter of necessity rather than choice. On March 21, 1946, the Los Angeles Rams signed Kenny Washington, who had been an All-American at the University of California at Los Angeles, and widely considered the best college player of his era. Both the Rams and the Dons of the AAFC were under pressure from African American civic groups and newspapers, who lobbied the Los Angeles Coliseum Commission to deny use of the stadium to any segregated team. The Rams signed Washington, and a few weeks later inked Woody Strode from Illinois, who played collegiately for UCLA.

In 1946 there were eighteen professional teams with 594 players. Each league had two African American players. In 1947 the total number of players increased to 664, with ten African Americans. At the end of the season, nine teams in the NFL and two in the AAFC had no African American players. When teams added black players, they were almost all ends, halfbacks, and defensive backs. In the NFL, none came from a black college, as there was an assumption that historically black colleges and universities (HBCUs) were lacking in talent.

On January 2, 1948, at the Vulcan Bowl in Birmingham, Alabama, "Tank" Younger of Grambling University became the first black player from an HBCU to be scouted by an NFL team. Rams scout Ed Kotel, the first full-time traveling scout in the NFL, talked to Younger after the game. The running back/linebacker then returned to Grambling to discuss the development with his coach, Eddie Robinson. Younger became the first player from an HBCU to sign with an NFL team. It was a small but significant advance for the NFL and a major advance for the Rams, who won three consecutive championships beginning in 1949.

The most sought-after African American player in 1947 was Claude "Buddy" Young from the University of Illinois. Both the New York Yankees and Los Angeles Dons were rumored to be interested in signing him. Young was interested in turning pro even though he had college eligibility remaining. Dan Reeves said that the Rams were not interested because of the NFL rule against signing anyone whose class had not yet graduated. In the end, Young signed with the Yankees of the AAFC at a reported $13,000 per year, well below the rumored offers.

By the end of the 1940s only twenty-six African Americans had been signed to play in the NFL or AAFC. Of those, many were on one-year contracts and signed as tokens. Only three NFL teams had African American players at that time: the Lions, Rams, and Giants. The AAFC contained only two teams that did not have African American players. The Browns had a larger number in 1947 than any other team, and their success owed greatly to that.[13]

Although the African American players became favorites with African American fans and with home-team fans, they were not welcomed with open arms in what was a segregated society. In some cases that included teammates.

On the Browns, where Paul Brown was in total control of his team, the head coach had a simple announcement for his players: "If you don't like playing with a black man, get out of here." When Motley and Willis hit the field in competition for the first time, they were greeted by ten thousand African American fans in the Cleveland crowd of more than sixty thousand. A week later the Browns traveled to Chicago to play the Rockets at Soldier Field in front of 51,962, the largest crowd ever for a professional game in Chicago. It was a game of racial incidents directed at Motley and Willis, marked by late hits, cheap shots, and racist verbiage. The Browns rallied around their men, and both players and officials expressed shock over the racist reactions.

Another major issue surfaced when the Browns were slated to play in Miami against the Seahawks. Behind the palm trees and the beaches, Florida was a southern state and Miami was a racist city. Florida law prohibited interracial competition, and there was no question that this law would be enforced. Motley received death threats, one of which read: "You black son-of-a-bitch, you come down here and run across the goal line, you'll be a dead son-of-a-bitch." Brown was criticized by some for not challenging the Florida law and the Miami welcoming committee, but there was no reason to put lives on the line in a place where threats of this type were not taken lightly.

This sort of behavior did not end soon. After the merger of the two leagues, the harassment of the Browns' players continued, and there was no inclination by the authorities in the NFL to put a stop to it. In 1950 Motley was still being kicked in the head and having his hands stomped upon during play. When African American player Len Ford joined the Browns, he quickly became known as the best pass rusher in the NFL. In a game against the Cardinals, Pat Harder was unable to block Ford. At one point after Ford ran by Harder, the frustrated Harder put his elbow in the side of Ford's cheek, crushing his cheek bone, breaking his nose, and knocking out several teeth. Ford required extensive surgery. For his trouble, Ford was penalized for illegal use of the hands. Paul Brown became furious and sent game film to Bert Bell, who agreed that Ford should not have been penalized and that Harder was the offender. Bell issued a statement saying that dirty play would not be tolerated, but in not immediately punishing Harder voided his own pronouncement.[14]

The New NFL

The end of the first season of the new NFL featured two playoff games, one in each conference, as the conference standings ended in a tie. The Rams beat the Bears 24–14 in front of 83,501 in Los Angeles, and the Browns beat the Giants 8-3 on a rock-solid frozen field in a game with no touchdowns, before a brave crowd of 33,754 fans. That set the stage for the Browns' first NFL title the following week, before an even smaller crowd in freezing temperatures in Cleveland.

The Rams and Browns had two of the best passing quarterbacks in professional football: Otto Graham led the Browns and Bob Waterfield led the Rams. Both teams had an excellent corps of receivers and a strong complementary running game. The game itself was decided in the last twenty-eight seconds, when Lou Groza kicked a field goal from sixteen yards out for a 30-28 Browns win. Bert Bell called it the greatest game he had ever seen.[15]

Two of the more interesting anomalies among players in the 1950s were Les Bingaman and Eugene Lipscomb, both of whom brought attention to the NFL. Bingaman was most noted for his size, which at 350 pounds was regarded as freakish. The Detroit defensive lineman was described as someone who specialized in "not moving." He played from 1948 to 1954 and made the Pro Bowl in 1951 and 1953. Eugene "Bid Daddy" Lipscomb, an African American, was a transforming figure in the fifties. At 6'7" Big Daddy had both speed and size and redefined the position of defensive lineman. He played for the Rams, Colts, and Steelers and became a beloved figure in Baltimore and Pittsburgh. He was a three-time Pro Bowl player. Big Daddy was known as a gentle giant. He also was a man who indulged heavily in sex, alcohol, and drugs. He died of a heroin overdose in 1963. For twelve hours at the funeral home in Baltimore people lined up four abreast to walk past the coffin and pay their respects to their hero who lay in state. Lipscomb's appeal and the growing mystique of the NFL, even in the literary world, was in evidence in 1967 when the *Atlantic* published the poet Randall Jarrell's "Say Good-bye to Big Daddy."[16]

As the NFL gained traction in the growing and expanding consumer economy, Bert Bell considered the merger his greatest achievement as commissioner. The economic uncertainties and anxieties of the late forties were fading, and the future was looking increasingly bright. Historian Craig Coenen believes that the war between the NFL and the AAFC enhanced the image of professional football, as it "affected the way in which people treated the sport nationally and teams locally." In the larger cities, successful teams drew well, and in some of them large fan bases were built. Professional football became another way for cities to claim major league status, more and more considered a mark of a successful city of consequence.[17]

Over the next three years, the NFL continued to make minor adjustments in their franchises. The Colts did not survive into the 1951 season, and then at the end of that year the New York Yankees franchise was sold to the league. In 1952 a twenty-one-man ownership group in Dallas was awarded the franchise. Most people thought Dallas would be an ideal location for a professional football team, but a combination of poor management and poor play led to the collapse of the Dallas Texans. The team played four games in the Cotton Bowl and the cumulative attendance could not crack the fifty thousand mark. At the half-way point of the season the undercapitalized owners walked out, and the NFL assumed operations of the team, which finished its schedule on the road.

The fate of the Dallas Texans was finally settled when Commissioner Bell announced that the franchise would be awarded to Baltimore if fifteen thousand season tickets could be sold. They were. The Baltimore Colts were resurrected, and Carroll Rosenbloom became the new owner. He hired Weeb Ewbank as his head coach, with Ewbank predicting a championship within five years. The year 1953 ushered in another period of league stability, as there were no franchise changes through 1959.[18]

The other franchise in jeopardy at the time of the merger was the Green Bay Packers. The Packers did not have the funds to compete in the player market of rising salaries during the AAFC war. Pressures built as many people argued that Green Bay was not a major league city and should not be in the NFL. Moving games to Milwaukee had been seen as a means of survival, but by 1948 average attendance in Milwaukee had dropped to twelve thousand, while attendance in Green Bay stood at thirty thousand per game. Still, some argued that the team should relocate to Milwaukee.

Facing the crisis, the team's board of directors issued five thousand shares of nonprofit, nondividend stock. Curly Lambeau opposed the stock issue and resigned from the board. Packer boosters went door-to-door, public rallies were held, and in three weeks all the stock was sold, raising $105,825. Local businessmen donated an additional $125,000, and the team sold ten thousand season tickets. In an act of God or man, just prior to the stock offering, the Packer-owned "Rockwood Lodge" training facility burned down, bringing $50,000 of insurance money and relieving the team of a drain on its revenues, as the lodge had become a financial liability. All of this was accomplished before the June 1950 NFL owners' meeting.[19]

The San Francisco 49ers was another of those franchises that looked shaky in the early fifties, although the study by Adelman and Linden shows the team turning a profit in both 1951 and 1952. In point of fact, the team had a good decade. The 49ers drafted Hugh McElhenny, who was named Rookie of the Year in 1953 when he recorded the best rushing average, the longest run from scrimmage, and the longest punt return in the league. He played in five Pro Bowls and was one of the most elusive runners in league history. McElhenny was a key member of the 49ers' "million dollar backfield" through the decade, joining the power runners Joe Perry and John Henry Johnson and quarterback Y. A. Tittle. All four became Hall of Fame members.[20]

Television's First Impact

Television was another new factor in the postwar world. Destined to transform the National Football League and the leisure time of Americans, television's early years were filled with doubt and anxiety. The first televised game was held on October 22, 1939, between the Philadelphia Eagles and the Brooklyn Dodgers. The broadcast reached anywhere from four hundred to one thousand television sets in New York City. It led quickly to a decision to begin televising Dodger baseball games throughout the season, but it was a false start, as the coming of war postponed any further development of electronics for nonmilitary uses.

In 1946 there were approximately twelve thousand television sets in the United States. By 1950 that number reached four million, with a potential audience of thirty million, or 20 percent of the population. In 1947 the Chicago Bears agreed with WBKB television to televise all six of its home games for a fee of $4,500. There were concerns that people would stay home and watch the games, but a doubling of gate receipts that year seemed to indicate quite the opposite. Nonetheless, in 1948 George Halas drew back and only allowed television for the final game of the season, against the Cardinals. Pabst Brewing paid $5,000 for the rights. The Bears experimented with a regional network of eleven cities, and they lost about $1,500 on the venture. In 1947 the Colts received only $50 per game for television rights. Two years later the Browns sold television rights to a local power company that was their chief radio sponsor for $5,000.

These spotty operations came and went, with no trends apparent. The first major experiment with television came in Los Angeles, where the Rams offered local rights for all their 1950 home games. To allay fears of the potential consequences, Admiral Television sponsored the telecasts, with the arrangement that they would make up any losses in ticket sales from the previous year. When attendance dropped 110,000, Admiral had to pay the Rams $307,000. The following year the Rams televised only road games and home attendance bounced back to 1949 levels.

The first network telecasts came in 1951. The Bears had a ten-city network that spread from Nashville to Minneapolis, and from Columbus to Omaha. Local stations sold advertising and the Bears picked up production and distribution costs. They lost money. On the national level Dumont was the only network interested in televising NFL football. In 1951 Dumont paid $95,000 per year to televise five games as well as the NFL championship. This arrangement lasted until 1955.

Most teams developed television networks in the early fifties, and the revenues they were able to generate varied widely. In 1953 the Rams received $100,000, while Green Bay generated only $5,000. That was the year Bert Bell promoted a rule passed in the NFL that no home games would be televised, and no contests could be telecast in a market where a home game was being played. This rule was challenged in court, but Judge Allan Grim of the U.S. District Court in Philadelphia ruled on the side of the NFL in November 1953.

By 1954 there were twenty-four million television sets in the country, and approximately two-thirds of the population had access to television. One of the problems facing the networks was programming to fill the Sunday afternoon "ghetto." The NFL was the solution. By 1956 all teams had some network arrangements with CBS, while NBC owned the rights to the championship game. Bert Bell sent out a memo to all league members urging them to present the best possible teams for television. The networks in turn were prohibited from showing fights and injuries because, as Bell put it, "We don't want the kids sitting in their living rooms to see their heroes trading punches. That doesn't teach good sportsmanship." Bell held the right of approval over all television contracts even though individual teams contracted their own games.[21]

All of this was merely prologue. The advertising community was in the process of discovering the potency of sports on television, and they were about to move into professional football. This arrangement turned out to be more potent than anyone imagined. Network executives were not much interested in sports, and they had to be dragged into it. Fortunately there was a serendipitous factor at work, as the advertising industry was centered in New York City, where the New York Giants were again becoming a force in the National Football League. The executives at the agencies were about to get a whiff of success from the men of the gridiron, and they found it intoxicating. Once they did so, it was a reasonably simple matter to take television along into this new world.

Ed Scherick of the advertising agency Dancer Fitzgerald had put together baseball's Game of the Week for Falstaff Beer. He looked at football and started by buying half of the spots on the Bears and Cardinals football network at $2,000 per game. Scherick called it the "greatest media buy in the history of television." When the beer people sought more spots, he went to CBS and sold them on it. Scherick, too, then moved to CBS. The pieces were falling in place, and it seemed as if it were raining money. Compared with what was to come, it was only a light mist.[22]

The Greatest Game Ever?

The 1958 NFL Championship Game between the Baltimore Colts and the New York Giants was played in Yankee Stadium on December 28 before 64,185 fans. Another forty-five million sat in front of their television sets. What viewers saw that day was the first championship game to end in a tie and go into overtime, one of the great finishes in football history. Baltimore led at the half 14-3, having turned two Frank Gifford fumbles into touchdowns. The third quarter featured a goal-line stand as the Giants threw Alan "The Horse" Ameche from the one yard line back to the five. The Giants then drove ninety-five yards for a touchdown. Four minutes later Gifford caught a pass for the go-ahead touchdown, making it 17-14.

With just under two minutes remaining in the game, Unitas etched his name into legend territory. The Colts got the ball on their own fourteen yard line. In the final minute of play, Johnny Unitas hit Raymond Berry on three passes over the middle for sixty-two yards, and the Colts had reached the Giants' seventeen yard line. With no timeouts, the field goal team came on, set up, and with seven seconds on the clock, Steve Myhra kicked the ball through the uprights for the game-tying field goal. Many of the players did not know what they should do next. A championship game had never ended in a tie. In 1947 a rule was put in place to handle this contingency. The teams would now play until someone scored in what was called "sudden death overtime."

The Giants won the coin toss and received the kickoff. They went three and out and punted to the Colts. In a series of brilliant passes by Unitas and punishing running by Ameche, the Colts moved to the Giants' eight yard line. Suddenly the television audience found itself staring at a black screen as a cable connection on the sidelines had come loose. Moments later the picture was restored, and the television audience hadn't missed a thing because a fan, perhaps overloaded with beer, had run on the field and was chased down by the police. In fact it was not a fan but Stan Rotkiewicz, a quick-thinking statistician working for NBC, who ran on the field to delay the game and save the day, while network technicians solved the transmission problem.

The game ended two plays later; a pass inside the one, and a power run from there put Ameche in the end zone. What has since been called "the best game ever" was over. It would be the topic of conversation among sports fans for days and weeks to come. Johnny Unitas was the latest hero in American sport, and the names of Alan Ameche, Lenny Moore, and Raymond Berry were spoken knowingly in animated discussions rehashing the amazing sudden-death finish. Thirty thousand Colt fans welcomed the team back to the city, although it is not known if the fan that drove his car into a telephone pole when Ameche scored was in the crowd. *Sports Illustrated* titled Tex Maule's game story, "The Best Football Game Ever Played," and Raymond Berry said simply, "It's the greatest thing that ever happened."

Michael McCambridge assessed the significance of the game: "By the end of the Colts-Giants game, a seismic shift in the American Sports landscape had clearly begun. In another decade, after another New York football team and its charismatic leader stunned the sport world, football was no longer the rebel, but the new king. And baseball was no longer the national pastime." Another person impressed by the game was Lamar Hunt. Although he always had an emotional interest in football, the Colts-Giants game sealed it, as he said to himself, "Well, that's it. This sport really has everything. And it televises well."[23] The ramifications of this impact came shortly.

Certainly the impact of this game was great, but as many have since argued, the National Football League was not "made" by this one game. Indeed the league had been growing in popularity over the previous three decades, and by the midfifties was a force in the sports world. This single game did not on its own awaken the NFL to the significance of television, although it may have awakened television to the significance of the NFL. This form of unscripted reality-based drama was ideal for television and its audience's insatiable appetite for dramatic and action-packed content.

New York Giant publicist Don Smith said that he found football fans were "violently partisan and devoutly involved," and that football easily "involved one's self, heart, soul, voice, and paycheck." According to McCambridge, fans identified with players like Johnny Unitas, who exuded toughness and a calm exterior, because the quality they "were seeing was similar to what Hemingway called grace under pressure and what test pilots referred to as 'the right stuff.'" If Unitas was not well known before this game, he certainly was after, and indeed he became a legendary figure of the fifties and sixties.[24]

Bert Bell showed early on that he understood the power of television and that the NFL must control it. The blackout policy was but one such indication. Ben Rader says that Bell created "an economic cartel," which he used in building the NFL's relationship with the television networks. In 1955, after watching a Colts-Redskins exhibition game, Commissioner Bell called the television announcer Bob Wolff in the middle of the night and pointed out to him that the NFL did not play "exhibition games" but rather they played "hard fought pre-season games." He told Wolff that there was no "tripping" in the NFL, only "tackling," and that a running back couldn't be "wrestled to the ground" because there was no wrestling in football. Otherwise, Bell told Wolff that he had done okay. A few years later Bell chose Wolff to voice the telecast of the Colts-Giants championship game. Bell also recognized the importance of the print and electronic media, which together gave the NFL $50 million worth of free publicity, while the NFL gave the public what it wanted: entertainment, presented as competition with suspense, as "On any given Sunday, any team in our league can beat any other team."

By the midfifties the networks and big advertisers were already on board with the NFL. Sunday afternoon audience share was thirty-seven, and by 1956 CBS was paying $1 million for TV rights, and NBC retained rights to the championship game. The NFL already had a television following. Teams including the Giants, Browns, and Redskins possessed something approaching national television contracts.

A few months before the Colts-Giants game, Bert Bell announced another significant rule change. Referees were instructed to call a timeout if nine minutes had passed in either the first or third quarter without a stoppage of play. It was the birth of the television timeout, and an indication of just how well Bell understood the new medium and his advertisers' needs.[25]

Nurturing the Macho Mythology

The print media too was increasing its coverage of the NFL prior to the 1958 championship game. The new sports magazine *Sports Illustrated* began publishing in 1954 and ran its first pro football cover in 1955, featuring Doak Walker and the Detroit Lions. In 1956 Tex Maule began covering the NFL for the magazine, as did skilled writers such as Jim Murray.

In 1954 the weekly news magazine *Time* published a cover story on the Detroit Lions and Bobby Layne. The story opened with a surprising comparison between college and professional football by claiming that on Sunday "fans who wanted to see football at its best turned out to see the pros." In stadia across the country football fans were learning "what dedicated sportsmen have been saying for years: that Saturday's college boys play a game, while Sunday's pros practice a high and violent art. After half a century of trying to capture the fans' fancy, pro football has finally made the grade." Time proclaimed a new "Era of Cash & Glory." The article dwelled on the roughness of the game, the toughness of Bobby Layne and his teammates, and the meanness drilled into players by the coaches. As a player was carried off the field with his groin ripped open by someone's cleats, a reporter was heard to say, "Pro football is getting like atomic war. There are no winners, only survivors."[26]

In profiling players in the fifties, the popular magazines presented them as men making a living from the game, not using sport to build character. As they were separated from "juvenile storybook values," writes Michael Oriard, they were more suitable as cultural heroes. And in a view which mirrored the public image of Bobby Layne, they might be "a hard-drinking, beer bellied quarterback whose coach tolerated his carousing as long as he showed up on time and alert for practice." This was especially true if they won. Bobby Layne was a hero who in no way resembled Frank Merriwell, the football hero of impeccable character in popular schoolboy novels.[27]

The press was impressed with the new, wide-open style of play fostered by coaches like Weeb Ewbank and Sid Gilman. Free substitution aided the change in style featuring specialization, expertise, and speed. But some of the press was critical of what they reported as violent and dirty play, something *Life* magazine called "Savagery on Sunday." Two innovations attempted to address this issue. One was a rule change, with the "down by tackle rule," which was designed to end piling-on tackling and the extra struggling by the ball carrier to get that extra yard or two. The other change was in equipment, as the Riddell Company put the face mask, developed by Paul Brown, into mass production as a standard part of the helmet.[28]

It is clear that prior to the 1958 Championship Game, the National Football League was growing in popularity, but it was a popularity laced with ambivalence. What *The Game* did was blow away that ambivalence and move the fans and media to a new level of respect, adulation, and intense devotion to the NFL, its teams, and its players. Economically the country was growing in areas that boded well for the NFL. Consumer spending was rising rapidly, businesses doubled the amount they spent on advertising in the decade, and suburbia was booming. An age of prosperity was clearly on, but as was the case in the immediate postwar period, there would be obstacles to fulfilling the promise that lay ahead.[29]

II

The Rozelle Era

4

Moving to Center Stage

The year 1959 was a major turning point for professional football in general, and the National Football League in particular. The NFL went through its first setback in the new struggle with its players, a challenge from a new league, and a change of commissioner. The ramifications of these developments over the next decade were earthshaking for the NFL in both a positive and a negative sense.

On the field 1959 was a memorable year. Vince Lombardi became the head coach of the Green Bay Packers, coming from the New York Giants, where as offensive coordinator he had developed a reputation as a motivator and innovator. He changed offensive line play and blocking techniques and significantly altered offensive play in general. Lombardi turned the losing Packer franchise into the dominant team of the sixties. He took the 1-10-1 team of 1958 and turned them into a 7-5 team in 1959 and then never looked back.

National media attention given to professional football increased in 1959. Thomas Morgan wrote "The Wham in Pro Football" for *Esquire* and attempted to explain the growing popularity of the professional game. Drawing on an essay by Dan Wakefield in *Dissent,* Morgan wrote knowingly about male rituals that bring glory to everyday life and the appeal of "controlled violence" in an "enervated society." American society was going through another of its periodic crises over male identity and the blurring of gender roles. Men needed to find a way to be men, and Morgan saw professional football as a male domain, comparing it to an "outdoor, stag poker game." It was "harder, faster, meaner and more acute" than the college game. It combined speed with a "brutal rhythm" and style. Football brought pleasure in "sanctioned savagery" to the boredom and dullness in the workaday world. Cold-war concerns over the softness and poor physical conditioning among Americans, as well as the moral corruption and self-indulgence prevalent in the expanding consumer culture, found corresponding expression in the political culture of the President's Council on Physical Fitness and the Kennedy family's "cult of touch football."

These concerns found another antidote in the constructed culture of pro football embodied in the person of New York Giants star Sam Huff, who appeared on the cover of *Time* on November 30, 1959. Huff was on his way to being named Defensive MVP in the NFL for the 1959 season. The title of the *Time* cover story laid it all up front: "A Man's Game." Laced with testosterone-tainted prose, the wordsmiths at *Time* wrote of "battle-tried" men who seemed "larger than life," embodying "sheer brute strength." The new emphasis on defense "epitomizes the raw strength and subtle scheming that lies at the heart of football." Brain and brawn must come together. The key figure bringing them together was the middle linebacker for the Giants, Sam Huff.

According to *Time* professional football was no longer the rowdy game of the factory towns of Pennsylvania and Ohio. It now had an air of gentility. There was no swearing in the Giants locker room, and in Cleveland Paul Brown demanded impeccable conduct from his players. Even the bookmakers saw the change and were convinced of the pro game's integrity. As for Sam Huff, although he could do his job with "brute force alone," he studied and prepared so that he knew where the ball would be at all times, and he would be there too. "You play as rough and vicious as you can," said Huff, because if "you hit a guy, you hurt him instead of him hurting you." There was a code that prohibited any "deliberate attempt to maim." Yet, even when played cleanly, "football is a game of awesome violence."

The next season, CBS television took football fans on a thirty-minute excursion inside "The Violent World of Sam Huff." Huff was wired for sound during practice and an exhibition game. The result was a CBS documentary filled with bone-crunching tackles, complete with a soundtrack of violence as "grunts, groans and hard hits could be heard in millions of living rooms." The *Time* cover story of the previous November came to life. The hits were real and savored by the camera and the narrator, Walter Cronkite, who although not yet the voice of God, was moving toward that status. The impact of the program was stronger than anyone anticipated and left a lasting impression on the nation, especially those middle-management softies in suburbia.[1]

The growing media attention was accompanied by growing attendance figures. The 1959 New York Giants drew an average of 65,026 to Yankee Stadium, a 33 percent increase over the previous season. Average attendance in the NFL grew each year from 1953 to 1959. Profits were up across the league, television ratings were increasing, and the AFL was about to open for business. The game was never more popular, and the popularity had only just begun to grow.[2]

A New Leader for a New Era

The death of Bert Bell left the NFL with an acting commissioner just as a war developed between the NFL and the new American Football League. It was a conflict that the NFL owners wanted and were determined to prosecute to the finish. Among those spearheading the NFL's effort was George Halas, who as a veteran of the AAFC war believed that strong action against the AFL was required. Halas, as head of the expansion committee, moved quickly, surveying his fellow owners on the issue of expansion while attending Bert Bell's funeral.

Before the owners dealt with expansion at the January 1960 meetings in Miami, they attended to the selection of a new commissioner. Halas held the key, as he was the deciding vote in that process. Seven teams supported Marshall Leahy, a San Francisco lawyer associated with the 49ers, who wanted to move league offices to that city. Eastern owners objected. Leahy had eight votes of the nine needed for election on three separate ballots. George Halas could have settled it all by voting for Leahy, but he knew expansion would be dead if he alienated either side on the vote for commissioner.

The meetings officially opened on Wednesday, January 20, preceded by four days in executive session, and then rolled on through the weekend without resolution. On Tuesday morning, January 26, after twenty-two ballots, Wellington Mara and Dan Reeves decided that it was time to find a compromise candidate. Mara and Reeves moved down their list, arriving at Pete Rozelle, the thirty-three-year-old general manager of the Rams, and youngest GM in the league. Paul Brown and Jack Mara liked the choice, and quickly Rozelle became the compromise candidate, and nearly as quickly

George Halas, Pete Rozelle, and Lamar Hunt at NFL Annual Meeting, March 22, 1971. AP Photo.

the new commissioner. In short order, expansion was approved. Dallas would enter the NFL in 1960 and Minneapolis in 1961, both cities with AFL franchises. AFL commissioner Joe Foss called the NFL action "an act of war" and promised a lawsuit and a congressional inquiry on antitrust grounds. A few weeks later Rozelle moved the NFL offices to New York.[3]

Lamar Hunt and the AFL

Before his death, Bert Bell had been involved in discussions with Lamar Hunt pertaining to Hunt's desire to purchase an NFL franchise, such as the Chicago Cardinals, and move the team to Dallas. Another option would be an expansion team. When those discussions failed, Hunt set out to organize a new league, envisioning a counterpart to the NFL with Bert Bell as its joint commissioner.

Hunt was typical of many football entrepreneurs and representatives of rising urban areas who looked on the National Football League with covetous eyes. By the late 1950s many of these potential owners were knocking on the door looking to join what was becoming an increasingly popular and exclusive club. Indeed the time seemed right for expansion. The economy was on the move and the demand for franchises was rising. The new sports theater of television was expanding, and as the demand for program content increased, television was beginning to take a further and serious look at sports. NFL owners, however, had no real interest in expanding their league, as rising demand and short supply of franchises was causing a rapid increase in the value of existing franchises.

Expansion was being discussed only because of the consideration of the "sports bill" in Congress, where under pressure the NFL found it convenient to pledge expansion with two new franchises by 1960. The bill had been passed in 1959 and gave professional sports limited antitrust exemptions for nonbusiness matters. With no real intention of fulfilling this promise, the league set up an expansion committee chaired by George Halas. Committee members made it a point to discuss expansion with city officials whenever the NFL played an exhibition game in a "potential expansion city." The charade was being played against an early 1959 owners' vote against any expansion for the foreseeable future. That would change abruptly.

This lack of vision within NFL leadership would soon be challenged and exposed by Lamar Hunt and "Bud" Adams, who put their oil money on the table in support of a new professional football league. At one point, said Hunt, "a light bulb came on" as it came to him that if he couldn't buy the Cardinals, and if the NFL was not going to expand, then why not start a new league?[4]

Indeed, why not? There were plenty of good coaches and quality players available. Thirty-six roster spots meant only 432 jobs were available for players in the NFL. With the growth of college football in postwar America and the demise of the AAFC, the supply of talent far exceeded the demand, something NFL owners liked, as it gave them more control over players and kept salaries down. The slow pace of desegregation in the NFL also meant that the untapped pool of talent in the African American community was very large.

Led by Hunt and Adams with their oil fortunes, it was clear that this new league was not going to be an underfunded venture. Hunt's father, H. L., was asked what he thought when after the first year of operations Lamar had lost one million dollars. H. L. pointed out that at this rate, Lamar would be broke in 123 years. There was money coming from other sources as well. Hotel magnate Barron Hilton in Los Angeles and Bob Howsman in Denver were men of some wealth. The team of Max Winter and William Boyer in Minneapolis were solid, and Harry Wismer in New York proved willing to spend his last penny on his team. Ralph Wilson, who had made his money in trucking, wanted a franchise in Miami, but when the Orange Bowl was not available, he settled on Buffalo.

What looked at first like an amicable coexistence between the two leagues quickly proved an illusion. Hunt and Adams were offered NFL franchises if they would drop their plans. In late August, Hunt received news that the NFL was going to expand by two teams, with Houston and Dallas the most likely candidates. He felt he had been stabbed in the back and that war had been declared. Hunt later said that his hope for cooperation with the NFL was "one of the more naïve thoughts in the history of American sports."

The NFL followed with an announcement that expansion would come in Dallas and Minneapolis, where George Halas had his owners in waiting. Houston was eliminated from NFL consideration because Rice University would not make their stadium available. The potential AFL owners in Minneapolis proved not as loyal as Hunt and Adams had been, and jumped ship when faced with a promise of an NFL franchise. News of the defection came at the AFL's November meeting in Minneapolis. The decision by Max Winter and his Minneapolis ownership group was facilitated by the local Stadium Commission, which would not sign a lease with the AFL, preferring to wait for the NFL. Oakland replaced the Minneapolis franchise in the AFL.[5]

New Life from a Near-Death Experience

Preparations for the 1960 season, the inaugural one for both the AFL and the NFL's Dallas Cowboys, began with the first AFL draft on November 23. This came shortly after the loss of the Minneapolis franchise and the addition of Boston. The new league was anxious to draft and get about the business of signing players ahead of the NFL.

Both leagues prohibited the signing of players with college eligibility remaining, but the desire to secure talent ahead of the other league trumped that rule. The first major signing battle between the leagues came over Billy Cannon of Louisiana State University. The Rams drafted Cannon and on November 30 brought him to Philadelphia under an assumed name, where GM Pete Rozelle negotiated several contracts. One was for a signing bonus of $10,000, one for $500 in travel expenses, and three contracts for each of three years at $10,000 per year. None of the contracts were signed, with the "understanding" that Cannon agreed to the terms. All this nonsigning signing was done to satisfy the power barons of the NCAA, who believed that signing a contract meant you were no longer an amateur, even though there were few amateurs playing football in the major colleges.

On January 1, 1960, at the conclusion of the Sugar Bowl, the LSU running back signed with the Houston Oilers and not the Rams. The Oilers offered a package worth $110,000, three times larger than his unsigned-signed agreement with the Rams. Cannon agreed to sign after the Sugar Bowl game, which he did beneath the goal posts, witnessed on national television by a waiting nation and Pete Rozelle. The Rams sued the Oilers, to no avail.

This was the beginning of a signing process that turned into a game of hide-and-seek. Players were taken off to undisclosed locations by one team and hidden from teams in the other league. The NFL created a special cadre of "baby sitters" whose job it was to keep a prized player away from the forces of temptation representing the AFL. The "baby sitters" became a part of the folklore of the war, which now seems amusing given how idiotic it all turned out to be. At the time, it was a high-stakes game involving something that could easily be termed "kidnapping."[6]

If the AFL was to survive and prosper, it would need more than millionaire owners and a league structure. It required visibility, credibility, and stability. Most critically it needed a network television contract to increase exposure and revenue. When the AFL organized, it adopted a television policy of revenue sharing first proposed for baseball by Bill Veeck in 1952, picked up by Bert Bell, and passed on to Lamar Hunt through Branch Rickey in 1958 in the Continental Baseball League.

Just when the AFL was organizing, the Gillette Company had $8 million in its sports advertising budget that it was no longer spending on boxing, while at ABC Roone Arledge was ready to launch the network's sports empire. In the end ABC agreed on a deal with the AFL for $8.5 million for local and national television for five years. The deal was contingent on the AFL selling 60 percent of the advertising spots for their games, which they did without much difficulty. The deal was sealed on June 9, 1960, and although it paid only $170,000 for each team in the first year, the value increased in each of the next four years to an average of $225,000 per season, a figure that exceeded the television income of the average NFL team.[7]

The AFL opened its first season in Boston on September 9, 1960, a Friday night, at the Boston University Stadium, where Denver defeated Boston 13-10. The NFL averaged 43,207 attendees a game, while the AFL drew 16,531. AFL franchises lost a collective $3 million in 1960 and $2 million the following season. Hope that relief would come through the $10 million antitrust suit against the NFL was dashed on May 21, 1962, when a federal court dismissed the case. Judge Roszel Thomsen ruled that NFL actions against the AFL, such as placing franchises in direct competition with the AFL in some cities, was undertaken not to ruin the AFL team but rather to open competition with them. If the AFL and NFL had been even marginally equal as competitors, the decision would have been more convincing. As it was, several AFL franchises changed ownership and the Chargers relocated from Los Angeles to San Diego before the 1961 season.[8]

Many perceived the new league to be more daring, more exciting, and simply more fun than the established and conservative NFL. Slowly a small and loyal following grew across the country, as football fans discovered the wide-open game of the AFL on their television sets. Nonetheless it was the NFL that offered the established and iconic star players. NFL television ratings exceeded those of the AFL, and NFL attendance passed the three million mark in 1962.[9]

The landscape of the NFL changed permanently with the coming of television, the AFL, and the commodification of nearly everything. Change and rebellion were in the air, some of it serious and some trivial, some lasting and some ephemeral. The style of the game changed, as did the racial makeup of teams, the relationships between players and coaches and owners, and the way in which the game was consumed via television. The biggest difference was the sheer amount of money that flowed over the NFL and the impact that had.

Each league produced its own heroes and memorable moments, and each league featured personalities that came to represent, at least in a superficial way, the divisions that had developed in the larger society. These heroes in turn exploited their celebrity and fame for their own advancement, speaking and acting to and for those who admired them. The culture wars, born in the 1960s, were played out in microcosm on the stage of professional football in front of an audience growing in size and intensity.

In 1962 the AFL Championship Game in Houston featured the Dallas Texans and the Houston Oilers before a standing-room-only crowd of nearly thirty-eight thousand. The Texans scored the first seventeen points of the game, then the defending champion Oilers scored the next seventeen. The game was settled after seventy-seven minutes and fifty-four seconds when Tommy Brooker of the Texans kicked a twenty-five-yard field goal. Inclement weather across the country may have been the catalyst for fifty-six million people to watch this game on television. The impact may have been comparable to the Colts-Giants 1958 overtime game, in that it was the first time many of the television viewers had witnessed an AFL game. Given the drama, many no doubt returned to watch another AFL game. Shirley Povich, columnist for the *Washington Post,* marked this game as the true birth of the AFL, writing, "The AFL was born at the age of three, so magnificent was this game." It was also the death of the Dallas Texans, who became the Kansas City Chiefs two months later.

If those first-time AFL fans who were captivated by the 1962 championship game tuned back in for the 1963 regular season finale between Oakland and Houston, they saw a game that seemed to the casual fan of the sixties to be a typical AFL battle, all offense and no defense. In the first half the two teams amassed a record seventy points, forty-nine of those coming in the second quarter. Seven touchdowns came via the air and three on the ground, with one of those a punt return. The game was tied at the half at thirty-five. Four more touchdown passes came in the second half, and the game was decided on a thirty-nine-yard field goal with 4:37 left in the game as Oakland won 52-49. Tom Flores of Oakland had seventeen completions, of which six were for touchdowns, while George Blanda completed twenty passes, five for touchdowns.

AFL fans came to admire the creative, daring, and wide-open style of play. Teams seemed to go for it on fourth down more than in the older league. In Kansas City Hank Stram used different offensive sets and motion in a multiple offense. There seemed to be more trick plays, more long bombs, and of course the two-point conversion that invited fans to second-guess the coaches. It should have been called the **A**lways **F**un **L**eague. In fact, statistical analysis debunks the notion that the AFL did not play defense, and it was the AFL that pioneered the bump-and-run pass defense.

The AFL had some of the great coaching minds in the history of professional football. Sid Gilman was known as an offensive genius. Weeb Ewbank was the only coach to have won championships in both the AFL and NFL. Lou Saban won two championships with Buffalo and was later the man who designed offenses for O. J. Simpson. Hank Stram of the Chiefs and Al Davis of Oakland became two of the great rivals in the final years of the AFL, carrying the rivalry into the NFL, and both had innovative football minds.

The AFL brought a number of innovations to football. In the matter of numbers worn by players, the AFL abandoned the NFL scheme of numbering by position. AFL players wore white cleats, popularized by Joe Namath in the midsixties, while the Kansas City Chiefs put their names on the backs of their uniforms, becoming the first in the big three professional sports to do so. Uniform style too could seem quite bizarre and odd to traditionalists, and even to some AFL fans. The AFL was credited with producing brightly colored uniforms and getting people to rethink uniform design. On the other hand, the 1960 Denver Broncos' brown and mustard-yellow uniform is generally considered the worst in the history of pro football. It was accentuated by brown and mustard-yellow vertically striped socks that were so ugly they were burned by their coach during a practice. The Broncos wore them for more than two seasons, seemingly before discovering just how ugly they were.[10]

Desegregation Gets New Life

The AFL provided leadership in professional football in the area of race. In 1963 the Dallas Texans drafted Junious "Buck" Buchanan from Grambling in the first round of the AFL draft. Eddie Robinson, the Grambling coach, said that this opened the floodgates for players coming out of black colleges. The AFL also had the first black middle linebacker, Willie Lanier of the Chiefs in 1968, a spot considered a "thinking position" because the middle linebacker was the defensive signal caller. Denver's Marlin Briscoe in 1968 and Buffalo's James Harris in 1969 became the first two black quarterbacks in the postsegregation era.

The AFL produced the first major act of protest over race. It came in January 1965 at the AFL All-Star Game in New Orleans. Black players were unable to get taxis and were shut out of nightclubs and restaurants on Bourbon Street despite guarantees from local officials that there would be no discrimination. The players were subjected to racial slurs and insults. Facing these issues, twenty-one black players met and voted to boycott the contest. After it was clear that they would not change their position, Commissioner Foss moved the game to Houston, where it went off without incident.

Michael Oriard argues that the AFL All-Star Game incident "marked the end of pro football's official accommodation with segregation," as it demonstrated that football had the power to effect an end to discrimination. The NFL would not use this power until 1991, when Phoenix lost its Super Bowl because Arizona voters rejected Martin Luther King Jr. Day as a state holiday. The AFL position on race didn't happen by accident, and many of the African American players and others have credited the AFL leadership on race to Lamar Hunt, league founder and owner of the Kansas City Chiefs. When the Chiefs won Super Bowl IV against the Minnesota Vikings, Kansas City had a team that was half African American, and that was no accident. Hunt gave complete backing to Chiefs' head coach Hank Stram. Both Willie Lanier and Bobby Bell believed that Hunt was the key to the AFL openness.[11]

If Lamar Hunt was a leader in the area of desegregation of professional football, Pete Rozelle was at best a follower. One of the most blatant examples of racist policy in the National Football League was the continuing segregation of the Washington Redskins and owner George Preston Marshall's insistence that his team would never have an African American player. It is generally accepted that Marshall was the person most responsible for the implementation of segregation in the NFL in the early 1930s. He said, "We'll start signing Negroes when the Harlem Globetrotters start signing whites."

In 1961 there were eighty-three African American players in the NFL, and Washington was the only team that remained lily white. As a result the Redskins and Marshall became a target of protests by civil rights groups at NFL meetings and at Washington home games at Griffith Stadium. The Washington press, too, was highly critical of Marshall's refusal to change.

Stuart Udall, the Secretary of the Interior in the Kennedy administration, was the key figure in forcing Marshall to desegregate his team. The Kennedy administration made a significant number of appointments of African Americans, and in early March 1961 issued an executive order creating the President's Committee on Equal Employment Opportunity. In this climate the segregation of the Redskins could not go on.

In October 1961 the Redskins began playing in D.C. Stadium. Because the stadium was financed with public funds and was located on National Park Service land, the Interior Department could deny its use to anyone practicing discrimination in hiring. When Udall notified Marshall that he must desegregate his team or lose use of the stadium, Marshall tried to laugh it off and went to the press to criticize Udall and the federal government. Marshall claimed that his team was southern, with a southern radio and television network, and players recruited from segregated southern white colleges. Somehow he seemed to think this absolved him of the need to change team policy.

Commissioner Rozelle reacted by trying to avoid the problem, saying this was a club matter and not a league matter. After Udall made it clear that the government was not backing down and NFL owners complained to the commissioner about the negative publicity, Rozelle met with Marshall and persuaded him to comply. Marshall announced that his team had no policy of discrimination, and he prepared a list of five players who he promised he would draft in December if they were still available when Washington picked. Udall agreed to the compromise, saying the Redskins would be allowed to field a segregated team in 1961 but no longer. In October picketing continued at the games, and the leading politicians in Washington honored the pickets and did not attend Redskin games. President Kennedy declined an invitation to a game.

There were other rumblings of change in the NFL in the early '60s. Jim Brown made it clear that he and his Cleveland teammates would not accept housing segregation during team travel, as did Philadelphia fullback Clarence Peaks. After Bobby Mitchell was traded to Washington he continued to speak out against quotas. Don Perkins spoke out against segregation in Dallas, both on the team and in the city's housing practices. At one point a number of African American NFL players called on Commissioner Rozelle to resign because of his insensitivity to racism in the league.[12] He, of course, ignored the call.

Final Battles and Settlement

Meanwhile the AFL-NFL conflict continued. The signing of Joe Namath by the New York Jets on January 2, 1965, set off a new phase in the war between the AFL and the NFL. The total contract for three years and one option year included signing bonuses and a Lincoln Continental, as well as scouting jobs with the Jets for two brothers and one brother-in-law. The Jets sold $200,000 worth of game tickets in the week following the signing. The football world was shocked by Namath's contract, and salaries were pushed upward across both leagues, with rookies the big winners.

For the AFL, the new players and the big money meant jumps in attendance. From 1963 to 1966 average attendance grew from 21,584 to 34,291, and the Jets as the big spenders were the big winners, with a 400 percent increase in attendance during that period. In 1966 the Jets averaged 59,395. Television ratings jumped as well, with a 7 percent increase for the NFL in 1965 and a 25 percent increase for the AFL.

The war included a battle over expansion. In 1965 the AFL announced that an expansion franchise was being awarded to Atlanta. Rozelle immediately ordered a poll, which not surprisingly indicated that the people of Atlanta would prefer to have an NFL franchise rather than the lesser brand. Next, as had happened in Minneapolis, the stadium board that controlled the leasing process would not sign a lease with the AFL if they could get one from the NFL. In short order, the NFL owners awarded a franchise to Atlanta's Rankin Smith for $8.5 million, and forty-five thousand fans stormed the ticket office to become season ticket holders. Smith was essentially guaranteed a profit. The AFL shifted their view south, first to New Orleans and then to Miami, where Joe Robbie and Danny Thomas led a syndicate that paid $7.5 million for a franchise. However, the racism evident in New Orleans during the 1965 AFL All-Star Game took that city out of consideration.[13]

The battle over players remained at center stage. In 1965 the two prizes were Gayle Sayers and Otis Taylor. The Kansas City Chiefs were involved in both cases. They signed Taylor, while Sayers signed with the Bears. Al Davis got the jump on everyone by signing Fred Biletnikoff *before* drafting him. Estimates were that signing bonuses in 1966 ran as high as $25 million. This madness finally pushed many toward a merger between the leagues.[14]

The end was near, but more bloodletting was needed and more ill will was generated, as was a great deal of intrigue and double-dealing before the end came. With the spending getting out of hand, in the spring of 1966 Tex Schramm contacted Rozelle about the possibility of a merger. Rozelle checked with the lawyers and was told that a merger would need an antitrust exemption from Congress. The commissioner appointed Schramm to represent the NFL in talks with the AFL, and naturally Lamar Hunt represented the AFL. Rozelle was not interested in a merger because he thought the NFL would win the war, but the owners were pressing him.

On April 4 Schramm and Hunt began a series of secret meetings. Schramm told Hunt that the NFL was ready for a merger, that all AFL teams would come into the new league, and that Pete Rozelle would be the commissioner. Two days later a new obstacle appeared when Al Davis was selected the new AFL commissioner following the resignation of Joe Foss. Hunt and Schramm continued their meetings in secret. By early May Schramm felt he and Hunt had made significant progress. Al Davis was feeling even better as he prepared for a fight, unaware of any negotiations. Hunt informed AFL owners of the talks and the news got a mixed reaction, with Davis the strongest opponent. Billy Sullivan and Ralph Wilson were added to the AFL negotiating team and things seemed to be moving toward a merger. Trust, not surprisingly, was a major issue.

On May 17 the issue of trust came back into focus as the Giants, desperate for a placekicker, broke the unwritten rule prohibiting signing players from the other league by inking Pete Gogolak of the Buffalo Bills. Pete Rozelle approved the signing on the grounds that Gogolak was a free agent. NFL owners were shocked by Rozelle's approval, which showed he had no interest in a merger. Lombardi called it a disgrace and told Mara that he had put the league in jeopardy. Al Davis was delighted and renewed his call for all-out war. The Raiders signed Roman Gabriel of the Rams, the Oilers signed John Brodie of San Francisco, and teams discussed other potential signings.

Rozelle then appointed a committee of owners to develop a merger plan. Lombardi and Rosenbloom told Schramm to inform Rozelle that it was time for a merger, and that they would like him to lead the process, "but we're *going*, with or without him." Rozelle was "stunned and furious" but after composing himself, and no doubt considering his future as commissioner, told Schramm, "If that's what they want, let's go do it." So the race was on to see if a merger could be in place before Davis succeeded in blowing the whole thing apart. On May 31 Schramm presented a plan that he and Rozelle had worked out, and he told Hunt it would be all or nothing. Hunt took the proposal to the AFL owners, who disliked many aspects of it, but in the end they relented.

The final issue was expansion. The new AFL franchise would draw players only from the AFL teams, while the payment for the franchise would go to the NFL. On June 5 those problems were ironed out, and on June 7 the NFL owners approved the plan. That night Davis was informed he would soon be out as commissioner. Schramm, Rozelle, Hunt, and NFL Executive Director Jim Kensil worked out a press release, which went out the next afternoon, June 8.

The terms of the agreement were few. There would be no relocation of franchises, the AFL would pay $18 million to the NFL over twenty years, and $10 million would go to the Giants and $8 million to San Francisco for territorial indemnity. Two expansion franchises would be added by 1968, one in each league. There would be a common player draft after the 1966 season, and interleague exhibition games would begin in 1967. A common regular season would start in 1970. In the meantime both leagues would continue their television contracts for the four years remaining on them, and each league would keep its own income. A world championship game would be played between the leagues beginning in 1966, and Pete Rozelle remained commissioner of the new NFL.[15]

Congressional approval would be needed for the merger. It would not be easy, despite the initial positive reaction from Senator Philip Hart of Michigan, who headed a Senate Anti-monopoly subcommittee and was himself a former minority owner of the Detroit Lions. The House Judiciary Committee was headed by Emmanuel Celler, who had been a key figure in passing the Sports Broadcasting Act of 1961, but he opposed the merger. When the Justice Department threatened a lawsuit without congressional approval, Rozelle told the press that the entire merger might be in jeopardy.

To get around Congressman Celler's opposition, Rozelle contacted Congressman Hale Boggs of Louisiana to see if something could be done. Boggs, whose popularity in Louisiana needed a boost because he had supported civil rights legislation, was told that if the merger was approved New Orleans would get the next NFL franchise. To circumvent Celler, Boggs attached the merger legislation as an amendment to a vital budget bill that was certain to pass, while Senator Russell Long of Louisiana handled the technicalities in the Senate.

A meeting was held between Boggs and Rozelle so that the commissioner could express his thanks to the congressman. There are differing accounts of this meeting, with Michael MacCambridge's the most colorful. Near the end of the meeting Rozelle told Boggs he didn't know how he could ever thank Boggs for his assistance. Boggs was taken aback: "What do you mean you *don't know* how to thank me?" he said. "New Orleans gets an immediate franchise in the NFL." Boggs then suggested that the vote could still be postponed, which stopped Rozelle in his tracks as he was leaving the room. Rozelle quickly responded, "It's a deal congressman. You'll get your franchise." By this time Boggs was irritated and uttered a line to Rozelle that no doubt through the years many others would have liked to deliver: "If it doesn't work out, you will regret this for the rest of your fucking life!" In 1967 the Saints came marching into the Crescent City.[16]

There was still work to be done on the merger. The three most urgent matters were the expansion of the NFL to New Orleans, preparations for the championship game, and the rules for the first combined draft. Voting to expand to New Orleans was a simple matter, because it was politically necessary. An enormous domed stadium was being built, ownership was in place, and the NFL did not share the qualms of the AFL over the racial climate in the city. On November 1, 1966, All Saints Day, Rozelle arrived in the city to announce that New Orleans had been awarded an expansion franchise. In mid-December John Mecom Jr., a Texas oilman, was introduced as the principal owner and president of the team that would officially become "The Saints" one month later. On September 17, 1967, the Saints opened their season at Tulane Stadium, losing 27-13 to the Rams in front of a crowd of 80,879 that roared when John Gilliam ran back the opening kickoff of the game for ninety-four yards and a touchdown for the Saints. It was not an omen.

In another story of league expansion, Paul Brown had been preparing to acquire an NFL expansion franchise for several years, and he had settled on Cincinnati as the best location. When Atlanta was awarded the fifteenth franchise in the NFL, Brown knew there would be a sixteenth, which he intended to get. Brown's ownership group was awarded the Cincinnati franchise a few months later, at a cost of $8 million.[17]

There were in fact many small issues that had to be resolved, and they were settled with little rancor. Roster sizes varied, the number of players allowed under contract varied, and there was no minimum salary in the AFL. Television contracts were different. Length of training camps differed by one week, as did the trading deadline. Waiver rules and procedures differed, as did penalties for gambling, which in the AFL resulted in a lifetime ban. Such simple matters as home jersey colors varied by league, and in addition the AFL teams had their names on the backs of the jerseys. Pension plans had different coverage and amounts. Playoff systems were different, as were the financing of the league offices. The AFL used the two-point conversion and the leagues used different balls.

The New League Takes the Spotlight

The Merger Committee took up the matter of a championship game at their first meeting in the summer of 1966. Among considerations was a name for the game. Lamar Hunt used the term "Super Bowl" inadvertently during the discussions, a term that came to him after watching his children playing with a "Super Ball." No one, including Hunt, cared for the name, and Rozelle had strong feelings against it. Lacking a catchy name, the first game would simply be the AFL-NFL World Championship Game. In the press, the electronic media, and on the street, the term "Super Bowl" came into use immediately.

The words "Super Bowl" did not appear on game tickets until Super Bowl IV, which still carried the designation "Fourth World Championship Game." Not until Super Bowl V was the designation World Championship Game dropped, and for the first time roman numerals appeared on the tickets. Hunt may have found it corny and Rozelle may not have liked it, but as is the way with language, common usage can trump all other considerations.

Rozelle hoped to stage the game at the Rose Bowl, but opposition from the Rose Bowl Committee, the Big Ten Conference, and the Association of Western Universities, as well as the rent demanded by the City of Pasadena, California, and Rose Bowl directors, prevented that from happening. As for television coverage, both networks were authorized to broadcast the game for a rights fee of $1 million each. Both networks promoted their coverage heavily in the weeks before the game. CBS charged $85,000 per minute for commercial time, while NBC offered one minute for $75,000. Attendance at the Los Angeles Coliseum was 63,036, which left more than thirty thousand empty seats. Television ratings were high, as sixty-five million tuned in, or about one-half of the televisions that were on in America, for a game whose outcome was a foregone conclusion, and a game not available in the country's second-largest television market.[18]

The first two Super Bowls held no surprises. The Green Bay Packers handled the best the AFL could offer and NFL superiority was validated. It was, however, the end of one era and the beginning of another. Super Bowl III was a sensational event and raised the AFL to the level of the NFL. The Jets, led by Joe Namath, beat the Baltimore Colts, a nineteen-point favorite to con-

Football—The New National Pastime. Joe Heller's Football Cartoon, "Football Season."©HELLER SYNDICATION All Rights Reserved.

tinue the NFL dominance. Indeed Rozelle had announced that the NFL was considering a change in the playoff format that would allow two NFL teams to meet in the Super Bowl. That issue died in Miami, along with a number of myths about the inadequacies of the AFL held by the NFL establishment in their smug self-assuredness.

From the beginning of Super Bowl week, Joe Namath was the big story. On Monday he got into a shouting match with Lou Michaels of the Colts at a Miami nightspot. He entertained the press with his comments and by playing the role of bachelor on the make. Supposedly Namath was asked by a reporter if he had taken basket weaving at the University of Alabama, and Joe replied no, it was too difficult, so he took journalism. This is one of those stories repeatedly told about Namath that may or may not have been true, and may or may not have taken place at Super Bowl III.

The greatest sensation came on Thursday night at the Miami Touchdown Club, where Namath was honored as Player of the Year. MacCambridge tells this version of the now legendary guarantee: Joe thanked the single girls of New York and his teammates for contributing to his success. At some point someone in the audience shouted, "We're going to kick your ass." Namath's response was, "Hey, I got news for you. We're gonna *win the game,* I guarantee it." No one took it too seriously, as it was just Namath running his mouth. One who did take him seriously was Vince Lombardi, who told reporter Jimmy Cannon, "This kid can beat them."[19]

He did.

The Jets dominated the Colts, and the game was not as close as the 16-7 score indicated. The Colts were 13-1 and considered by many as one of the greatest teams in NFL history, while the Jets were regarded as the third-best AFL team. The Jet defense picked off four Colt passes, Matt Snell ran for 121 yards and caught four passes for forty yards, while Namath passed for 206 yards, going 17 for 28. The Colts did not score until 3:19 remained in the game.

Namath's performance was sweet for AFL supporters, who savored any and all victories over their senior partner. The AFL was regarded as a second-rate football league by the football establishment. Everyone in the AFL resented this view, none more than the Chiefs' head coach, Hank Stram. In the first year of exhibition games between the two leagues, Kansas City thrashed the Chicago Bears 66-24, leading at the half 39-10, with the only Bears touchdown coming on a kick return. After the last touchdown by the Chiefs, Stram went for the two-point conversion, as he had a special resentment of George Halas, who referred to the AFL as "that damn Mickey Mouse league."

Super Bowl IV was truly special for Hank Stram and the Kansas City Chiefs, as they totally dominated the Minnesota Vikings. Stram was wired by NFL Films, and when the film was released his unbounded joy was a sight to see and hear. It was also proof positive that the two leagues had achieved parity, and competition up and down the leagues was strong. Super Bowl III had not been a fluke. It was the tenth anniversary of the AFL and the last game played by an AFL team. If Rozelle had been secretly pleased by the Jets' win over the Colts, then he was even more so after Super Bowl IV. When he presented the Super Bowl Trophy to Lamar Hunt, Rozelle no doubt thought back to the first AFL game he had attended with Hunt in Kansas City in November 1966. Hunt called this victory "a satisfying conclusion to the ten years of the American Football League."[20]

When the merger was first announced, the two leagues maintained their separate identities. Expansion franchises were added to each, with the final step being the end of the AFL and the setting up of two conferences, the AFC and the NFC. From the start there were differing views of the new configuration. The AFL-NFL Championship Game had proven attractive to the public, so why not retain the identities of the two leagues within the new format?

After Super Bowl III the issue of realignment was still not settled. At the 1969 annual meeting, the Merger Committee made a proposal that things should not change. Rozelle was comfortable with that, and there was no objection by NFL owners. For Paul Brown there was a major problem with the decision. At the joint meeting of the two leagues, Brown said that he only had accepted an AFL franchise in Cincinnati with the understanding that there would be a merger of the leagues. He did not want to be in a conference where he would be consistently on the short end of a 16-10 vote and where the AFC influence would be limited. Rozelle made it clear that there would be thirteen teams in each conference, and that meant three NFL teams would be required to move to the AFC. There were no immediate volunteers.

When a special meeting was held in May, Rozelle let it be known that it would continue until restructuring was settled. For the first three days the leagues met separately. It was finally decided that three teams from the NFC would move to the AFC. The owners took a one-week recess, and Rozelle continued talking with individual owners. The meeting reconvened on May 7. In the midst of this, Art Modell was rushed to the hospital with stomach problems. The days dragged on. Finally at 1 A.M. on Saturday May 10, Rozelle called the press together and announced that three teams were moving to the AFC: Pittsburgh, Cleveland, and Baltimore. The key people in the decision were Art Modell, Art Rooney, and Carroll Rosenbloom.

The AFC was divided into three divisions, with Baltimore in the East along with Buffalo, the New York Jets, Boston, and Miami. In the Central were Cincinnati, Cleveland, Pittsburgh, and Houston, and the West had Kansas City, San Diego, Oakland, and Denver. The fans in the three affected NFL cities were angry, but they would get over it. The three teams each received $3 million to ease their pain.

Finally, in January 1970 at Super Bowl IV, the new NFC alignment was agreed upon. The owners considered nine plans, discarded four, but failed to reach an agreement. In the end the five plans were put in a hat and Rozelle's secretary, Thelma Elkjer, came into the meeting and pulled a piece of paper out of the hat: Plan Three. In the East would be New York, Washington, Philadelphia, Dallas, and St. Louis; in the Central Chicago, Green Bay, Minnesota, and Detroit; in the West San Francisco, Los Angeles, New Orleans, and Atlanta. Inequities in travel expense and gate receipts would be balanced by compensation. This configuration pulled out of a hat lasted for thirty years.[21]

The final sorting was nearly completed, and the 1970 season began with realignment in place. The NFL was about to depart into a new era ushered in by Monday Night Football in a realigned league. Television coverage and money would jump to undreamed-of levels, labor issues would become chronic, and lawsuits would abound. Rozelle's magic would be severely tested by a myriad of elements in the new NFL.

The NFL was driving professional football from respectability to the pinnacle as the number-one spectator sport in the nation, the new national pastime. Heroes and characters seemed to be everywhere as subjects of public admiration and adoration.

A Troubled Decade

The decade of the sixties can be characterized by an assault on what David Zang termed the "American One Way." This is the notion that in America and for Americans there was only one truth on any subject, and that particular truth alone held the floor in public belief and commanded conformity by all. In some ways the "American One Way" was a product of the cold war that demanded cultural conformity and unity against communism. In some ways it is linked to the Puritan concept of a "city on a hill" and American exceptionalism. The "American One Way" took a beating in the 1960s in every nook and cranny of American life, including within the culture of the National Football League.[1]

From the beginning Pete Rozelle established his authority as commissioner and built his image as a leader with vision, a ruthless negotiator of formidable skill, and a commissioner who had tight control over his league. As the quintessential public relations man, Rozelle placed image at the top of his priority list for the league, and he saw himself as a defender of the "American One Way."

In retrospect some cracks in the facade of the NFL surfaced in Rozelle's first years as commissioner, although at the time it was not obvious. Indeed the commissioner's leadership seemed to belie any such possibility. Nonetheless, three of the dominant personalities of the decade—Jim Brown, Joe Namath, and Vince Lombardi—illustrate the fissures of change that were forming across society and across the league. Each represented one shard of the breakage produced when the "American One Way" shattered under the pressures of political and cultural change.

The Authority

Early in 1963 Pete Rozelle made what he called the most difficult decision of his tenure as commissioner, although what made it difficult may not have been as obvious as it seemed. For two years Rozelle had received reports about players gambling and having connections with gamblers. In addition there were reports, along with plenty of evidence, that Baltimore Colts owner Carroll Rosenbloom was a high roller, bet on NFL games, and had indirect connections with organized crime. In January 1963 reporters pressed Rozelle on the rumors of a gambling scandal. On January 9, he confirmed the rumors.

That same day, Rozelle interviewed Green Bay Packer halfback Paul Hornung, who initially denied then admitted to gambling after failing a lie detector test. A few days later the NBC Evening News aired an interview with Detroit Lions lineman Alex Karras in which he admitted betting on NFL games. Both Karras and Hornung were suspended for the 1963 season, and Lions coach George Wilson and several of his players were fined for betting on the 1962 championship game.

Simultaneously the commissioner was dealing with gambling charges surrounding Rosenbloom, as well as more serious issues. Rosenbloom was the business partner of Louis A. Chesler, an associate of Mafia kingpin Meyer Lansky. Chesler controlled three companies in which Rosenbloom had an interest. In 1958 Chesler and Rosenbloom advanced money to Mike McLaney, a professional gambler, to purchase the Hotel Nacional and Casino in Havana, Cuba. Rosenbloom supplied $200,000 for this purpose. In addition to their business associations, Rosenbloom and Chesler were betting partners.

Rozelle has been charged with using the Hornung and Karras case to cover up the Rosenbloom issues. The suspensions meted out to Hornung, Karras, and other players and coaches were not applied to Rosenblooom. The commissioner did not explain why a suspension should be applied to players and not owners because it could not be explained. As historian Michael Lomax concluded in his study of the affair, Rozelle had established a double standard for players and owners. Rosenbloom was every bit as guilty as the players and probably more so. To Michael Oriard it is clear that Hornung and Karras were scapegoats for the larger problems around the league.

Rozelle's action was a message to fans that "they could trust him to safeguard 'the integrity of the game,'" a phrase Oriard finds simultaneously potent and meaningless. What this meant was that the game should be free of all corruption in reality, but more importantly that it should "appear uncorrupted to the public." For Rozelle, as with all good public relations types, "reality and image are indistinguishable."

If this is what Rozelle hoped to achieve, he could not possibly have done better. The press focused on the players and praised Rozelle for his decisive and principled actions. Tex Maule in *Sports Illustrated* called Rozelle a "strong commissioner" and not just some "glorified secretary." Arthur Daley of the *New York Times* praised him for not trying to soften the blow but facing it head-on. *Sports Illustrated* underlined it all by naming Rozelle their "Sportsman of the Year," the first time a non-athlete was so honored. Rozelle hired James Hamilton, a former intelligence officer for the Los Angeles Police Department, as full-time head of security for the NFL and expanded the NFL's surveillance unit. The objective was to instill the fear of God, or of Rozelle, into the players.

In the end the gambling issues never were resolved. A decade later *Business Week* reported that there was a feeling that pro football tolerated gambling, and the responsibility for that was laid directly at the feet of the commissioner. Ron Powers found irony in the entire affair: "What Rozelle and the NFL people never seemed to fully grasp, is that the public didn't care about this connection."[2]

Another test of Rozelle's authority came when George Halas verbally assaulted game officials following a Bears' game in San Francisco in 1964. Rozelle handled the incident quietly but firmly and established his authority over a league founder, and did so without publicly humiliating Halas. Rozelle also had a test of authority with George Preston Marshall over television policy and quietly won that one as well.[3]

Misstep

For all of his public relations savvy Pete Rozelle's one major mistake in his first years as NFL commissioner came in a public relations blunder of considerable proportions. On Friday, November 22, 1963, President Kennedy was assassinated in Dallas. For the nation, and for Rozelle, it was a traumatic event. The immediate question was what to do about the games scheduled for Sunday afternoon. Many public events were cancelled, including a large number of college football games scheduled for the weekend, and the AFL cancelled its games.

Rozelle decided the games should go forward. Owners Art Modell and Art Rooney (and in some accounts, Dan Rooney) called the commissioner to urge cancellation. Rozelle called presidential press secretary Pierre Salinger, who encouraged his friend to have the games proceed. There were no contests scheduled in Dallas or Washington, Salinger argued; the president would have wanted the games to go forward. In announcing his decision, Rozelle noted that it was traditional in sports that athletes perform in times of great personal tragedy, and "Football was Mr. Kennedy's game. He thrived on competition."

This may have been the only case when the AFL achieved higher approval ratings from the public than the NFL. Many NFL owners and players were distressed by the decision and didn't want to play. CBS refused to televise the games and did not pay for them. The scene at the stadiums varied widely across the country, with a somber atmosphere in some locations and a sense of release in others. Rozelle took a beating in the newspapers, where he was described in the most uncomplimentary terms of his career. However just a few months later *Sports Illustrated* chose him as "Sportsman of the Year," describing the decision as an act of courage. Other Rozelle confidants and biographers have subsequently supported the decision to play.[4]

NFL Films

NFL Enterprises had been in existence since late 1959 and was operated by Roy Rogers, Inc. By 1962 it had grown into a profitable business, and one year later Rozelle convinced the owners to create "National Football League Properties, Inc." to serve all the teams in the NFL in the "areas of youth sports competitions, publishing, advertising and merchandising." Standardization of policies and products was one of the first results. This proved to be a financial bonanza as well as a way of further advertising the league and its teams.

The following year Rozelle brought NFL Films in-house as a promotional vehicle for the league and a means of glamorizing the game while presenting it to the public. NFL Films was the creation of Ed Sabol, an amateur filmmaker, art major, and former football player. He bought the rights to film the 1962 Championship Game from the NFL for approximately $3,000. Sabol's success in creating highlight films of games was followed by the creation of team highlight films.

At the NFL spring meetings in 1965 the owners decided to buy Sabol's company, Blair Films, and rename it "NFL Films" with Sabol as its director. Soon Sabol's crews filmed all games using two or three cameras for each. This led to the development of the "NFL Game of the Week" sponsored by American Express and distributed by CBS. Sabol used the camera eye, slow-motion footage, tight close-ups, and melodramatic narration by the booming voice of John Facenda. The soundtrack of classical music was punctuated with grunts, groans, and collisions, while the use of hand-held cameras focused on hands, faces, and the football, giving the films an artistic and majestic quality.

Michael Oriard called NFL Films "pro football's troubadour and epic poet." Michael MacCambridge summed it up with these words: "And so began the profligate documentation that would bring about the self-mythologizing of pro-football." If, as one of the cinematographers said, the goal was to create "reality as we wish it was," then certainly NFL films exceeded beyond anyone's wildest dreams. In its technical artistry it presented "a hyperrealism that is at once larger than ordinary life and more 'true' than the football we watch with our own eyes."

NFL Films and NFL Properties transformed professional football into a "life-style choice," from "something to do, to something to experience" and from a Sunday activity into "a seven day week part of the popular culture." The NFL wasn't just selling a game, "it created a full-force public relations strategy" to bring the game to what C. Wright Mills called the new America, "a great salesroom, an enormous file, an incorporated brain, and a new universe of management and manipulation," the world of the booming consumer culture where not only things, but also heroes and events, were consumed largely through television.[5]

The public relations apparatus was given another outlet at the beginning of 1963 when the Pro Football Hall of Fame opened in Canton, Ohio. Eleven of the sixteen inaugural members were present: Mel Hein, Curly Lambeau, Red Grange, Cal Hubbard, Earl "Dutch" Clark, Don Hutson, Johnny Blood-McNally, Sammy Baugh, George Halas, Ernie Nevers, and Bronko Nagurski. George Preston Marshall was ill and not present. Joe Carr, Bert Bell, Tim Mara, Jim Thorpe, and Pete "Fats" Henry were posthumously inducted. The NFL now had a national shrine to rival the Baseball Hall of Fame and Museum in Cooperstown, and soon the pilgrims were making their trek to the sacred place where pro football was born.[6]

Jim Brown and Race

Jim Brown was among the greatest players of his or any other era. He dominated the running game. He led the league in rushing as a rookie and in eight of his nine seasons. He gained 12,312 yards in his nine-year career, a record that stood for eighteen years. In his final season in 1965 Brown gained 1,544 yards, the second highest total of his career, scored seventeen touchdowns, and was league MVP for the second time. His last game, although nobody knew this at the time, was the Pro Bowl, in which he scored three touchdowns, gained sixty-four yards, and was named game MVP for the third time.

Jim Brown was chosen by the Cleveland Browns in the 1957 draft as the sixth overall pick. Coach Paul Brown was considering quarterbacks Len Dawson and John Brodie, but both were gone before Cleveland drafted. Instead,

Jim Brown and Muhammad Ali on set of *The Dirty Dozen,* August 5, 1955. AP Photo.

he turned to the powerful and graceful runner out of Syracuse University. It was a transformative choice, as Jim Brown led Cleveland to the Eastern Conference title his rookie year. The Browns remained a force throughout Brown's relatively short career.

Brown was a runner of extraordinary talent with remarkable lateral movement and tremendous acceleration, along with great speed and strength. He was nearly impossible to bring down even when the opposition was allowed to do anything they chose to stop him, including "punches to the ribs and kidneys, often in full view of game officials." He was kicked in the groin, his fingers were deliberately bent backward, and he suffered an unknown number of concussions. "I have never seen an athlete be as physically abused and still play at such a high level, as Jim Brown," recalled former Cleveland owner Art Modell. "Things were done to Jim that today would lead to players getting arrested." Through it all Brown retained a coolness that was a "learned and calculated response" to the abuse, both physical and verbal. He was known as a very quiet man, but his silence was really a means of maintaining focus.

As time passed, Jim Brown found it more difficult to remain silent, especially off the field, where he was expected to be docile. Black players were expected to be quiet in the face of the racism they faced, and never comment on the racial turmoil in society. If they did, they risked their jobs. Within a few years Brown left this role behind as he organized his black teammates into a politically active group. "They were a group of rabble-rousing, women-chasing partiers whose influence and organization skills spread across the league from team to team."

Brown was fully aware of the ten player quota per team and the general rule that black and white players were not allowed to room together. If there were an odd number of black players on a team, one would be given a separate room, even if there were an odd number of white players. Many white coaches and fans believed that blacks did not have the "intellect or vigor" to play professional football. Jim Brown was aware of and irritated by these views and was determined to disprove them.

Brown was increasingly vocal about racism in the NFL and throughout America. He was increasingly quoted in the media, made appearances on television, had his own radio show, published his autobiography, and became a controversial figure. The FBI too became interested in Jim Brown and began to keep a file on him.

After Art Modell purchased the Cleveland Browns, Jim Brown and Modell became close. Both came to believe that the game had passed Paul Brown by and he needed to be removed as coach. Jim Brown and many of his teammates felt that because of Coach Brown's inflexibility, Cleveland was losing games they should have won. As the relationship between Jim Brown and Art Modell grew, the relationship between the two Browns deteriorated, not so much over race as over the changing world, including the changing football world.

Paul Brown believed in total control by the coach, both of the team's operations and the players. He expected unquestioned loyalty and deference from his players and embodied the "American One Way." Over time that loyalty became something that Jim Brown and many other players could not give. Finally the players went to Modell with their views. Modell was looking for an excuse to fire Brown without having to take all the heat for the action. The stage was perfectly set and Modell fired Brown.[7]

Coach Brown's successor and longtime assistant Blanton Collier analyzed the Cleveland offense and moved to implement change. Jim Brown's rushing yardage doubled as he produced an NFL record during Collier's first season. In the second year the passing of Frank Ryan to receivers Paul Warfield and Gary Collins produced an offensive juggernaut and an NFL championship.

Jim Brown organized a support system for the black players who came into the Browns organization. He tutored them in professional behavior and policed them when they violated team standards. In 1964 Brown emerged into full public view as a militant as a result of the publication of his autobiography, *Off My Chest*. He wrote bluntly about his racial views and candidly assessed a number of football personalities, something that simply was not done by players, let alone black players. When asked if he was a black Muslim, Brown said no, but he approved of their principles and many of their actions.

Away from football Jim Brown created the Black Industrial and Economic Union, an organization designed to promote black businesses. It spread across the country and eventually attracted Ford Foundation funding. He started a film career that extended beyond his playing days, which allowed him to retire from football well before anyone expected. Brown was also known for his association with white women, which offended the establishment much more than the fact that he was cheating on his wife. He was sued for assault by a young woman, and when that case failed, she sued him in a paternity case, which also failed. But each of these cases became part of the public rap sheet repeated through the press over and over again.

In November 1965 Jim Brown was the subject of a *Time* cover story. It was generally complimentary and recognized his great talents and achievements on the field, but at the same time managed to include any number of racial stereotypes extant in the culture. After noting that Brown won the Hickok Belt as the 1964 Professional Athlete of the Year, *Time* added: "Jimmy seems to be shooting for still another title: Most Controversial Athlete of the Year. Flashy, arrogant, casually indiscreet, he drives a red Cadillac Eldorado," owns more suits than he can count, and "does not care much for people in general," nor does he "care what they think of him." Brown was "well known to the toughs and prostitutes" of Cleveland, sympathetic to the black Muslims, and critical of Martin Luther King Jr. The charges brought against him by women were mentioned.[8]

The '60s were a time of considerable turbulence in America. Cities were enduring "long hot summers" of violence and rioting. The civil rights movement was near its peak and in the media the terms "black power" and "white backlash" were used with increased frequency. The antiwar movement was well underway and the counterculture of sex, drugs, and rock 'n' roll had arrived. Words like *freedom* and *rebellion* were tossed around with abandon and were met by a call from others for order, restraint, and discipline.

To some in the NFL Jim Brown was somewhat menacing and represented an end to both the docile athlete and the compliant African American. One consequence was that Brown became a lightning rod for the NFL establishment and the white sporting press, who were filled with anxiety in this time of uncertainty and changing values. Brown had a complexity about him that defied the stereotypical categories by which the sporting world dealt with both athletes and African Americans, especially those of extraordinary talent. The only reassurance he offered was to Cleveland fans, who longed for a winning football team and a superstar to lead it.

When the volatile decade opened there were sixty-one African American players in the NFL, and in 1961 that figure rose to eighty-three. African Americans made up 10.5 percent of the U.S. population but 16.5 percent of NFL players. By 1968 the figure stood at 28 percent and in 1975 42 percent. The year 1982 was the last in which African American players were a minority in the NFL. Players faced discrimination wherever they were, on or off the field, but the numbers continued to move in the same direction. Quarterbacks remained white, while receivers were more and more likely to be black. Larry Csonka and Jim Kiick in Miami were among the last of the white running backs. As late as 1968, other positions not open to blacks were center and middle linebacker.[9]

By the end of the decade African American protest in sport was everywhere, and in 1968 Jack Olsen at *Sports Illustrated* wrote a story on the issue of racial discrimination in the NFL. Many denied it could exist, but he found otherwise. Olsen noted that quotas were a routine fact of NFL life. Each owner had a maximum operating number for blacks on their roster, but no one spoke of it publicly. Quarterbacks were not only white, but in 1966 eleven of the fifteen starting quarterbacks were from the South or Southwest, and although it would be denied universally, black receivers wondered if this tendency toward racism explained why they were not receiving as many passes as they expected. There were other positions that seemed to be reserved for whites. On a typical weekend there were no African Americans starting at quarterback or center, and of the thirty-two starting guards, twenty-nine were white. At linebacker forty-five of forty-eight NFL starters were white. The linebacker, reported Olsen, had to be white because the position required the player to be able to perform a number of different functions and, most importantly, to exercise judgment in a very responsible defensive position.

What positions would the African American play? On defense the cornerback required speed, the commodity that most black players had in quantities greater than whites. A retired linebacker told Olsen that cornerback was not a brains position and little judgment was required, so it was the perfect position for African Americans. On any given weekend in 1967 three-fourths of all cornerbacks in the NFL starting lineups were African American. One white player told Olsen, " . . . the prejudice is there. The league reeks of it. The way teams are composed. The way the locker room is laid out. The way Negroes are criticized more than whites. The way they're not supposed to know how to play certain positions. The way white players are allowed to boss them around and criticize them." A black journalist told Olsen that the teams "don't recognize the black man's mind." They only see the beauty and strength of the body. They "will tell you they don't discriminate, but they do."

Olsen found that the black professional athlete had two major complaints. First, he must be significantly better than his white counterpart; and second, after his playing days were over, there was no place for him in the game. Olsen noted that although only 25 percent of players in the NFL were black, 40 percent of the NFL all-star team was black. Despite this success, there was no room for African Americans in the front office.[10]

The contents of Olsen's article seem remarkable viewed in retrospect. Perhaps "remarkable" is not the right word, and "comical" would be more appropriate if the subject were not racism. Nonetheless it accurately represented prevailing views. Over the next few years there would be a not-so-subtle shift as more positions opened to African Americans. The Kansas City Chiefs' roster in Super Bowl IV was 50 percent African American, and this was not lost on the world of professional football when the Chiefs demolished the Minnesota Vikings.

When the changes came and African Americans approached a majority in professional sports, the assumptions of white superiority would no longer hold. New explanations of the sports universe were needed. *Sports Illustrated* once again stepped forward as Martin Kane's probing article, "An Assessment of 'Black Is Best,'" appeared in the magazine's Super Bowl Issue on January 18, 1971. This turned out to be an incredible mix of serious-sounding physiological science, rehashed anthropological racial theories, geographical differentiation, and pop racial explanations that anticipated the alcohol-enhanced theories expounded by Jimmy "the Greek" Snyder. There were explanations based on tendon, muscle, and body fat, as well as the black athletes' possession of "hyperextensibility." The story explored climate and its relationship to physiology, and differentiations were made between East Africans and West Africans. Black athletes were quoted on such theories as "survival of the fittest" in the slave trade and breeding practices on the plantations. The conclusion seemed to be that African Americans were possessed of superior speed and power, and this was the key to understanding their superiority in certain sports. Kane's piece even included a discussion of African American inferiority in swimming.

Reactions were mixed, with some *SI* readers dazzled by the brilliance of Kane's revelations. Others saw it as one more rollout of tired racial theories masking as science. Dr. Harry Edwards at San Jose State University wrote an extended response in the *Black Scholar* of November 1971. Edwards systematically dismantled the assumptions and conclusions of Kane's piece, and stressed social and economic conditions as the dominant factors in the emerging majority presence of the African American athlete in sport. Edwards warned that such thinking as found in the *SI* article allowed whites to continue to deny the intellect, character, and hard work of African Americans.[11]

Jim Brown's impact on the NFL was multifaceted, but none was any more important than his role as a catalyst in this evolving discussion of race and the changes in racial policies. By the end of the 1960s those changes were just beginning to make an impact, and they were irreversible—and this was the case in both the NFL and within American society.

Joe Namath: Rebel with No Particular Cause

Joe Namath represented another kind of change and rebellion in the 1960s. From the moment of his signing by the New York Jets for $400,000, he was regarded as something different. No one had ever before provoked a professional football owner to cough up this sort of money. In what seemed like a flash, he became "Broadway Joe," perhaps the first true celebrity in professional football, or at least the first since Red Grange. He took on the playboy persona as if he were born to it, and then cultivated it with meticulous attention to detail. He was rebellious, wore white shoes, and defined "cool." He had long hair and sideburns and later a Fu Manchu mustache.

For middle America and those still clinging to the "American One Way," long hair on men was an ultimate transgression, something approaching the sign of the devil. It provoked an intensity of response from the defenders of values that is difficult to capture in retrospect. Clearly Joe Namath was a major problem, a rebel with or without a cause, although it probably didn't matter which it was. In his actions he echoed Marlon Brando's character in *The Wild One*, who when asked what he was rebelling against responded, "Whatta ya got?" Namath's hair carried political and cultural meanings associated in the mainstream with the antiwar movement and the new drug culture, and that was enough to stir controversy.

John Bloom notes that in their highlight film of Super Bowl III, NFL Films chose not to frame the narrative as the AFL defeats the NFL, but rather as a duel of male images won by Namath over Johnny Unitas. It was the future versus the past, with a victory for the countercultural view of masculinity. Namath's image did not square well with football's celebration of the tradi-

Broadway Joe—Jets/
Patriots Game at Shea
Stadium, November 11,
1973. AP Photo/Richard
Drew.

tional. Unitas embodied that masculinity. The contrasting images were woven
deeply into the fabric of the film, and in the end Namath's victory affirmed
the possibility that masculinity could come in a new form.

Dan Jenkins wrote about Namath's lifestyle in *Sports Illustrated* in the fall
of 1966 in a piece titled "The Sweet Life of Swinging Joe." The sweetness
included the women in the nightclubs "wearing their miniskirts, net stock-
ings, false eyelashes, long pressed hair, and soulless expressions." Namath was
in his element as "he slouches against the wall . . . a filter cigarette in his
teeth, collar open, perfectly happy and self-assured . . . sorting out the winners from the losers." Jenkins captured "Joe Willie Namath at play. Relaxing.
Nighttiming." The article described Namath in his penthouse "that features a
huge white llama-skin rug, an Italian marble bar, an elaborate stereo hookup,
an oval bed that seems to increase in size with each glance, a terrace, and a
couple of roommates . . ." As Michael Oriard put it, even Namath's hedonism
was tame: "booze and broads" rather than "dope and hippie chicks."

Just how serious a rebel Joe Namath was became clear in December 1968,
the morning after his appearance on *The Tonight Show,* when he agreed to
shave off his Fu Manchu. Team and league officials had been telling him to
get rid of the mustache because it was not good for the game. "Namath didn't
like anyone telling him how to wear his hair. But there was a higher princi-
ple at stake here: money." It was a "watershed moment in sports marketing.
Broadway Joe was like pornography for admen; he gave them hard-ons." He
could sell football or hair products for men. "He was changing the generally
accepted idea of the American athlete. In the not too distant future, athletes
would be judged not by their play but by the merchandise they moved." The
fee from Schick for shaving the mustache was $10,000, or about $10 a hair.

In the off-season of 1969 Namath's legend continued to grow. His autobiography was published: *I Can't Wait Until Tomorrow . . . 'Cause I'm Getting Better Looking Every Day."* He appeared in a film with Ann Margaret. Both enhanced his celebrity image and stirred the discussion of the topic "Joe Namath—rebel icon or curse of the permissive society?" For Tex Maule, the keeper of the sacred NFL trust at *SI,* it was clear that Namath had become "the folk hero of the new generation" as well as a great quarterback. "So the era of John Unitas ended and the day of Broadway Joe and the mod quarterback began. John is crew cut and quiet and Joe has long hair and a big mouth . . ."[12] It was a new world dawning. It too proved irreversible.

It is claimed that institutional structures with an economic hold on people can bring deviant individuals under control by applying leverage at the proper pressure points. In the case of Joe Namath, the commissioner of the NFL was presented with an opportunity to subdue the rebel in 1969. Following Super Bowl III Namath acquired an interest in a New York nightclub, Bachelors III. Because gamblers and mobsters frequented the club, Rozelle ordered Namath to sell his interest. Rozelle made it clear that Namath's integrity was not in question, but the NFL's image was threatened. Refusing to comply, Namath held a tear-filled news conference and retired from football.

Basically, as Oriard points out, this was another chance for the commissioner to stand up for the "integrity of the game" on the cheap. Such a vague and nebulous concept allowed the commissioner to wield control over those of his choosing, and in the process reinforce the notion that he was in control and the game was safe in his hands. That there were as many gamblers in NFL league meetings as there were at Bachelors III went largely unnoticed. Matters were settled within a month, as Namath agreed to sell his interests in the club and Rozelle welcomed this important human asset back to professional football. For Namath the affair enhanced his reputation as a rebel, although not a martyr, and gave his rebellious fans another reason to denounce the Establishment.

In 1969 *Playboy, Esquire,* and *Newsweek* all published profiles of Namath. He was more than just a football hero now, but he was more of a style rebel than a political one. He "rocked" the NFL in the '60s, and then in the '70s "the NFL absorbed him and his iconoclasm to attract and hold a new generation of fans." Namath's trajectory illustrated, as did so much of the rebellion of the '60s, the absorptive capacity of the consumer culture that Herbert Marcuse identified in *One-Dimensional Man.* Just as the peace symbol was turned into mass-produced jewelry, Namath become a highly marketable commodity for the New York Jets and NFL Properties. When his knees gave out, it only added to his appeal. He became "a wounded god, almost classically tragic," or as Murray Kempton put it: "He is most immortal in his mortality."[11]

Joe Namath had only one more level to rise, and that came in Super Bowl III with his "guarantee" of victory. He could not only play on bad knees, but he performed miracles too.

Vince Lombardi and a Troubled Tradition

In the milieu of American popular culture and in the public imagery of the NFL, a counterbalance to the rebels was needed, someone who represented the traditional values and the illusion of stability in a changing world. What the league needed was a highly successful person who could lead, inspire, and wield authority in the old-fashioned way, a stern father figure who continued to affirm the "American One Way."

Vince Lombardi was that man.

Lombardi first attracted attention as an assistant coach with the New York Giants, where he became known for his offensive coaching skills. With Tom Landry, the defensive coach, the two men created a powerhouse in New York. When the Green Bay Packers were looking for someone to take them out of their self-induced misery in the late '50s, nearly everyone suggested Lombardi. After some hesitation over moving to Green Bay from New York, and after securing full control over the team, Lombardi accepted the position as head coach and general manager. Results came immediately. In 1958

Vince Lombardi, 1960s. AP Photo/NFL Photo/Vernon Biever.

the Packers were 1-10-1. The following year, Lombardi's first season in Green Bay, the Packers were 7-5 and he was selected NFL Coach of the Year.

In 1960 the Packers won the Western Division as Paul Hornung set an NFL scoring record with 176 points. They lost the championship game to Philadelphia, the only time in his career that Lombardi lost in the title match. In 1961 Bart Starr emerged as quarterback and field leader of the team, and the Packers beat the Giants 37-0 in the championship game. The following year, the Packers missed a perfect season by one game as they lost to the Detroit Lions on Thanksgiving. In 1963 Hornung served his gambling suspension but the Packers still had an excellent season, finishing just behind the Bears. Hornung returned the next year, but the Packers had a mediocre season. In 1965 the Packers were back as NFL champions, and then in 1966 and 1967 they won the NFL title and the Super Bowl. Both of the latter NFL title games were tight ones with Dallas, and the game in '67 reached legendary status as the Ice Bowl. During Lombardi's tenure the Packers were 9-1 in postseason play. Twelve members of his Packer teams are in the Hall of Fame, along with Lombardi himself.

As Lombardi's Packers started winning, the national story became Green Bay, the little town that could, always an attractive theme in sports writing. But as the wins mounted, the story shifted to Lombardi. The first story line was how this man went to football Siberia and transformed a team of losers into winners. He made good trades and excellent draft picks, and used the power of his will to instill confidence, backbone, and above all toughness, both physical and mental. It was about discipline and repetition. Football was a violent game, but it was also a simple game involving blocking and tackling, and those who excelled at these basics, promised Lombardi, would win. He preached stoicism, an ability to deny pain and to overcome fatigue which, he said, "makes cowards of us all."

The year 1962 ended on an even higher note when Lombardi was *Time*'s cover story, "Vinnie, Vidi, Vici." The great man was on the cover standing in front of the Packer bench, with fans providing the background. A banner across the upper left proclaimed: "The Sport of the '60s." Inside, the prose was very *Time*-like: ". . . some 40 million Americans are enraptured by a modern day spectacle that even the Romans would enjoy." This was professional football, a game of "special brilliance, played by brilliant specialists." It was a game both simple and filled with complexities, at once mesmerizing and action-packed, with thrills presented at breakneck speed that leave the fans "literally limp." And in Green Bay, Wisconsin, devoid of Romans, the fans were convinced that they had the greatest team in the world, led by the greatest football coach in the world.[14]

With the *Time* cover story, Lombardi entered the category of "legend." From humble beginnings in Brooklyn, the son of an Italian American butcher, he played college football at Fordham, absorbed the lessons of a Catholic education, and was a member of Fordham's Wall of Granite. He worked his way up the football coaching ladder starting with high school, then working as assistant to Red Blaik at West Point, and then to the Giants, building his reputation as he went. Vince Lombardi saw the game in simple terms: "Football is two things. It's blocking and tackling. You block and tackle better than the team you're playing, you win." Any contradiction to *Time*'s analysis of complexity seemed lost on Lombardi, or perhaps just to the editors at *Time*.

Lombardi sometimes screamed so much that he lost his voice. He had a vocabulary that could make a sailor blush. Lombardi accepted nothing but a total effort by his team, and anyone who crossed him would no longer be a Packer. Fear was a major motivational tool. Lombardi could be simultaneously sentimental and brutal. He talked of the importance of God, family, and the Packers, and as he moved to national prominence he would add "nation" to that pantheon.

Leonard Schecter's *Esquire* profile of Lombardi was decidedly different in tone from the *Time* cover story. Titled "The Toughest Man in Pro Football," Schecter's article described Lombardi's methods as involving torture and sadism. Lombardi didn't want to see any acknowledgement of pain from his players, as he worked to "prevent injuries after they happened."

Lombardi was offended and angered by Schecter's piece, preferring to think of himself in other terms. To Lombardi football was about character and about what he called football's fourth dimension: "selfless teamwork and collective pride which accumulate until they have made positive thinking and victory habitual." He believed in fair play but not good losers, as good losing was "a way to live with defeat." He saw himself as a teacher, and not just of the techniques of football.[15]

By mid-decade as his team was executing a three-peat of championships, Lombardi grew impatient with the youth rebellion and breakdown of order in the streets. Politically he was a liberal, a friend of the Kennedy family, particularly Robert and later Ethel. Culturally he was a conservative. Sex, drugs, and rock 'n' roll did not mesh with his Catholic or his Italian American upbringing.

Lombardi was in increased demand as a speaker, especially within the business world, where executives loved football and convinced themselves that Lombardi's leadership style could translate to the board room. On the surface this was an attractive thought, but on close examination it was simply preposterous. His first talk in the business world was to the American Management Association in early 1966. *Time* reported that the audience was "almost spellbound" as Lombardi spoke about leadership. It became a standard speech adopted from the views of Red Blaik and Ignatius Loyola and organized into Seven Blocks. These included the importance of competition, the need for discipline, the centrality of character and will, and naturally the analogies between football and life. It played well in the boardrooms where business executives loved being associated with the jock culture.

Some talked about the coach as a political candidate, and Richard Nixon toyed with the idea of Lombardi as a running mate in 1968 until he found out that Lombardi was an admirer of Robert Kennedy. A football coach as a political leader was an idea that still seemed questionable, if not absurd, even in this decade of changing values. In the late sixties, as Lombardi became more strident in his attacks on the counterculture, he was in even greater demand as a speaker. But even then Lombardi was not totally reliable as a defender of tradition, as he was a strong advocate of racial equality and gun control and was critical of the authorities at Kent State after the 1970 shootings.

Still, in his final year in Green Bay, he supported the idea of a group of Green Bay women to stage "Pride in Patriotism Day" at Lambeau Field. Flags were draped all over the stadium, fifty thousand additional flags were distributed to fans, and the St. Norbert College Choir sang "This is My Country" and "God Bless America." The game was nationally televised and Pete Rozelle sent Lombardi a one-word telegram at the half: "wonderful."

By the late sixties football was clearly the national pastime. In 1969 William Phillips in *Commentary* called football the secret vice of the intellectuals. The game offered respectability to "the most primitive feelings about violence, patriotism, and manhood." Michael MacCambridge found that football could be characterized increasingly as the game of "Nixon's Silent Majority and Barry Sadler's 'Ballad of the Green Berets.'" President Nixon's obsession with football added to that view, and Vince Lombardi's elevation to national icon confirmed it.[16]

The popular images of Vince Lombardi and Joe Namath were in large part constructions of the media, but they were constructions that carried weight. Michael Oriard argues that these men symbolized football in the United States. Lombardi represented the NFL of the sixties; Namath represented the NFL of the seventies. They encapsulated "opposed values at the heart of football itself since its beginnings—violence and discipline on the one hand, artistry and self-expression on the other." These are the ancient archetypes, the "Apollonian and Dionysian principles in opposition: work and play, control and abandon, pain and pleasure, deferred and instant gratification." At the end of the decade "Lombardi was football's past, and Namath its present and future." It was no accident that while Lombardi was greatly admired by President Nixon, Namath was on Nixon's "Enemies List."

Vince Lombardi was in fact an old and traditional type, the "impassioned tyrant" that was as old as the college game. Football and military training had come together to give us the toughness of "Bear" Bryant and Woody Hayes, and the strict discipline of Paul Brown and Red Blaik. Lombardi brought these values together in one man and one place.

Namath was the future, and it was sealed in Super Bowl III when the Jets shocked the NFL with their win over the Colts. Lombardi knew this as well as anyone and it bothered him. Marie Lombardi reported that near his death, Vince called out from his sleep, "Joe Namath! You're not bigger than football." Perhaps not, but for many he was bigger than Vince Lombardi.[17]

The Perfect Television Game

The engine that powered the new National Football League was television. All else seemed to derive from it, as for three decades television provided at least half of the annual revenue flowing into the league. It was the Great Enabler for the league, the owners, the players, and for all those ancillary enterprises associated in any way with the NFL.

While television money was important, perhaps even critical, to the AFL, it became increasingly important to the NFL. During the '60s the NFL and television developed a relationship in which the senior partner was not always easy to identify. Was television dependent on the NFL? Or was the NFL dependent on television in a way the AFL clearly was? Or were these two partners locked in an embrace that both enjoyed, and which neither could afford to terminate?

As was made clear during the 1950s, the embrace was an enticing one. The NFL provided television with dramatic content at an inexpensive rate, while television provided the NFL entrée to the American home and psyche. It seemed like a win-win situation as these two new entertainment entities grew together. It was reality television before there was such a genre.

Pete Rozelle came from a public relations background and seemed to have a genius for dealing with television, and indeed with all media. He built upon the foundation laid by Bert Bell and quickly established the NFL as the senior partner in its relationship with television. His adeptness and growing reputation served the NFL very well and created an aura of awe around the commissioner. When Rozelle relocated the NFL offices to Rockefeller Center, he placed the NFL at the epicenter of Madison Avenue and the television networks, and adjacent to the money men of Wall Street. The move was a claim to status and power, and a message to all that the NFL was ready to operate at the highest levels of the new economy.

Rozelle seized control of the NFL, creating a clear sense that all league business ran through his office, and all owners were obliged to rally around the league rules and regulations. David Harris called this "League Think," and it built upon Bert Bell's notion that the individual interests of the teams were best served by financial sharing, a notion first put to the test in building the business relationship with television.

In a number of accounts, Pete Rozelle is credited with the idea of a unified national television contract with shared revenue. A recent biography of Bert Bell indicates that Bell was the first to propose the concept, and that he persuaded the key major-market owners—Halas, Mara, and Marshall—to support it. In his autobiography George Halas indicates that he, along with Bell, Mara, and Marshall, proposed revenue sharing. As the plan developed, Bell died of a heart attack before any action was taken, and nothing more happened until Rozelle was chosen commissioner. Actually, television revenue sharing was first proposed by baseball's Bill Veeck and was picked up by both Bell and Lamar Hunt. Behind this policy was a belief that, across the nation, many fans would be NFL fans, not simply supporters of particular teams. In the end, regardless of whose idea it was, this first television contract, argues Michael Oriard, "more than any other single factor . . . made the NFL what it has become."[1]

In late April of 1961, the commissioner reached an agreement with CBS on a two-year deal worth $9.3 million to broadcast all NFL regular-season games. Shortly thereafter the U.S. Department of Justice filed a civil suit over the contract, arguing that it violated antitrust law, and that the ruling by Judge Grim in 1953 allowing the blackout did not give the league the authority to negotiate a collective television contract. The NFL asked for a rehearing, and that request was denied.

The commissioner then sought relief in the U.S. Congress. Using his political contacts, which included presidential press secretary Pierre Salinger, as well as Carroll Rosenbloom's Kennedy connections and help from a number of other sports organizations, Rozelle proved effective. The NFL argued that an antitrust exemption was needed for the television contract so that the American public could watch the NFL every week, making it sound like a constitutional right.

In early September the House Judiciary Committee complied with the Sports Broadcasting Act of 1961 that allowed professional and amateur sports leagues the right to sell their television contracts collectively. It passed both houses of Congress with ease, and President Kennedy quickly signed the bill into law. In short order CBS and the NFL re-signed their $9.3 million contract. The lesson was clear. The NFL was dependent on government at all levels as a "powerful enabling but non-profit-sharing partner." Ron Powers saw this episode as "the first step in what would become a lifelong obsession of Rozelle's: the license to do exactly what he thought was best for the league, and for network television . . ." It might be said "A Czar Is Born."

From the start of his professional life in New York, Rozelle cultivated well-connected, powerful, and brilliant men: Herb Siegel, chairman of the board of Chris Craft, who was regarded as an "astute media man"; Jack Landry, the senior vice president at Philip Morris, which owned Miller Beer and became a major sponsor of NFL football; David Mahoney, chairman of the board of Norton Simon, a Park Avenue public relations firm; and Bob Tisch, president of Loews Corporation. This power quartet kept Rozelle informed on media developments and advised him on television network negotiations. In return, Rozelle offered good seats to NFL games and invitations to his parties. The other major player close to Rozelle was Bill MacPhail, the head of CBS Sports, whom some argued Rozelle both used and exploited in the NFL's dealings with the networks.[2]

Rozelle's Numbers

Rozelle developed the NFL's media relations and moved to exploit the media and manipulate the public, politicians, and anyone else deemed worthy of manipulation. The commissioner redesigned the NFL public relations apparatus with the help of Jim Kenzil, an Associated Press writer who became one of Rozelle's closest advisers.

Understanding the insatiable American appetite for numbers, Rozelle hired Elias Sports Bureau to pump out a never-ending stream of statistics for media and public consumption. *Sports Illustrated* fell under the commissioner's charms as it grew in tandem with the NFL. Tex Maule, in covering the NFL for *SI*, wrote in the reverential tones that came to permeate the magazine under Rozelle's watchful eyes.[3] This was the beginning of a process of change within the NFL, the world of sports television, and American culture.

The sixties was a watershed decade for sports and television. ABC's decision to develop sports as a central part of their programming moved the other networks in the same direction. The result was a sharp increase in the hours of sports on television, a quantum jump in rights fees, and a repackaging of sports to fit the needs of television. The influx of undreamed-of amounts of money into sports further transformed the sports culture. The battle over money led to an enhanced role of unions in professional sport, which in turn led to further conflict and disruption.[4]

The 1964 NFL television rights auction illustrated the growing power of the NFL, as well as the Machiavellian skills of the one man everyone seemed to trust, and no one should have. Rozelle proved a ruthless negotiator. All three networks were invited to submit sealed bids to this auction. Both CBS and ABC had inquired if Sunday doubleheader telecasts would be acceptable. Rozelle replied in the affirmative. NBC did not ask, and Rozelle did not volunteer the information to NBC because he felt it would be "unethical for me to reveal a rival's plan."

At each of the networks, the sports executives convinced the top levels of management to go to extremes to get this contract. Rozelle disingenuously claimed the bids were opened in random order. First came NBC's bid at $20.6 million, or $10.3 million per year, a significant increase over the expiring CBS contract. Next, ABC offered $26.4 million, or $13.2 million per year including doubleheader broadcasts, nearly triple the old contract. Certainly no one would go higher. The CBS bid was the winner, at $28.2 million, or $14.1 million per year. The announcement took the air out of the room, as it was the largest sports contract ever and almost seven times higher than the previous contract.

Tom Moore at ABC was certain that CBS had knowledge of the ABC bid the night before. Rumors circulated concerning inside information. Color commentator Pat Summerall recalled that he was with Bill MacPhail at CBS late in the week when MacPhail got a call from Rozelle, who told MacPhail to resubmit the offer because the commissioner did not want NBC to get the contract. NBC moved immediately to sign the AFL. The final number was $42 million for five years, a figure that ABC had no interest in matching. As a result, within about a week both leagues had new television contracts.

Rozelle was even more impressive in the negotiations with CBS over the 1966 contract. Many assumed that Rozelle had no leverage on CBS, as no other network was bidding. What the commissioner presented to CBS was the NFL option to create its own television network unless it got what it wanted from CBS. The network agreed to pay $37.6 million for two years, plus $2 million for the two championship games. Shortly after the deal was sealed, CBS learned that there was going to be a merger, and that the championship games for which they were paying $2 million were only preliminary contests to the AFL-NFL championship game. Rozelle's close friend Bill MacPhail asked why no one told him about the pending merger. The commissioner's friendly reply was "because it was our business and nobody else's."[5]

The 1970 NFL contract produced a stratospheric jump when a four-year agreement was signed between the NFL on one side and CBS and NBC on the other. Ultimately, the total package came to $142 million. The breakdown was $10 million for the Super Bowl, with each network getting two telecasts. The regular-season rate was $33 million per year, with CBS paying $18 million for the NFC and NBC paying $13 million for the AFC. The variance in price resulted from the differences in the television market sizes as well as previous Nielson ratings. The NFL had already signed an $8.6 million deal with ABC for *Monday Night Football*. This brought the total package to more than $46 million annually, or $1.76 million per team per year. It was a nice way to begin the life of the new NFL, but this was only a preview of the riches that lay ahead.[6] In Churchillian language, it was the end of the beginning.

The *MNF* Factor

The 1970 inauguration of *Monday Night Football* was transformative, as *MNF* quickly became a pop-culture phenomenon well beyond a mere football game. It also transformed the presentation of the NFL on television.

Rozelle had previously convinced CBS to televise five games on Monday night. Ratings were poor. Among the television people, only Roone Arledge believed that prime-time football would be successful. Most television executives were unwilling to upset their prime-time schedules and were uncertain about how advertisers would react. ABC had nothing to lose, as it was trying to challenge the other networks in prime time. With neither CBS nor NBC interested in a Monday game, Arledge and Rozelle began discussions in 1969. After initial hesitation ABC executives signed on, fearing that if they did not they would lose local affiliates to the Hughes Television Network, who wanted *MNF*.

Most television critics and historians agree that Roone Arledge and his vision was critical to the success of *MNF*. He was a rising star at ABC sports when he sent his now-legendary memo around the network in which he argued that the techniques used in other programming could be applied to football. He wanted to reach the female audience as well as males, and stressed the need to capture the pageantry of the game. He would use six cameras rather than three, and put cameras on jeeps, on platforms, and in helicopters. His use of the handheld camera and more sophisticated sound equipment gave the ABC telecasts a raw and more authentic feel. Television historian Ron Powers claimed that Arledge's style derived from "a high respect for the power of *story* over human imagination, a probing visual intimacy with the subject matter, a relentless, even obsessive preoccupation with the smallest detail . . ." Above all, Arledge knew that football was entertainment and treated it as such. It was no longer the CBS and NBC "game in the cathedral."

The first game revealed the new look. Arledge used nine cameras, including handheld cameras for sideline and reaction shots, split screens, end zone replays, and halftime highlights with the improvised narration by Howard Cosell. The three men in the booth were Keith Jackson for play-by-play, Don Meredith for ex-player analysis, and Howard Cosell for analysis and opinions. The interplay between Cosell and Meredith developed quickly and became the centerpiece of Tuesday morning discussions of the games. *MNF* was an immediate hit. It achieved a thirty-five share on opening night and a consistent Nielsen rating of eighteen, which translated to sixty million viewers. The average share in the first year was thirty-one. *MNF* occasionally reached into the top ten of prime time.

Cosell had an ability to irritate almost everyone, and fans of each team in a game felt he favored the other team. By the end of the first season Cosell and Meredith had developed a "shtick" in which Dandy Don played the role of the "good ole boy" and Howard that of the "big-mouthed New York Jew." In counterpoint, these two were perfect for those bored with football by the time Monday night rolled around. Roone Arledge, *MNF*'s creator, understood that fans were looking for entertainment, not just another game. Under his direction *MNF* offered melodrama and entertainment, with a little football on the side.

The Meredith-Cosell dance became an extremely popular part of the entertainment and brought Cosell a deluge of hate mail. At one point a Denver bar held a weekly raffle in which the winner was given a brick to throw at a television when Cosell's image came on screen. Cosell had a very high Q-rating as a highly recognizable public figure, with extremely high approval and disapproval ratings. The only thing that didn't seem to work well in the format was Keith Jackson, whose strong association with college football made it feel as if you were watching a perpetual Oklahoma-Nebraska game. (After one year of Jackson, Arledge replaced him with Frank Gifford.) Part of *MNF*'s appeal was its unpredictability. Late in a 1972 game in the Astrodome, with the home team getting hammered and the majority of attendees already in their cars heading home, the camera panned the crowd, settling in on what appeared to be a sleeping, scruffy-looking character. His eyes opened, and he shot his middle finger directly into the camera. Without missing a beat,

Meredith said simply, "Number one in the nation, and number one in our heart."

Fans learned to be creative with signs to get their faces or messages on camera. The most elaborate of such ploys came in 1980 in Tampa, where a large group of people held up a bedsheet with the words, "ABC and the BUCS." When the ABC cameras focused on the message, the sheet was dropped to reveal a second sheet that read, "Howard Sucks." The camera went elsewhere. Silence followed. It was the only time in the history of *MNF* that Cosell was at a loss for words.

It was remarkable just how much the habits of the nation were transformed. The football weekend had been extended, reducing some of the gloom at the start of the workweek. The ratings made *MNF* the king of Monday-night television. Fans gathered in bars and homes to watch the games and wait for the next outrageous or hilarious thing to happen. NBC and CBS could not compete, and at times gave up trying.

Monday Night Football enjoyed a 555-game run at ABC. The team of Meredith and Cosell ended when Cosell announced his departure at the end of the 1983 season, and ABC let Meredith go the following year. The heyday of the Cosell-Meredith team in fact was even shorter, as Meredith left after the 1973 season to pursue a career in television movies at NBC. He returned in 1977 but the Howard and Dandy Don magic did not. While Meredith was in exile, only former player Alex Karras added rather than subtracted in the booth. Karras's most memorable line was uttered when the camera focused on the shaved head of Otis Sistrunk. It was a cold night and steam was rising from his dome. Karras announced that it was Otis Sistrunk, "from the University of Mars." It was so memorable that the Oakland media guide listed Sistrunk's college as "The University of Mars" for the remainder of his career as a Raider.

From this point onward, various combinations came and went, with the exception of Frank Gifford. He remained with *MNF* through 1997, although his role changed from play-by-play to color commentator in 1986 when Al Michaels took Gifford's previous position. Michaels retained that job to the end of ABC's *MNF*. Analysts came and went, but only John Madden, while working with Pat Summerall at CBS and FOX and then with Michaels on *MNF*, attained similar renown to Frank, Howard, and Dandy Don.

MNF helped transform the way in which Americans watched football and other sports by turning announcers into stars and celebrities, and sport into entertainment. Prime-time sports became common, and ultimately the rule, as the World Series of baseball went to prime time in 1971 and the Olympics in 1972. *MNF* was a gathering point and a cultural phenomenon. Movie theaters were near empty on Monday nights, but bars were more crowded, and increasing numbers of people called in sick on Tuesday or came to work tired and/or hungover.

One of the market segments that the NFL long sought to exploit was the female viewer. *MNF* made an important step in that direction. Over more than three decades of *MNF*, the female audience for professional football grew to the point that by the early twenty-first century, females constituted half of the NFL audience. The NFL in turn did what it could to encourage this development by offering "NFL 101 Workshops" for women, ultimately reaching more than ten thousand participants. At one Atlanta workshop in 2004, 75 percent of the women attending indicated they played Fantasy Football. The Punt, Pass, and Kick competition drew more than a million girls each year. In 1994 the NFL hired Sara Levinson, former co-president of MTV, as the new president of NFL Properties, another indication that "NFL football was no longer your father's Sunday pastime." In a September 2004 Harris poll, 30 percent of women surveyed indicated that NFL football was their favorite sport, a larger percentage than the combined total for NASCAR, Major League Baseball, and the National Basketball Association.[7]

Once the merger was completed and realignment a reality, Pete Rozelle turned his attention back to the money machine that was television. New contracts needed to be negotiated and new ventures launched. The relationship between the NFL and television was about to take off. Television revenues were still a relatively small portion of gross revenues at 27 percent, while ticket sales were 61 percent of gross. Franchise values were increasing rapidly. A team worth $1 million when Rozelle became commissioner was valued at $15 million in 1973, and in that year only two teams were reported to have lost money. In 1974 things got better as the new television contract rose to $252 million, a sharp increase from 1970, bringing nearly $2.4 million per team per year.

Four years later a new four-year contract came in at $654 million, or $6 million per team per year. Many considered this an astounding amount of money until the next contract was signed in 1982. The total exceeded $2 billion for five years, at $427 million per year. This came to a tidy $14 million per team per year, which was close to what CBS had paid for the entire 1964–1965 package. This contract marked the first time that television money surpassed ticket sales as a revenue source. It also prompted Raiders owner Al

Davis to say, "Any dummy can make money operating a pro football club," a proposition that has become self-evident over the years.

The networks were also doing very well from their NFL connections. In 1981 *Time* estimated that CBS earned $25 million from the NFL broadcasts. Television ratings were at record levels. ABC paid $650 million for five years for *MNF*, which included prime-time games on Thursday or Sunday. It also paid $17 million for the rights to Super Bowl XIX. NBC quickly agreed to pay $590 million for their rights to the AFC. The CBS negotiations were a bit more difficult, but Rozelle had his trump card ready. He told CBS that he wanted $730 million, and when CBS hesitated, Rozelle went to ABC and asked Roone Arledge if ABC would be interested. It was. Rozelle immediately took that news back to CBS, who agreed to a "compromise price" of $665 million.[8]

The next contract in 1987 did not contain the kind of increases that had marked the previous deals. With the addition of ESPN to the mix, the overall price tag did go up modestly. ESPN bought into the NFL by taking on Sunday night games in the second eight weeks of the season, which in the short run was a bigger boost for ESPN than the NFL.

The Blackout

The rapid rise of television as a powerful medium was demonstrated in another way. The NFL blackout rule had been in force since 1950, when Bert Bell invented it. In 1953 the courts affirmed its validity. The blackout rule prohibited the televising of any home games, or those games of another team, into the territory of a home team, defined as a seventy-five-mile radius of the home city. As the NFL gained popularity on television and in the stands, there was growing fan dissatisfaction with the rule. If a game was sold out, why should the fans that could not get tickets be required to travel seventy-five miles to view a home game? Indeed, many did just that.

As the Super Bowl established itself, the same issue was raised. The seventy-five-mile rule was applied to any Super Bowl location, and so the game would be blacked out in the host city. This seemed unwise and self-defeating from a public relations perspective. It also raised questions about a city subsidizing an event of this magnitude with taxpayer money, and then having to face the reality that the taxpayers could not see the game. The issue came into focus at Super Bowl V in Miami, when Ellis Rubin, a Miami attorney, pressed the issue in the courts.

This was but the first episode in Rubin's campaign that ultimately attracted national attention. The NFL's position was clearly stated by Don Weiss, who arrogantly spoke for power: "Because we owned the rights to the games, we had every right to decide if, when, and where they would be televised." That taxpayer's money was being used to stage the games mattered not to Weiss, Rozelle, or the NFL.

The blackout issue remained a public irritant, particularly in NFL cities where sellouts were common and tickets hard to come by. Change, when it came, was not so much a matter of the NFL and Rozelle finding enlightenment as it was simply a case of pure power politics. When the Washington Redskins came to prominence in the early seventies under Coach George Allen, many Washington politicians and power brokers became avid fans. Tickets were very difficult to acquire.

The first break in the blackout policy came when the commissioner lifted the blackout for the 1972 Super Bowl in Los Angeles, when the Miami Dolphins completed their perfect season by defeating the Redskins. When the Fan-in-Chief in the White House, President Nixon, made it clear that he desired repeal of the blackout rule, Rozelle looked for compromise. The blackout would be lifted any time all seats in the stadium were sold within seventy-two hours of kickoff. As the 1973 season approached, legislation to that effect sailed through both houses of Congress and was signed by the president in what seemed like record time. The law was in effect for three years and when it expired, the NFL made no attempt to reinstate the blackout.

The impact of the end of the blackout was exactly as everyone but NFL officials anticipated. More games were now available to the fans of a home team, and this created more fans along with higher television ratings, which meant higher advertising fees for the television networks. It also created a new term, "no-shows," the body count for those fans who had tickets but did not attend a game. This no doubt created a new betting opportunity in some quarters.[9]

Cultural Power and the Media Revolution

In the late '70s the NFL made a major move into the premium cable world with the debut of *Inside the NFL* on Home Box Office (HBO). This was another step in spreading the artistry of NFL Films and satisfying a seemingly insatiable appetite for highlights and talk about the NFL. The show ran without commercial interruption and offered analysis by former players and coaches, along with prognostications. Ed Sabol's films, with all of their beauty and violence set to music, as well as unique camera locations and sound recording, made the HBO program another major showcase and promoter of the NFL.

Throughout the '70s and into the 1980s the popularity of the NFL continued to surge. In Washington the Redskins became a focal point for the political culture, with tickets at a premium. Divorce proceedings came to a breaking point over custody of the Redskin tickets, and wills were contested on the same subject. To have a "prime seat at a Washington Redskins game on a Sunday in Washington was for many of the rich and powerful more important than an invitation to the White House itself." The only thing better was to be in the owner's box, where Jack Kent Cooke basked in the glow of celebrity and power. The numbers of people watching the Redskins on television raised Nielsen ratings as high as seventy, and two Washington movie theaters offered the games on the big screen, covering their costs on concession sales.

Washington was not exceptional in terms of fan interest for the local team, and national interest continued to grow as well. In 1980 the League of Women Voters scheduled two of the presidential election debates for Monday night, apparently not aware that the NFL owned Monday night television. The debates were moved to Tuesday. It was also the year that the NFL began sending its televised product onto the international scene. In 1981 NFL television ratings hit a new high, as did attendance and interest in the Super Bowl. There were seemingly no limits moving forward.[10]

Terry O'Neil recalled that when he was a producer at CBS, one of the priorities was to "mythologize" the NFL. O'Neil claimed this was not manipulation, but rather "we simply got so intimate with the people, rivalries, and emotions of our conference we couldn't help but communicate them." Cowboys' quarterback Roger Staubach said he just felt that CBS was always "more into the game than anyone else." It could have been that the coverage had this character because, as O'Neil was told by Van Gordan Sauter when he came to CBS, professional football subsidized CBS sports because everything else either broke even or lost money. The NFL "covers the losses and provides our yearly profit." Sauter pointed to the "deeply embedded masculine culture in the networks" that led "the suits" to go most anywhere for a major event such as the Super Bowl. The prize NFL contracts were a sign of their status in television world.[11]

The world of television sports was at a crossroads in the late 1970s and early '80s. There were forces emerging that transformed the television industry and in turn impacted sports. The change can be dated from September 7, 1979, at 7 P.M. EDT when the Entertainment and Sports Programming Network (ESPN) began broadcasting out of Bristol, Connecticut. Initially regarded by some as a mad experiment, it grew rapidly and now dominates television sports.

To a considerable degree the future of ESPN was tied to the NFL. Initially offering highlights of games on a daily basis for multiple sports, ESPN began to develop shows featuring the NFL and making use of NFL films. One of the early programs featured Chris Berman, Paul McGuire, Terry Hanratty, and someone from a Las Vegas sports book named Austin. They talked about the upcoming games, showed some highlights, and then picked against the spread. It was highly entertaining, appeared to be improvised, and had an irreverent touch to it. It may have been a spin-off of Berman's character, "The Swami," who made his NFL picks on the overnight 3 A.M. version of *SportsCenter*.

In less than a decade ESPN became the first cable outlet to air NFL football live. Before ESPN, the major networks aired an average of eighteen hours of sports per week. That number quickly doubled and then continued to climb. Network hours were of course supplemented by cable hours, as national and regional sports networks popped up everywhere. Soon sports on television were omnipresent. This meant more dollars chasing after more sporting events, which became no more than programming to feed the insatiable appetite of the sports cable networks and their viewers. There seemed to be more and more highlights feeding the sports "news" programs that saturated cable and then satellite services, the latter being NASA's contribution to sports television.

The National Pastime and Obsession

For the National Football League the growth of television coverage not only increased the bottom line in the industry, it also expanded the visibility of teams and athletes both on and off the field. Through his stint at *MNF*, Howard Cosell was fond of saying that he would "tell it like it is," a phrase that became a staple of the national language, and not just in sports. By the end of the '80s such a declaration in the face of the information explosion seemed quaint, as cable networks rushed to tell it like it might be, or it could be, or how you might wish it to be. Athletes were now celebrities, and the NFL was ground zero for the creation of new celebrities and the cross-breeding of celebrities. Even the sports television hosts became celebrities. In a different twist, Michael Oriard wrote: "The awestruck fan sees the athlete as larger than life, the hip-ironic fan sees him merely as life-size, or smaller."

ESPN also changed the way sports were reported. It was criticized for creating a style that critics called "sports lite," with its emphasis on highlights that featured the sensational play or the flamboyant personality. It perfected, as Oriard says, "the art of storytelling for short attention spans." It glorifies pro football players and at the same time "deflates them with hip irony that characterizes our so-called postmodern culture, particularly the youth oriented part of it." While irony had always been present, Oriard argues that *SportsCenter* "brought irony closer to the center." Keith Olbermann once joked that he and Chris Berman were in prep school together and "took the same class in Wise Ass Sportscasting." If so, Dan Patrick and company perfected a style of self-promotion and fawning condescension perfect for dealing with celebrity athletes.

Television had an impact on other media, especially print, that had to change how it approached football, as well as all sport. Fans no longer relied on daily and weekly newspapers for results and game reporting. Television did that better than print could ever hope to do, delivering the results in a rapid fashion. The print media needed to develop another role. For some it would involve increased coverage of the personal lives and foibles of the players, while for others it meant a focus on legal and economic issues. *USA Today* ramped up their data presentation, introduced charts and graphs in color, and color photography. At *The Sporting News,* once known as "The Bible of Baseball," football pushed its way in and *TSN* moved to serve the NFL and college fans with more coverage. In addition *TSN* developed supplemental coverage of the NFL with highly popular newsletter subscription services for each of the NFL teams.

There have been many reasons offered for the success of the NFL on television and for its larger success across the nation. Michael Oriard sees football as a game that makes little sense in terms of the rules we live by, and this accounts for the power of its appeal "not just to the working stiffs wearing dog masks and barking in the end zone seats in Cleveland, but also to TV executives and CEOs in luxury suites." Others find the appeal within the testosterone factor and the violence, as clearly the game appeals to the infantile masculinity of many of its male fans. Marshall McLuhan found a perfect connection between the nature of football and nature of television technology and its interplay in the brain.

All of these factors were in play, but there was more. As a game, football reflects as well as any other the collective American culture in the second half of the twentieth century. The characteristics described by William Whyte in *The Organization Man,* and that David Reisman termed "other-direction," seemed to mesh perfectly to make football the new national pastime. The people-oriented team players of postwar urban America were given direction from others in their group. They responded well to conformity, authority, and organization.

American society had come to depend on this type of individual and this sort of behavior. Jerry Kramer in *Instant Replay* offered an excellent portrait of professional football as this other-directed game: "Assembly lines, computers, automated factories with their intricate precision movement of parts, mirror to modern man his society and his expected life-style. Professional football is this man's game. With its intricate and precision movements of eleven men, each one of whom must perform his small task so that the team can succeed, it reflects the ideals of the other-directed society."[12]

By the middle of the 1980s there was some concern in the NFL about what was happening in the television market. *MNF* had lost a bit of its luster, but the Super Bowl ratings continued to grow. The downside, if it can be called that, stemmed from the fact that the game seemed less and less important. A holiday atmosphere was growing around the Super Bowl, and the commercials began to attract more attention than the game. However, in 1985 and 1986 ratings records continued to fall, and *MNF* became the longest-running prime-time series in the history of television. Each year it seemed some new television ratings or audience records were set.

The Illusion of Declining Television Power

Despite all the record ratings in both 1983 and 1984, ratings for the regular season were down and advertisers were unhappy. There was even talk at the NFL meetings of cutting back on television. Teams faced the prospect of losing money, and there was little chance, reported Dan Rooney, that television was going to bail them out of their difficulties. Much of the difficulty owed to labor strife, and there were growing divisions among the owners.

Oddly enough, ESPN reported its first profit in 1985, with *Sunday Night Football* as their most important property. As a result, Getty Oil was able to sell ESPN to Capital Cities/ABC for $278 million, even though Getty reported that it had lost $67 million on the sports network. A decade later, when Disney purchased Capital Cities/ABC for $19 billion, the ESPN property was considered a key acquisition. By then ESPN had added ESPN2, ESPN Radio, and the ESPY Awards. *ESPN the Magazine* was launched in 1998. By 2001, according to the *Sports Business Journal,* ESPN was worth approximately $20 billion and was "the cash cow that drives Disney."[13]

In the late '80s and the '90s the boom in sports talk radio increased the stake many fans felt they had in their favorite NFL team. In this forum fans could take to the airwaves and tell the world what they thought about the new quarterback, the play calling last week, or the lack of imagination in the offensive scheme. Players, coaches, executives, and owners were praised and criticized with abandon by anyone who had a telephone and an opinion. Sports talk demonstrated the fan strength achieved by the NFL as fans talked about the NFL in and out of season.

The growing popularity of the NFL Draft as a "happening" was clearly related to sports talk, where the draft was a subject for year-round discussion. The draft may be the biggest, most popular nonsporting event associated with the NFL. The only real rival to this dubious title would be ESPN's two-hour special to announce the schedule for the upcoming season some six months before the season actually begins.

There are different accounts as to how the NFL Draft on ESPN came into existence. In one version, Commissioner Rozelle approached Chet Simmons at ESPN about covering the draft. The second account has Chet Simmons approaching the NFL. Rozelle's reaction was to wonder why anyone would want to do that. In one version, Rozelle was the man of genius and vision, and in the other it was Simmons.

The NFL Draft became a major hit in short order. Fans began showing up in big numbers, led at first by the fans in New York. They came wearing their team gear, cheering on their favorites, and ultimately passing instant judgment on the choices being made. Soon the draft moved to the weekend and to a larger venue. In 1984 Mel Kiper Jr., and his now-famous hair, appeared for the first time on the ESPN draft show, as he has every year since. Within a few years, Kiper became a year-round fixture at ESPN. Commercial time on the draft telecast sold out, ratings were escalating, and within twenty years the NFL Draft had more viewers than many college football games. Draft previews developed into a nearly year-round phenomenon on both radio and television. Then with the coming of the NFL Network, the whole thing was replicated on a second cable network. From there it went to another elec-

Saturating the Television Market. TANK MCNAMARA©2013 Millar/Hinds. Reprinted with permission of UNIVERSAL UCLICK. All Rights Reserved.

tronic destination, the Internet, and then to wireless electronic devices and platforms everywhere.

Finally in 2010, the seventy-fifth anniversary of the draft, the event moved to prime time with the first round on Thursday night and the second and third rounds on Friday night, with the other rounds on Saturday during the daylight hours. Radio City Music Hall was jammed for the event, top college players and their families were present, and the television audience on Thursday reached 7.3 million people, an increase of about two million viewers since 2009.[14]

The New Electronic Age

Television ratings, contracts, profits, and franchise values presented some paradoxical realities moving through the 1990s and into the twenty-first century. From 1981 to 2005, ratings went from seventeen in a more or less steady drop to ten and one-fifth. This could lead to pessimistic conclusions, but other information pointed in another direction. The NFL still offered advertisers the best opportunity to reach a general audience. Sunday afternoon games had higher ratings than prime-time programming on the networks. In sports programming, the NFL boasted twenty-two of the top twenty-five-rated telecasts, including all of the top ten. In addition the NFL continued to deliver the advertisers' preferred demographic. Television decision makers had to face a difficult question: which was more costly, having or not having the NFL?

The networks concluded that it was more costly not to have an NFL contract than to overbid for one. By the turn of the century, half of the league revenue came from television. This is one of the major reasons why NFL franchise values continued to rise. The price of an expansion franchise was $206 million in 1993 and rose to $700 million in 1999. *Forbes* reported that NFL franchise values increased eleven times faster than the S&P 500 between 1998 and 2006, as franchise values jumped 212 percent. In 2005 the average NFL team had an operating income of $30.8 million, up from $5.3 million in 1997. Even the lowly Arizona Cardinals, who suffered through nearly twenty years of losing, operated at a profit.[15]

The new technologies grew rapidly in the '90s and in the new century and further impacted the relationship of the NFL to the media. The advent of the personal computer opened up many new contact points between the fans and the NFL, the fans and teams, and the fans with one another. The NFL developed its own Web site, as did each individual team. Fans could go to these sites and find statistics, analysis, biographical material, the league and team histories, audio, and video. Tickets could be purchased there, as well as team merchandise. The Super Bowl had its own site. The fans of each team set up chat rooms and Web pages to discuss the teams, the players, the coaching, to call for the firing of coaches or changes in quarterbacks, or simply to spread gossip and rumor. The functions on these sites seemed to grow almost daily. Radio and television broadcasts became available on a subscription basis, as did the opportunity to become a team "insider." The NFLPA developed its Web site, where its side of labor issues and labor history were told. And it goes on and on. Players themselves developed their own sites, as did fans who developed electronic fan clubs.

In September 2000, NFL.com and team Web sites received 5.4 million unique visits, not simply hits. By 2004 this figure rose to 14.5 million and in 2005 to 16 million unique visits. The NFL generated revenue from Internet arrangements with AOL, CBS Sportsline, and Viacom. Ad sales were shared equally across the league. This allowed the NFL, its teams, and its players to send their message directly to fans without the interpretation or spin put on it by journalists. It has created a strong brand loyalty and has produced in recent years $3.5 billion in merchandise sales and additional millions in advertising revenue. The Internet technology has extended the NFL's reach across the globe, and it is directed not just at Americans living abroad but to fans from all nations.

Satellite technology made a strong impact in several areas. Most obvious has been the creation of "NFL Sunday Ticket" in association with DirecTV. Not only does it give the fan access to any game being played, but also such extras as multiple screens, a Red Zone channel that picks up any action that reaches inside the twenty yard line, and channels devoted to such special features as unique camera angles. DirecTV customers can download highlight packages to their digital video recorder (DVR) and receive all games in high definition (HD). The NFL enrolls subscribers to wireless and broadband broadcasts and a fantasy football program using NFL footage. Sprint contracted for exclusive and original NFL content for mobile phones, which included game updates, highlights, statistics, live video, and video on demand. And for those who lack some of these toys or who want all the games available by radio, especially for the automobile, there is Sirius Satellite Radio, which relays local radio broadcasts via satellite and offers NFL Radio when games are not ongoing.

Indeed radio has remained a significant player as a provider of access to NFL games. In 1980 CBS signed a four-year national radio deal with the NFL giving them radio rights to twenty-six regular-season games, including the Monday night game, and ten postseason games. Record radio audiences were registered for *MNF*. In 1985 NBC outbid CBS for twenty-seven regular-season and ten postseason games. In 1987 CBS was back, outbidding all others for a forty-game package over the next three seasons. Renewals between CBS Radio and the NFL continued until 1997 when Westwood One, a CBS property, signed a three-year deal for radio. The Westwood One connection has continued since, with the most recent contract worth $15 million per year. This contract included all games, preseason, regular season, and postseason, including the Super Bowl. On the Internet, "NFL Field Pass" now allows access to local radio broadcasts of games for a nominal subscription fee, and "NFL Talk Radio" is now offering a wide variety of podcasts.

The personal computer and Internet technology produced a major expansion of fantasy football. In a sense there has always been fantasy sport, played mostly by children using their creative impulses to fill a summer's day plagued by the horror of "there's nothing to do." There were also board games that had some of the fantasy qualities to them. Sometime in the late 1950s Wilfred Winkenbach, a part owner in the Oakland Raider organization, developed fantasy games for golf and baseball using statistics from the players in actual competition. In 1962, along with two writers at the *Oakland Tribune*, he turned to football. What started as modest and simple manually run leagues was transformed by the Internet into highly sophisticated operations played across the globe by individuals for money, or run by Web sites for various forms of reward. All major sport- and football-related Web sites now run fantasy football games of some variety.

The world of video games produced various pro football products, the most popular or visible being the Madden game, to which the former Raider coach and network analyst lends his name and perhaps some of his expertise. The release of "Madden NFL" is a major media event in and of itself, as it has become a singular honor for those who grace the cover of each year's version. Many cover players have suffered season-ending injuries that year, a phenomenon known as the "Madden Curse." The game can be played on an X-Box 360 and the current version of Playstation. Developed in 1989 for Apple Computers, it was known as "John Madden Football." It is now the product of EA Sports.

Satellite television facilitated the growth of sports bars. They offer multiple screens for NFL games. As clientele developed, many sports bars came to specialize by catering to the fans of particular teams. Both the Internet and local newspapers provide guides for fans to locate the sports bar in their area where they can be guaranteed of seeing their favorites, and share the experience with fellow fans. All across the world NFL fans found locations to watch the NFL in action.[16]

On January 16, 2003, the National Football League announced the hiring of Steve Bronstein as executive vice president of media and president and CEO of the NFL Network. Bronstein was a major figure at ESPN and a former executive at Disney. *Business Week* described the development as "evidence of the faster march into showbiz." The NFL Network, a twenty-four-hour cable network devoted to the league, began operations on DirecTV in November 2003. The network featured game highlights and replays, historical game highlights, documentaries, and talk and analysis programs, including lengthy pre- and postgame programming, live coverage of the draft, and the NFL combine preceding the draft. Late in the season, Thursday and Saturday night games were carried live, as well as games from NFL Europe. NFL Films became a major provider of content for the network.

The agreement with DirecTV, along with agreements with other smaller carriers, gave the channel considerable distribution. However, disputes with Comcast, the largest cable television provider, and other major cable carriers meant that large numbers of NFL fans did not have access to the NFL Network. The conflict involving cable charges and network placement on the cable menu, particularly with Comcast, moved into the courts and led some U.S. senators to raise the specter of a review of the antitrust exemptions in the Sports Broadcasting Act.[17]

Some have wondered if this media growth will ever stop. The answer seems to be no. In 2006 *Forbes* reported that although ratings seemed to be falling, NFL football remained the ratings king in prime time. Nearly three out of four Americans watched an NFL game during the 2006 season. When television contracts between the NFL and the three major networks were renewed for 2006, the league raked in an average of $2 billion a year through 2011. When ESPN picked up the *Monday Night Football* contract for eight years, they did so at double the rate previously paid by ABC.[18]

Finally, the significance of television and other media could be seen in the development of media training within the NFL teams, by the NFLPA, and by individual agents, contractors, and consultants. Everyone realized that television is where the money is, and that it is the lifeblood of the National Football League. Television fueled the league, shaped the league, and altered the game. The medium has been exploited unmercifully by the NFL leadership, who understood the relationship between television and the NFL, and how to gain and retain the upper hand in that relationship.

Any assessment of the impact of television on the NFL must take into account the impact of money and what that has done to the game. Michael Oriard described a tremendous change in the NFL, as it has gone from being a sports organization to become an entertainment and marketing group. The NFL regards itself as a brand, and pro football has become a product to be marketed. Oriard wonders what has happened to the football team and the players, who seem no longer to be the focus. Ben Rader thinks that television has "trivialized the experience of spectator sports." The essential drama of sport has been sacrificed to the needs of entertainment, and the sports themselves have been "contaminated with a plethora of external intrusions."

If one pays close attention to an NFL broadcast, you cannot help but notice that everything seems to be sponsored by something, with this process accelerating each year. If you attend a game, you are struck by how much time passes when absolutely nothing is going on, as timeouts for commercials are extended further and further. This in turn has increased the length of games. Some wonder how serious these problems are, and at what point the sports experience becomes secondary to the entertainment experience.[19]

7

The Cartel

When a joint business enterprise, or a cartel in the case of the National Football League, has great success in terms of massive revenues and considerable profit, one might envision a world of happiness and contentment. One might expect that as the pie grew, and as each piece of the pie got larger, those who fed off the pie would be grateful for their good fortune. In the NFL, where the term "revenue sharing" developed a sacred aura over the years, where dedicated owners had pulled together for decades to produce this successful sports enterprise, surely the achievement of prosperity that enriched one and all would be hailed as a stellar accomplishment.

So it was, to a point.

A sports cartel was defined by James Quirk and Rodney Fort in a paraphrase of Ambrose Bierce's definition of a Christian as: "a benevolent association that is organized to further the interests of sports fans, insofar as this is not inconsistent with extracting the maximum amount of money from them."[1] One small problem with cartels is that individual members, seeing the profits, have a tendency to look at their piece of the pie and imagine that it could be even bigger. They often believe they grow the pie more than others and deserve a larger piece. The magic word in this process is "more," and the word never heard is "enough."

The initial success of the NFL accelerated the search for more sources of revenue, ways to elaborate the product, and ways to spin off new ones. Although these activities often led to the expansion of the pie, at other times they could lead to conflict with "revenue sharing" and conflict within the cartel.

In 1973 the average per team gross revenue was $6.2 million. The average operating profit was $900,000 a year and only two teams lost money. This was not a huge business enterprise but it did represent considerable growth over the previous decades of the NFL.[2] Over the next two decades sports franchise values rose at the heady rate of about 22 percent per year. In the 1990s the rate per year decreased, but it remained in double digits. NFL franchise values followed the pattern at least until the late 1980s, when rising salaries and flat television revenues briefly slowed the trend. By the late 1990s the NFL average franchise value reached $205 million, and seven of the ten highest valued teams in professional sport were in the NFL.[3]

The Stadium Game

Increased television revenues, along with franchise movement and stadium construction, pushed team values upward. In addition average franchise values spiked when two expansion franchises were priced well beyond the preexisting market values.[4] If a team owned their stadium, the total value of the franchise increased. If the team didn't own the stadium, team revenues could be supercharged by generous contract arrangements with the governmental entities that built the structure. New revenues came through increased ticket prices and sales, heightened concession sales, and such innovations as luxury boxes, premium seating, and seat licenses, all of which sent revenue streams overflowing their banks.

The building of new stadiums by local and state governments was encouraged by a desire to acquire or keep an NFL franchise and thereby capture or retain the title, "Major League City." This is one of those ephemeral titles that developed currency in the second half of the twentieth century. Part of its power stemmed from urban boosterism and part from growing enchantment with spectator sports. Starting with the AFL in the 1960s the opportunities to acquire these markers of civic greatness became easier for two reasons: expansion, and the willingness to move a franchise for a price. For sports leagues a delicate balance needed to be maintained between supply and demand, so that becoming "major league" was possible but not too easy. As an added benefit, limiting franchises gave NFL owners the leverage they needed to extort their communities by threatening to leave for greener pastures.

That there is very little evidence that being "major league" has any real or measurable value seems to matter not one bit. One study of metro areas between 1958 and 1987 found no significant difference in per capita personal income between those cities that had or did not have a major league team. There is no evidence that a major league franchise makes a city more desirable or attracts new businesses, or in any way alters the economic status of a city. Many studies indicate that per capita income falls when sports franchises come to a city. The Kansas City Federal Reserve found that the value of new jobs and tax benefits of an NFL franchise for a city is about $40.3 million per year. This falls well short of covering the costs to a city that run to $100 million per year. Jobs gained versus jobs lost tend to cancel each other, and in most cases a stadium does not offer optimum land use. As for fans coming and spending money in a city drawn specifically by a sports team, this is generally not the case. Game attendance is generally tangential to the main motive to come visit a city.[5]

None of this seems to have mattered to anyone. In 1970 the Cincinnati Bengals moved into Riverfront Stadium and the Steelers into Three Rivers Stadium. The following year five teams moved into new stadiums. The majority of these were joint baseball and football facilities. Between 1972 and 1975 four teams moved into new stadiums. In 1976 both the Giants and Jets moved to the New Jersey Meadowlands but retained the name "New York." From 1974 through the end of the Rozelle era in October 1989, twenty-three of twenty-six franchises played in new or refurbished facilities.

In many ways the most impressive and most influential of all the new facilities in the early postmerger years was Texas Stadium in Irving, which opened in 1971. Dallas owner Clint Murchison was a pioneer. He was the first to play the suburbs off against the city. When Dallas officials did not give him the new stadium he wanted, Murchison talked with Irving politicians, where he owned a piece of land, and got what he wanted. Irving provided financing of the $25 million project by issuing thirty-five-year bonds. The construction contract was awarded to the Murchison-owned J.W. Bateson Co. Stadium management was awarded to Texas Stadium Corporation, a subsidiary of the Dallas Cowboys; concessions went to another Cowboys subsidiary; and the exclusive right to sell liquor went to the Cowboy's Stadium Club. Insurance was purchased from Kenneth Murchison Co., which had been founded by Clint Murchison's late uncle and in which Clint owned an 8 percent stake.

Clint Murchison further developed a concept that was already nearly a century old. A. G. Spalding built eighteen luxury boxes, containing armchairs, in his new stadium in Chicago in 1883, and Walter Camp provided luxury boxes for the wealthy at the Yale-Princeton game in the early 1890s. The luxury boxes in Texas Stadium were called "circle suites" and marketed as something akin to a second home. Anyone wanting a suite was required to buy $50,000 in stadium bonds, twelve season tickets at $1,300 per ticket for thirty-two of the next thirty-five years, and twelve memberships in the Stadium Club at $300 per season. The suites were basically an empty shell that were furnished by the owner according to their taste, or as was the case with many, their own tasteless[...]. The minimum cost over the thirty-two years was $643,400. The suites sold quickly as corporate money rushed in, owners clutching their tax write-offs as business expenses for the entertainment of clients.

The *Dallas Morning News* described one of these 172 suites adorned with "blue velvet Louis XIV couches, gilt armchairs, blue velvet draperies, mini-bar with leather armrests, tufted velvet love seats, crystal chandelier hanging from a vaulted gold ceiling, and hand-painted French panels concealing closed-circuit television sets for instant replays." Within ten years the suites were selling for $600,000 ($2,343 per square foot), and as time passed more suites were added, bringing the total to 379. In the early '90s they sold for around $1.25 million. Those who purchased stadium bonds saw nothing even remotely comparable in their rate of return.[6] Lessons were learned across the nation.

In 1975 the Louisiana Superdome opened, dwarfing the previous "Eighth Wonder of World," the Astrodome. The Minnesota Vikings convinced the state legislature to subsidize the construction of a domed stadium, for which the Vikings paid only 12 percent of the cost. The lure was keeping the Vikings in Minneapolis and revitalizing downtown. The first goal was achieved, and across the league such scenarios were replicated.[7] Dolphins' owner Joe Robbie conned both season ticket holders and the City of Miami. In New York, Giants owner Wellington Mara carted off millions in his deal with the New Jersey Sports Authority for a stadium in the Meadowlands.[8]

Expansion

Expansion was closely related to the stadium and movement issues. During the hearings before Congress to secure the Football Merger Act in the midsixties, Pete Rozelle testified that if the Merger Act was approved it would ensure expansion of the league all across the land. He promised two franchises by 1968, with many more to follow. The New Orleans Saints were on the field in 1967 and the Cincinnati Bengals followed in 1968. "Many more" failed to materialize, despite ever-growing demand. Four cities were quite active in their pursuit of an NFL franchise: Memphis, Phoenix, Seattle, and Tampa. A 1973 study commissioned by the NFL Expansion Committee and conducted by the Stanford Research Institute found that twenty-four cities were possible locations for NFL franchises.

When the NFL did not deliver on expansion, Rozelle heard from congressmen representing the powerful interests of projected expansion cities. Opposition to expansion came from those who understood the math of shared television revenues, and realized that one-twenty-sixth of something was larger than one-twenty-seventh of the same something. As David Harris notes, expansion of a monopoly is a delicate business in that there is a balance between the risks of overexposure and leaving a demand gap so large that someone might seek to fill it.

When Gary Davidson announced the formation of the World Football League in October 1973, it was clear that some thought the gap existed. The NFL responded in April 1974 when the Expansion Committee recommended two cities for entry into the exclusive club of the NFL, Tampa and Seattle. After considerable argument, the league set the price at $16 million each. Choosing ownership for the two cities proved difficult because the NFL was preoccupied with labor issues. Not until the end of 1974 did Rozelle announce that Tampa's ownership group was headed by Hugh Culverhouse and Seattle's by Herman Sarkowsky. Commissioner Rozelle let it be known that more would follow, and the league would move from twenty-eight to thirty teams. It took two decades for that to happen.[9]

Movement and the Courts

Under Pete Rozelle the movement of franchises was tightly controlled and impossible without his consent. Al Davis, along with the Los Angeles Municipal Coliseum Commission (LAMCC), challenged this control both on the ground and in the courts. The background of the Davis challenge involved Carroll Rosenbloom's dealings with the LAMCC, his desire and his decision to move the Rams to Anaheim, and Davis's discontent in Oakland, particularly over the condition of the Oakland Coliseum.

The relationship between Rozelle and Rosenbloom was an old and often rocky one. Trouble surfaced between them during the Hornung-Karras gambling scandal when Rosenbloom felt Rozelle had betrayed him by pursuing an investigation of his activities. Another issue involved Rozelle's voiding of a free-agent signing by the Rams, prompting Rosenbloom, at a league meeting, to threaten to get even with the commissioner. At a more petty level Rozelle, Rosenbloom, and Davis squabbled over Super Bowl ticket allotments and Rosenbloom charged Rozelle with ticket scalping.

Facing a decline in attendance and a decaying stadium in a decaying neighborhood, Rosenbloom requested and received league permission to move to Anaheim in 1978. The LAMCC applied for a new franchise and initiated a lawsuit against the NFL, charging the league with violation of the Sherman Anti-Trust Act by requiring unanimous league consent before a franchise could

Al Davis—NFL Annual Meeting, March 3, 1980. AP Photo.

move. The saga took another twist when in April 1979 Rosenbloom drowned while swimming in the Atlantic Ocean at his Florida home. The ownership of the Rams passed to his wife Georgia, who it was assumed would turn the team over to Rosenbloom's son, Steve. She did not. Instead she purged all of Carroll Rosenbloom's loyalists from the Rams front office. Within a few months she married Dominic Frontiere and then hired a personal public relations firm.[10]

Within the NFL Al Davis was regarded as an eccentric owner whose hostility to Rozelle had its roots in the AFL-NFL merger. Rozelle was irritated by a number of things, as Davis blocked his policy changes and defied the commissioner on several occasions. Davis had a long and impressive football resume and a reputation as a brilliant football mind. He became head coach and general manager of the Oakland Raiders in 1961. His habit of wearing silver and black, the team colors, spread to the fans. One of his players recalled that Davis had once told him: "Let me just say this, young man, anything good in this life is worth cheating for."

Rozelle came to the conclusion that Davis was a threat to the league, and moved to isolate him by turning several owners against Davis. At times, feelings ran high. During the 1982 league meetings in Phoenix, one owner placed a parrot at the check-in door. It was trained to say "Fuck you, Al Davis" whenever someone entered the room.

Davis was unhappy with his lease and the condition of the Oakland Coliseum, and looked to Los Angeles. He was also willing to defy the league and move the Raiders without league approval. Following discussions with Rozelle, the LAMCC concluded that the league would not permit any team to move to Los Angeles and that expansion was not in the cards.[11]

Negotiations between Davis and Los Angeles moved forward and received a boost when Peter Ueberroth, chairman of the U.S. Olympic Committee, assured Davis that the money for Coliseum improvements would be there, as the Olympic Organizing Committee agreed to an advance on rental fees. By late December 1979, final terms were near as the LAMCC and the NFL sparred in the courts, and Davis sparred with the Oakland Coliseum Board.

The LAMCC sought a reactivation of their *LAMCC v. NFL* suit and an injunction to prevent the NFL from taking actions to stop the move of the Raiders. Oakland reinvigorated its attempt to keep the Raiders by making a new offer to Davis. In February the mayor of Oakland and Davis had come to an agreement on a new lease, but when the Oakland Coliseum Board unilaterally changed its terms, Davis declared negotiations dead.

On March 1 amid a climate of threat and tension, Davis appeared at the office of the Los Angeles mayor, Tom Bradley, to announce the move. Rozelle with some hyperbole called it "apocalypse now" and Art Modell, applying a standard he would later fail to meet, declared that the league had "a strong moral obligation to Oakland for its previous support."

The NFL sought a restraining order and asked that Davis be removed from control of the Raider franchise. Davis was ahead of the game, sending Rozelle a telegram on March 6 informing him that the Raiders had already moved. When the vote was finally taken on the move, NFL owners voted twenty-two against, five abstentions, and one absent. More legal maneuvers ensued when Davis came with a suit of his own for $160 million in damages under the Sherman Act and joined the *LAMCC v. NFL* case. Davis named three people in his action: Pete Rozelle, Georgia Rosenbloom, and Gene Klein. Game on.[12]

For the next year the focus was on a public relations campaign involving the individuals named in the case. It got quite ugly. Bill Robertson referred to Klein as Rozelle's "hatchet man" and lap dog, while Rozelle referred to "Ayatollah Robertson" and called him "Al Davis's lackey."

Next on the public flogging rack was Georgia Frontiere. She married her seventh husband in a ceremony in Jacksonville presided over by Tampa Bay Bucs owner Hugh Culverhouse in his capacity as notary public. Steve Rosenbloom claimed that Culverhouse was running the Rams franchise. Rozelle saw no problem with this, and many owners were also untroubled as they felt that Georgia Frontiere had no mind for business. One owner dismissed her as a "crazy cunt," whose head rattled when she shook it yes or no.[13]

The trial finally opened in March 1981 and was expected to last four months, hear one hundred witnesses, and ring up legal fees of $5 million. The league position was that the procedures for moving in the NFL constitution were "valid, not anticompetitive, and a reasonable rule for leagues to have for the betterment of fan loyalty and stability." The NFL denied that the individuals cited in the suit were involved in a conspiracy, and claimed that the NFL was exempt from the Sherman Anti-Trust Act because the league was "a single economic entity with a unitary product and [therefore] could not conspire together to commit an antitrust violation." This latter argument was the opposite of what the NFL argued when defending themselves from charges of colluding to hold down player salaries. On that issue the NFL claimed that it was an entity of competitors and not a single economic entity.

All the principal witnesses performed well. Davis was the most impressive, taking on the NFL lawyers who questioned him in shifts. The judge told Davis he was the best witness he had ever seen. A number of the NFL's witnesses seemed to help Davis more than the NFL. Eagles' owner Leonard Tose tried to get Rozelle and Davis to settle, but Rozelle would not agree to meet Davis. Tose concluded that the problem was "nobody had balls enough to take Rozelle on."

After Davis testified, the trial lost its glamour. Two rulings by the judge were significant. First, when the NFL asked for a dismissal, the judge did not grant it, but he did dismiss the conspiracy charges against Rozelle, Frontiere, and Klein. On July 24 the judge made a second key ruling that the NFL could not be treated as a "single entity" for the purposes of the lawsuit. This cut out the heart of the NFL defense.

The case went to the jury on July 29 and deliberations went on for two weeks. On August 11 one juror, Tom Gelker, was found to have connections to football. The jury was deadlocked 8-2, with Gelker one of the two. Two days later the judge declared a mistrial. Davis charged that Gelker had been an NFL plant. Rozelle said he would have preferred to win, but was pleased the NFL didn't lose, and then attacked the Los Angeles media for being pro-Davis.[14] Another attempt at an out-of-court settlement was fruitless, as Rozelle would never settle with Davis. Rozelle also headed to Congress to seek a broad exemption from the Sherman Anti-Trust Act for the NFL and other sports organizations along the lines of the baseball exemption. For the most part there was little said publicly in the interim.[15]

The second trial began on March 30,1982. It was shorter and simpler than the first because the LAMCC dropped the conspiracy charges and the elimination of the NFL single entity defense. Both Davis and Rozelle repeated their testimony, with little variation. On May 7 the trial went to jury, and after six hours of deliberation it ruled in favor of Davis and the LAMCC, finding the NFL in violation of antitrust law and in breach of its contractual duty of good faith and fair dealing with Davis. Rozelle announced immediately that the league would appeal. Davis called it "justice rectified."

Within a few weeks the NFL got more bad news, as the jury awarded Davis $11.5 million in damages and the LAMCC $4.9 million. In an antitrust case damages are tripled, and so the total cost to the NFL approached $50 million plus another $10 million in legal fees for the plaintiffs. Added to the total were league legal fees. The damages ruling was appealed and the damages reduced. The Los Angles Raiders began league play in the fall of 1982.

In trying to assess the final outcome of the case, it can be said that Rozelle was the loser. His control of the NFL was severely eroded and his power considerably reduced. For Davis the victory was personally sweet but over the longer run could be described as Pyrrhic. The Raiders never were able to build a strong fan base and fan loyalty in Los Angeles. On the Coliseum, improvements never came. The money tree of pay television failed to materialize. Following the 1983 season the Raiders won Super Bowl XVIII and made the playoffs through 1985. From the mid-80s on, mediocrity hit the franchise, save one playoff year in 1990. Finally, after the 1994 season, Davis took his Raiders back to Oakland.[16]

Owners Unleashed

One of the many dramatic stadium and relocation stories developed over several years in Baltimore. Carroll Rosenbloom had built the Baltimore Colts franchise into a successful enterprise. However, when the Los Angeles Rams became available after the death of Dan Reeves in 1971, Rosenbloom wanted to acquire the Rams. The taxes incurred selling the Colts would have been high, so he arranged for Robert Irsay to buy the Rams from the Reeves estate for $19 million. Then Rosenbloom and Irsay traded teams, with Irsay receiving an additional $4 million.

The trade proved costly for Baltimore. Robert Irsay had made his fortune in industrial air conditioning and heating. He lived in Chicago and had no attachment to the city of Baltimore or the Colts. Irsay quickly alienated the community. As early as 1977 the City of Indianapolis was courting Irsay and the Colts. A delegation from the city, including the mayor, told the Colt owner that they were considering building a downtown stadium that could seat sixty-two thousand.[17] In 1979 Irsay was shopping himself and the Colts to the city of Los Angeles. Over the next few years he dangled the Colts before Los Angeles, Phoenix, Memphis, and Jacksonville. This left Baltimore scrambling to keep the Colts by repeatedly enhancing their offers to Irsay.[18]

Once the Davis Case ended and the lid was off on franchise movement, Irsay intensified his efforts. Super Bowl week in early 1984 was indeed super for Irsay. He held secret negotiations with several groups in Phoenix and it appeared he was close to agreement there. At the same time he ordered five moving vans from Mayflower just in case. He then returned to Baltimore to negotiate with the mayor. At the same time, he reopened negotiations with Indianapolis and Phoenix, all the while continuing discussions with Baltimore and Maryland officials. After both Baltimore and Indianapolis made extravagant offers, Phoenix withdrew from the circus.

Indianapolis promised new luxury boxes, offered a ten-year loan at 8 percent, a $2.5 million line of credit, a new $4 million training facility, the first $500,000 of luxury box income for twelve years, 50 percent of suite income after that, exclusive rights to sell programs and novelties, and a guaranteed income from ticket sales of $7 million for twelve years. The Maryland Senate countered by passing legislation that would allow the city of Baltimore to use the right of eminent domain to prevent the Colts from moving. At this point Irsay put the moving vans in motion. It was a beautiful scene, this tribute to cutthroat capitalism, and one that the people of Baltimore would not forget and later replicate, doing unto others what was done unto them. Eleven moving vans made a quiet midnight exit from Maryland filled with office furniture, file cabinets, and the private records of the Baltimore Colts.

Meanwhile in Indianapolis, the football fans celebrated. On April 2, 1984, seventeen thousand Colt supporters came to a rally at the Hoosier Dome. There they heard some words of great significance from Robert Irsay: "It's not your ball team. . . . [I]t's mine and my family's ball team and I paid for it and I earned it."[19] This was more candor than any owner had ever offered on the realities of the NFL and its relationship to fans and communities.

The Mayflower moving van was an excellent symbol for the new NFL. This was not so much for all the moves that did occur, but for those that were threatened for the purpose of extorting cities and states into building bigger and better stadiums for the rich elite who owned a piece of the NFL Money Machine. It also symbolized Rozelle's loss of control over the owners.

Rozelle's power was eroded further by his insistence on his version of "ownership rules." All franchises must have a 51 percent owner and there would be no corporate or public ownership. There was never any league agreement reached on these rules. In May 1972 Rozelle offered a resolution prohibiting NFL owners from ownership of other sports franchises. When owners rejected the resolution, Rozelle introduced a resolution against ownership of a team in a major sport. Anyone holding an interest at the time could not increase their ownership stake and would be required to make a "best effort" to divest. The resolution was accepted in 1972 with the proviso that it had to be renewed annually. What constituted a "best effort" remained unclear, but it was understood that no one should be expected to sell at a loss or below market value.[20]

The ownership issue illustrated Pete Rozelle's insistence on securing his policies, preferably in the league constitution. In late June 1978 the commissioner offered another and more severe constitutional proposal aimed at those league members who owned franchises in the North American Soccer League: Williams, Hunt, and Robbie.[21] Personal animosities, conflicting business interests, mercurial personalities, tax issues, family issues, and enormous egos spun around the ensuing battle. The most formidable opponent for Rozelle was Washington Redskins' part-owner Edward Bennett Williams, who accurately and forcefully predicted that Rozelle's policy would precipitate a lawsuit from the NASL and cost the NFL in damages. Although the majority of owners supported Rozelle's ownership policy, as long as it didn't affect them, the division that was let loose damaged Rozelle's veneer of infallibility. One by one, the owners became disillusioned with the commissioner's leadership.

The *NASL v. NFL* trial began in New York City in April 1980. The NFL defense was built on the notion that it was a single economic entity and therefore exempt from Sherman Act coverage. The NASL argued that the ownership policy was designed by the NFL to reduce competition between sports leagues, and that there was a limited market in which to obtain sports ownership, capital, and skill, and the NFL was trying to limit access to that market. The judge found in favor of the NFL on both issues raised by the NASL, but the Second Circuit Court of Appeals overturned the decision two years later and the Supreme Court denied further appeal. The court banned any ownership policy amendments forever, however long that might be.[22]

Philadelphia

In addition to the lawsuits and the confrontations over league policy, several owners found themselves facing financial problems that threatened their control of, or possibly even the loss of, their teams. Leonard Tose was in this position in the spring of 1977. When he entered the league as Eagles owner in 1969 his assets were put at $12.5 million. By the end of 1976 they were $2.5 million and dropping. He had lost $2.5 million in his trucking business in the previous three years. His combined salary from his trucking and football ownership was $100,000 annually, or the cost of his personal helicopter. To cover his extravagant expenses, Tose charged them off to the Eagles, and as a result the team lost $1.3 million in 1976 despite having one of the best attendance figures in the NFL. Tose once said he would be dead before his money ran out, but as David Harris noted, "When making that prediction Leonard Tose seriously underestimated his own skill at losing money."[23]

Rozelle and other owners did their best to save Tose, but after several rounds of failure and threatened bank foreclosures Tose sold his team for $70 million. This covered his debts and allowed him to walk away with $10 million and a guaranteed income of $1.5 million for ten years. He spent the first month on the French Riviera sans helicopter.[24]

Cleveland

In Cleveland troubles aplenty dogged owner Art Modell. His wheeling and dealing damaged his reputation as a man of character and made the Tose problem pale in comparison. In 1982 Modell faced a lawsuit from one of the Browns' minority owners, Robert Gries, who charged that Modell had received $4.8 million by having the Browns purchase Cleveland Stadium Corp. for $6 million, when its book value was $385,000. Modell used the sale of Cleveland Stadium Corp. to the Browns to get himself out of debt. The surprise was that the previously unknown Gries owned 43 percent of the team.

In April the other principal client of Stadium Corp., the Cleveland Indians, sued Stadium Corp. charging fraud on the Indians' concession revenues, amounting to $1.25 million. In June a second suit by the Indians against Stadium Corp. and the Browns charged that their refusal to negotiate with the Indians was a violation of the Sherman Act. That night Modell suffered a severe heart attack.

In 1984 Gries won both the first and second suits and Modell was ordered to repay his former partner. These developments, along with the rejection by voters of a referendum on a new stadium, thwarted Modell's plan to use the new stadium as a way out of debt. It led instead to Modell's flight into exile in Baltimore, where in 1996 Modell's team began play as the Ravens.[25]

Dallas

If there was one franchise that seemed secure, it was the Dallas Cowboys. When the Cowboys entered the NFL they were owned by Clint Murchison and run with complete authority by Tex Schramm, a close confidant of Pete Rozelle. Schramm in his heyday had more power than any non-owner or owner in the NFL. Clint and John Murchison were partners, and when John died in 1979 the partnership ended when a liquidation of "Murchison Brothers" took place. Considerable debt and a loss in a lawsuit brought by a nephew necessitated the sale of the team. One of the conditions was that Schramm, who handed the sale, would retain total control of football operations. H. R. "Bum" Bright, an oilman and chairman of the Texas A&M trustees, offered $86 million for the team and the stadium lease. Bright was the largest single owner of the team at 17 percent. Rozelle's 51 percent owner rule did not seem to apply, as he approved the sale.

The Bright years were anything but. In Bright's five years of ownership the Cowboys were 36-44 and a dismal 3-13 in 1988, the final year. Bright's fortune was in decline and in 1988 his banking operations were declared insolvent and taken over by federal regulators. Soon the Cowboys were back on the market. Among interested buyers were Jerry Buss of the Lakers, Don Carter of the Dallas Mavericks, and some seventy-five others, including Jerral (Jerry) Jones.

Jerry Jones—Arlington, Texas, July 24, 2009. AP Photo/Donna McWilliam.

Jerry Jones emerged as the leading candidate as he impressed Bright: "The more I got to know him, the more I knew he was the right man to own the Cowboys." Bright hoped to get $180 million in the sale, but reports were that Jones paid $90 million for the team, $50 million for the stadium lease, and assumed a $10 million mortgage on Cowboys headquarters. Jones financed the purchase himself. Approval of the sale came early in 1989.

The days of Schramm and Landry were numbered as Jones promised to put his fingerprints on every aspect of Cowboy operations. Jones announced that Schramm would continue to be an important part of the Cowboys, but he would move to the background behind the owner. Jones, not Schramm, would represent the Cowboys at league meetings.

One of the first major decisions was the removal of Tom Landry after twenty-nine years as the one and only coach of the Cowboys. Landry was stunned, Schramm was in tears, Rozelle compared it to the death of Lombardi. At the press conference announcing the changes, Jones talked of his anguish at the decision, comparing Landry to Bear Bryant and Vince Lombardi. He called Landry an angel of competitors. Jones then talked about Jimmy Johnson, Landry's replacement, saying that he would not have bought the Cowboys unless Jimmy could be his coach, even though he also said that Johnson "couldn't carry Tom Landry's water bucket." Bob Lilly, who played for Landry for fourteen years, summed it up. "It's the end of an era, our era. A lot of old Cowboys are crying tonight."[26] Lilly was prophetic, and the meaning of his comments spread across the franchise and the league.

Sometime in the late 1980s the commentator and writer Beano Cook felt similar winds of change moving through the NFL ownership ranks. There was a time, noted Cook, when a handshake was all that was needed in the NFL. The owners, the majority of them Catholics and trained by nuns, "fought like hell with one another but when a deal was made, that was it. A handshake. No lawyers. You know that when Art Rooney gave his word, that was it." It was the same with many others, but now that was nearly gone. Cooke told Rozelle that the NFL now reminded him of the Roman Empire.[27]

8

Unraveling

Though the loss of the court case to the LAMCC and Al Davis ensured a decline in Pete Rozelle's ability to control NFL owners, there were other signs that the omnipotence of the commissioner was waning. One such sign was his failure, once again, to get an antitrust exemption from Congress, something the NFL had already failed to achieve in the courts. It was the drug issue that more than anything careened out of control, especially in the '70s and '80s. The commissioner did demonstrate effective leadership in handling the challenge by the new United States Football League (USFL).

The Quest for Antitrust Exemption

Looking for a way out of the LAMCC case in late 1981, Rozelle decided on a strategy that displayed poor judgment, arrogance, or perhaps a little of each. The commissioner decided to go back to Congress and seek an antitrust exemption that would be retroactive in character and thus void the LAMCC suit against the NFL. As he had done with the Football Merger Act in the mid-60s, Rozelle looked to entice/bribe members of Congress with potential NFL franchises for their districts or states. He told Congress that in the current uncertain legal climate, there could be no expansion, even though the league wanted to expand and many cities desired teams. The expansion ploy was aimed particularly at Sen. Howard Baker of Tennessee, who was heading up the Memphis effort to get an NFL franchise.

Appearing before the House Judiciary Committee in early December, the commissioner argued that the NFL needed to be able to control franchise location and relocation, and revenue sharing needed to continue without fear of legal consequences. Also at stake was the ability of the NFL to make and enforce its own rules and prevent franchises from abandoning cities without cause.

The NFLPA expressed their concern to the Judiciary Committee over the implications such a law would have for labor questions. Former San Francisco mayor Joseph Alioto called it the worst kind of special interest legislation, which was "giving even arrogance a bad name." He charged that football franchises were being sold for votes. It was Rozelle's obsession with Al Davis that led to his insistence on the retroactive provisions of the legislation.

In May, following the verdict in the LAMCC case, Rozelle turned again to Congress. Three House members, two from California, introduced the Major League Sport Community Protection Act of 1982. The Senate version of the bill contained an antitrust exemption for the NFL on revenue sharing and franchise relocation, and it was retroactive in its coverage. Hearings on the Senate bill did not go well, as Al Davis, Bill Robertson of the LAMCC, and Ed Garvey of the NFLPA all testified against it. When the NFLPA went on strike in the midst of the hearings, any possibility of passage was dead, as Congress did not want to be seen as interfering in a labor dispute. In 1984 the Sports Community Protection Bill resurfaced but in a form unacceptable to the NFL, because it required any franchise move to be approved by an arbitration board. The NFL wanted no part of an independent board controlling any of its activities.

If nothing else, the commissioner was persistent. In 1985 he promised two expansion teams for passage. The following year he returned with a "compromise" bill that would subject the NFL to certain criteria for moves, but give the league the power to deny moves and approve new owners by a ¾ vote as well as control over television revenues. This bill was killed by a threatened filibuster led by Sen. Albert Gore Jr. of Tennessee, who wanted a minimum of six expansion teams. Gore argued that the bill would free the NFL to ignore both fans and market forces.[1]

Throughout Rozelle's losing efforts in Congress, the opposition to his power grew among NFL owners. Jack Kent Cooke became a force both inside the league and inside political Washington. He led a group that commanded up to eight votes in league meetings, and therefore had the power to block league governance changes.

Owners expressed concern over excessive legal fees and courtroom losses and the lack of accountability for Rozelle's $18 million budget. Most owners had never seen Rozelle's contract. At league meetings in March 1983 the Cooke faction forced the reading of Rozelle's contract, revealing a salary of $700,000 per year plus $25,000 per year in deferred salary. Hugh Culverhouse of the Tampa Bay Buccaneers was one owner that remained steadfastly loyal to Rozelle, and his influence brought the Super Bowl to Tampa in 1984, making it the smallest city with the smallest stadium to host the game. Culverhouse's power stemmed from the fact, as David Harris concluded, that in the new age of accountants and lawyers in the NFL, Culverhouse was both.[2]

The USFL Distraction

On May 11, 1982, four days after Al Davis's victory over the NFL, the United States Football League announced its arrival. Its founder was Donald Dixon, a New Orleans antiques dealer who had been a lobbyist on the AFL-NFL merger and had tried to convince the NFL owners to form a developmental league with spring competition. Chet Simmons of ABC was commissioner of the USFL, and Peter Hadley of the NFL was head of football operations. It was a spring league set to begin play in March 1983, and quickly secured a television contract with ESPN and ABC.

Rozelle predicted that the new league would play, spend too much money, and go deeply into debt, and then when they were about to go out of business they would sue the NFL. It didn't take long for them to spend a lot of money, as the New Jersey Generals signed Heisman Trophy winner Herschel Walker out of the University of Georgia following his junior season in Athens. Walker's contract was worth $3.9 million over three years, with incentives potentially increasing it to $4.5 million. It was a sensational signing and major headlines for the USFL.

Perhaps the most difficult development for the NFL came when Eddie DeBartolo Sr. became owner of the USFL Pittsburgh franchise, while his son owned the San Francisco 49ers. NFL owners and Rozelle found having father and son as owners in the rival leagues an untenable situation. Given the outcome of the Davis case, there was nothing that could be done to Eddie Jr. as an NFL owner, whose position was that there was no problem as father and son operated separately.[3]

In its second year the USFL expanded to eighteen teams, and new owners like Donald Trump entered the league. Trump purchased the New Jersey Generals, and along with Eddie Einhorn of the Chicago Blitz followed a strategy of suing the NFL and then settling the case by getting their own franchises in the NFL. The USFL schedule moved to the autumn, in direct competition with the NFL. When the USFL could not get a television contract, they sued the NFL for $1.6 billion.

Several NFL owners were concerned when a legal consultant ran a mock trial and it ended in a USFL victory. Some owners wanted to settle, but NFL legal counsel Paul Tagliabue recommended against it, arguing that the USFL case was a sham and settling it would only encourage other leagues to form and then sue.[4]

The 1986 trial was an ordeal for some, particularly Rozelle, while it was high entertainment for others. Testifying against the NFL were Donald Trump, Al Davis, and Howard Cosell. The cross-examination of Cosell produced the most entertaining moments of the trial. When NFL co-counsel Frank Rothman, who once had represented Cosell, commented that he was not as smart as Cosell, Howard replied, "We have learned that long ago." When Rothman told Cosell that if there was a question Howard did not understand, he should say so, Cosell was quick to answer. "If you ask a question that I don't understand, you will have the biggest story of the century." On the truthfulness of NFL owners, Cosell said, "Not in recent cases involving actions of the National Football League, Sir."

The most damaging testimony came when USFL chief counsel Harvey Myerson introduced a document identified as the Harvard Study. It had been developed at the request of the NFL Management Council by Michael Porter, a professor at the Harvard Business School, who had first presented the results to a seminar of sixty-five NFL executives in early 1984. The study contained three recommendations. First, try to force ABC to discontinue its USFL contract by giving ABC poor MNF match-ups. Second, entice powerful USFL owners with promises of NFL franchises. Third, try to bankrupt the weakest franchises in the USFL, thus damaging league credibility. This was coupled with the so-called Donlan memorandum, which argued for the NFL to drive up the salaries of the lowest-paid players to increase pressure on the new league.

On July 26, 1986, the jury, after five days of deliberation, found the NFL guilty on one of nine counts brought by the USFL. The jury awarded $1 to the USFL, and with triple damages that came to $3. The NFL was also ordered to pay all the USFL court costs. A court of appeals upheld the ruling two years later.[5] This was the classic definition of a Pyrrhic victory for the USFL.

From mid-decade on, Commissioner Rozelle had at least one other event in his life that was pleasant. In January 1985 he was elected to the Pro Football Hall of Fame and inducted in ceremonies in Canton, Ohio, on August 3. At the induction ceremony the Reverend Peggy Ecia of Canton's Unity Church gave the invocation. She thanked God for providing a wonderful day and prayed especially for those to be enshrined. "We know that you have chosen them, you have selected them. We know you have guided them through the years. . . ." Tex Schramm introduced Rozelle and enumerated his achievements. Rozelle was warmly received, and he gave a rather subdued speech in which he was both nostalgic and reflective.[6]

The Drug Issue

Through the years Rozelle, ever conscious of the league's image, dealt cautiously with issues of drugs and questionable conduct. The majority of these cases involved players, in part because players were more numerous and publicly active than owners, and in part because Rozelle did not have significant disciplinary power over owners. Then too he was reluctant to take on the group that hired him over issues of personal or public conduct.

The use of illegal and performance-enhancing drugs in sports was not new, and it was an issue that seemed a constant in the NFL. Amphetamine use went back to the late 1940s and steroids were found in the NFL by the 1960s, having migrated in from the body-building community. The first systematic use of steroids at the team level came in the AFL with the San Diego Chargers of 1963. Prior to training camp Head Coach Sid Gilman informed his players that they would be lifting weights. Alvin Roy, director of the Charger weight-training program, explained that he had learned a great deal from the "Rooskies" while working as a U.S. Olympic trainer. Among the things he learned was that weight-training combined with dianabol, an artificial form of testosterone, helped players assimilate protein and build their strength rapidly. Quarterback John Hadl said that within a month the offensive linemen were beginning to look like "Popeye." The Chargers went on to sweep through the AFL to the 1963 championship behind their overpowering offensive line

In 1969 San Diego defensive lineman Houston Ridge suffered a career-ending injury and sued the team for giving him drugs that made him more susceptible to injury. The case was settled out of court for $265,000. Ridge was one of the players who were given steroids before reporting for training camp. He weighed in at 275 pounds after playing at 210 pounds at San Diego State. San Diego was by no means alone, as the 49ers experimented with dianabol in 1963, and its use had reached down into the high-school level.[7]

In 1971 Ken Gray of the St. Louis Cardinals filed a $3.5 million lawsuit charging that the team physician and trainer had deceived Gray into taking "potent, harmful, illegal and dangerous drugs" so that he would perform more violently. The case was settled out of court. The following year Bernie Parrish found that the stimulant dexedrine was the capper to the pregame meal for the Cleveland Browns and was available from the team trainer, Leo Murphy. Parrish first used drugs while at the University of Florida, and once he started, he never played another game in college or the pros without them. Parrish charged that bad drug mixing was common in the NFL and misuse and malpractice went "undetected and unchallenged within the structure of professional football."[8]

Other critics, including players and former players Dave Meggyesy, Chip Oliver, and Rick Sortun, commented on the drug culture in the league and attacked the culture of the game itself. In 1969 *Sports Illustrated* published a three-part series by Bill Gilbert in which he concluded that there was a widespread culture of drugs in sport. In 1971 Jack Scott published *The Athletic Revolution* denouncing the NFL for its misuse of drugs.[9]

In 1973 Arnold Mandell, a practicing psychiatrist and co-chair of the Department of Psychiatry at the University of California at San Diego Medical School, spent a season with the San Diego Chargers at the invitation of owner Gene Klein and head coach Harland Svare. Mandell wrote about his experiences in an article in *Psychology Today* in 1975 and in his book, *The Nightmare Season,* published in 1976. Mandell was exposed to the intensity of professional football and to the widespread use of amphetamines and other drugs in the game. Over the course of the season, Mandell tried to convince players to move away from dependency on drugs by making certain they had access to clean drugs and taking players through a process of decreasing dosage. Success was limited. Mandell advocated a program of urine testing similar to that used in the Olympics and in European football (soccer). Rozelle refused, fearing that it would send the wrong message about drugs in the NFL and create a public relations problem for the league. In the end Rozelle attempted to discredit Mandell by accusing him of being a drug supplier to the players.

Mandell and others who studied the NFL concluded that drugs were an integral component in setting the level of violence, and therefore one that could be calibrated. For those who controlled the game, violence was part of the product, while drugs were only a public relations problem. They were a medical aid, and addiction was not a concern. When the NFL singled out the San Diego Chargers as a problem issue, Mandell and others felt that this was convenient scapegoating. When Mandell's medical records ended up in the hands of NFL security, he realized just how powerful the commissioner's office was.[10]

On June 14, 1982, *Sports Illustrated* contributed further to the discussion when it published a cover story on Don Reese, who had played in Miami, New Orleans, and San Diego. Reese detailed his cocaine addiction that began in the mid-70s when he was a first-round draft pick of the Dolphins. He tried cocaine during his first week at training camp and claimed that cocaine use was widespread in the NFL. Reese maintained that his coaches and the own-

Bill Walsh—San Francisco, January 19, 1985. AP Photo/Rusty Kennedy.

ers knew this and chose to ignore it. His NFL career ended in shambles, his marriage was destroyed, and he was deeply in debt to drug dealers.

NFL officials reacted to the *SI* article on Reese by blaming the messenger and dismissing the message. Rozelle wrote to the magazine two days after the article appeared, arguing that these problems were societal and not unique to the NFL. Then two days later he conceded in an interview in the *New York Daily News* that drugs might be a bigger problem in the NFL than in society at large.[11]

When Bill Walsh evaluated his 49er team in 1982, he saw problems beyond the strike. He found complacency. Players were no longer willing, or had a need, to make the personal sacrifices necessary for success. Distractions seemed to be everywhere, and his team was losing its edge. It was the cocaine that was sweeping through the NFL and devastating Walsh's 49ers.

Cocaine, wrote a San Francisco columnist, was "God's way of telling you you're making too much money." The drug was available at team parties and in hotels before the games. Reportedly, nearly half the team was using. NFL security and the San Francisco police gave Walsh reports throughout the 1982 season indicating that more than one-half of the regulars from the championship team were abusing cocaine, and it was negatively affecting performance. Walsh later explained that his personal code would not allow him to go public with his knowledge, and indeed he publicly and repeatedly denied that his team had drug issues. He later admitted, "Some of our key players didn't show up to play and cocaine was the reason why."[12]

Drug use was clearly an issue and had been for some time. In 1986 Rozelle, citing his responsibility as commissioner to "protect the integrity of the game," announced that each player would be given two unannounced drug tests during the 1986 season. The NFLPA filed a grievance citing the existing agreement on drug testing in the Collective Bargaining Agreement (CBA). One test was permitted during the preseason physical exam, and after that tests would be given only for reasonable cause. Labor arbitrator Richard Kasher declared the commissioner in violation of the CBA. Among those pleased with Kasher's decision were the NFLPA and the American Civil Liberties Union, who agreed that Rozelle's actions were a hypocritical public relations move. Mark Murphy, assistant to players' union representative Gene Upshaw, said the ruling meant that Pete Rozelle could not move unilaterally to do whatever he or the owners wanted him to do.[13]

The steroid problem also intensified. According to Michael Oriard, one of the reasons for the growth of steroid use was a small but significant change in the pass blocking rules in 1978. The new rule allowed offensive linemen to extend their arms and open their hands on pass blocking. This put an emphasis on holding your ground in pass blocking, which in turn increased the importance of size and strength. The new technique resulted in bigger offensive linemen who could simply smother the smaller defensive pass rushers. That in turn meant that the defensive linemen, in response, got bigger. In 1985 there were seventeen players in the NFL weighing more than three hundred pounds. In 2002 that number reached 331, and three years later it exceeded five hundred. It would be naive to assume that all of this bulk appeared solely from natural development in the weight room.

Related to the issue of size, violent collisions, and drugs, a number of occupational hazards began to appear among football players. The NFLPA commissioned the National Institute for Occupational Safety and Health to look at the medical records of seven thousand NFL players between 1959 and 1988. It found that linemen were 52 percent more likely than the average American to die of heart disease and three times more likely than players at other positions. These findings were confirmed in later studies. Also, the Living Heart Foundation found that linemen were 54 percent more likely to have an enlarged heart than other players, and half the linemen had "metabolic syndrome, a group of risk factors for cardiovascular disease that includes obesity, high blood pressure, low levels of protective cholesterol, and insulin resistance."

Not only drugs and steroids but the physical demands of pro football took a serious toll on players. According to the *Jobs Related Almanac* of 1988, professional football jobs ranked a low 247 out of 250 when considering working conditions, income, and security. Major changes in salary in subsequent years couldn't push the ranking any higher than 204. Surveys of former players found that they suffered from emotional as well as physical problems. In a *Los Angeles Times* survey in 1988, 54 percent of former players reported they had emotional problems ranging from "periods of despair and adjustment to serious thoughts of suicide."[14]

Commissioner Rozelle in late 1988 finally discovered that steroids might be a problem in the NFL, and that steroids might harm the health of those who used them. Ira Berkow of the *New York Times* thought this discovery came at a remarkably late date considering that the public press, the sporting press, and international governing bodies of sport had been discussing the problem for several decades. Of course, wrote Berkow, Rozelle had known all along, and as usual it was the "commissioner's public relations timing" that was "impeccable." In announcing a new, tougher steroid policy, the commissioner said, "We've been trying to educate ourselves on the matter of steroids for some time and we feel like we know enough about it to move ahead. We know the dangers of steroids to the body and we want to do all we can so that players enjoy a quality of life after their football careers."[15]

The notion that Rozelle was genuine in these statements defies all credulity. For the commissioner the primary concern was always public perception. It took precedence over concern for the players, the integrity of the game, the views of the medical profession, or concerns of the law. Rozelle's late arrival to the steroid issue was one more indication that he had not only lost control over the league, but that he had lost his way as commissioner.

With mounting criticism, Rozelle would soon exit stage left while it was still possible for him to depart on his own terms, and with the praise of a gullible public. The commissioner was growing weary and tired from having fought all these battles, as well as the biggest battle of all, that with the players.

9

Labor Conflict

It may seem ironic that the professional sport that had by some measures the poorest working conditions of them all was, in the end, perhaps the most difficult in which to organize a union. Some have attributed this to the nature of the game, in which nameless-faceless components could be easily replaced; others point to the solidarity and tenacity of the early ownership generation. That solidarity has been attributed to the owners' status as outsiders in American life: Catholics, Jews, and immigrants. The solidarity might also have been the result of several decades of struggle for survival, during which mutual assistance had been critical.

The struggle between management and labor was long and divisive, preceding and postdating Rozelle's reign as commissioner. Many owners who joined the league in the 1950s and 1960s were businessmen who had succeeded in a union-free environment, and came into the league hostile to unions. Some also brought union-busting experience with them.

The authoritarian world of football, where coaches demand total submission of the individual to authority and to the team, within an atmosphere of paternalism at times bordering on abuse, was a world in which unions seemingly made no sense. The logic was simple: Coach knows best, coach hates unions, therefore unions must be bad. Organizing players in this world was very difficult and further complicated by the rapid personnel turnover. In those days before instant communications, players were scattered across the country, and that added to the difficultly.

Prelude

Beginning in the midfifties players faced a new reality of lower salaries in the midst of increasing prosperity for the league. The merger of the NFL and

All-American Football Conference reduced the number of professional teams from eighteen to twelve, and the supply of players on the market drove salaries down. The reserve clause further stripped the players of any leverage on salaries. Recruitment by Canadian Football League teams did not offset the decline. In 1954 Otto Graham, the star quarterback of the Cleveland Browns, had his salary cut by one-third.

By 1959 players' real wages were less than in 1949 while, for example, Green Bay Packer revenue was up 140 percent. In 1956 player salaries consumed 32 percent of revenue. Over the next fifteen years the players' share dropped to 20 percent. In that same time frame the owners' share rose from 9.4 percent to 50 percent of revenue. Another player concern was the long, nine-week training camp, during which players received only room and board. The four to six exhibition games when players were not paid their regular salaries could net the owners as much as $100,000.[1]

It is not surprising, then, that there was a move to organize the players. It began in Cleveland, where Paul Brown's iron-fisted control of the players' lives, and tight-fisted control of salaries, led to dissatisfaction. In 1954 players Abe Gibron and Dante Lavelli contacted Creighton Miller, who had been on the Cleveland Browns staff in 1946. As a result, in November 1956 the National Football League Players Association (NFLPA) was formed. At the first meeting, the players called for recognition of the group, a minimum salary of $5,000 per year, a uniform per diem for players, a rule requiring teams to pay for players' equipment, a provision for the continued salary payment for injured players, training camp pay, pay during the period between the end of camp and the opening of the season, and shorter training camps. The owners invited NFLPA representatives to attend league meetings in January 1957. Then, as if to make a point, neither the commissioner nor any owner sat down with them at the league meetings.[2] The owners offered a few crumbs to the players, such as an opportunity for them to draw a fifty-dollar advance on their salaries for each exhibition game; if a player did not make the roster, he would not have to pay back the money. The arrogance of power was a heady thing.

In 1949 Bill Radovich, a Detroit lineman, filed an antitrust suit against the NFL. Three years prior, Radovich jumped from the Lions to the Los Angeles Dons of the AAFC, and he played for the Dons for two seasons. In 1948 he was offered a minor league contract as player-coach with the San Francisco Clippers of the Pacific Coast League. The PCL had an affiliation with the NFL and it had blacklisted Radovich for signing with the Dons. When informed of the blacklisting, the Clippers withdrew their offer. In 1949 he sued the NFL. A California Federal Court ruled against Radovich. He appealed and in February 1957 the U.S. Supreme Court ruled 6-3 that professional football was subject to antitrust law. It then sent the case back to a Court of Appeals. The ruling also called into question the legality of both the college player draft and the reserve clause. The case was finally settled out of court, with Radovich accepting $42,500.

Congressional hearings into the matter of antitrust and sport were held in July 1957, at which the NFL owners took a beating in front of the Judiciary Committee. Seeking damage control, Commissioner Bert Bell, on his second round of testimony, announced recognition of the union on the spot. He promised to enter negotiations with the NFLPA. However, NFL bylaws required ten of the twelve teams to ratify this action, and Bell was able to muster only nine votes. Both official recognition and negotiations were blocked. The NFLPA then threatened the league with a $4.2 million lawsuit if formal recognition was not granted.

Commissioner Bell announced that the NFL accepted the $5,000 minimum salary, an injury clause in contracts, and a fifty-dollar payment for exhibition games. Owners still refused union recognition, although Bell claimed that the terms being offered were an implied recognition. It was a delicate dance of technicalities. Another threatened lawsuit in 1958 led to the creation of a benefit plan for the players, including hospitalization, medical and life insurance, and pensions at age sixty-five. Implementation was, of course, in doubt.[3]

The Rozelle-NFLPA Conflict Begins

The sixties were marked by the coming of the American Football League (AFL), a new commissioner in Pete Rozelle, and a growing frustration and then division within the ranks of the NFLPA. In these years the NFLPA learned not to trust the commissioner or the owners, but they never were able to mount an effective opposition.

Bernie Parrish was active in the Players Association as a player representative of the Cleveland Browns, and later took a leadership position in the organization. The NFLPA achieved little, as it sent all of its proposals to Pete Rozelle, who supposedly presented them to the owners. Parrish found the practice "to be as stupid as its sounds," and learned that often the NFLPA proposals never reached the owners. Parrish claimed that Creighton Miller, legal counsel to the NFLPA, made no attempt to challenge the college draft or the reserve clause even though judges in the Radovich case questioned their legality.

Divisions in NFLPA leadership hindered progress by the players, while the arrogance of the commissioner and the owners further aggravated the labor-management relationship. In 1963 it was discovered that the owners took 10 percent off the top of the net revenue from the championship game before calculating the 70 percent for the players. Four years after the Retirement Plan and Trust Agreement was instituted, the NFL still had not supplied the NFLPA with a copy of the document. In 1963 the association discovered that anyone playing out their option and signing with the AFL would forfeit their pension under terms of the plan.

On the issue of product endorsement, Rozelle sent an "exclusive-agents contract" to all players, naming the commissioner as the exclusive agent for every individual. In the middle of this dispute a story broke that Rozelle short-changed the Players' Benefit Plan on television money even as he took money from broadcast revenue for coaches' pensions. After calling for Rozelle to be fired by the owners, Parrish laid plans for a strike in August 1965. The commissioner and the owners in turn lobbied the players and player representatives, and in the end, under pressure from Rozelle and the owners, only half of the player reps supported Parrish.[4]

At one point Parrish contacted the Teamsters and sought their help in organizing the American Federation of Professional Athletes as an all-sports union. The attempt failed when the AFLPA, under the leadership of Buffalo Bills' quarterback and future U.S. congressman Jack Kemp, refused to join such an organization. In January 1968 Dan Schulman, a Chicago labor leader, replaced Miller as NFLPA director. Schulman announced that the NFLPA was now a union and that the owners immediately recognized it as such, thereby heading off the Teamster option. John Gordy of the Detroit Lions became the new president of the NFLPA and a year later was replaced by John Mackey of the Baltimore Colts.

Despite their recognition of the NFLPA, the owners would not bargain with the organization. Also despite the AFL-NFL merger, the two player associations did not merge, and this split gave the owners a wedge in dealing with the players. When the NFLPA offered new pension proposals in 1968, the owners refused to talk. This led to strike preparations by the players aimed at the training camps. Before there could be a strike, the owners took preemptive action and locked out the players. It was the first work stoppage in professional sports history.

Settlement came quickly, and on July 14, 1968, the first collective bargaining agreement was reached. The owners agreed to put $3 million into the pension fund within two years, far from the $5 million demanded by the NFLPA. There was little change on minimum salary and no change in exhibition game pay of fifty dollars. The retirement age remained sixty-five, and the recognition of the commissioner as arbitrator with absolute power to rule on disputes was reaffirmed. The NFLPA found it difficult to resist this settlement, as the ten AFL teams accepted the owners' terms without hesitation. For the owners, the issue was control, and they clearly had retained it.[5]

Mackey and Rozelle

After the completion of the merger and realignment of the NFL and AFL, it was clearly past time to merge the two player associations. In any merger the original NFL teams and players would hold a strong majority, and it was clear that the NFL players would not accept the leadership of Jack Kemp in the new organization. John Mackey was elected president of the consolidated NFLPA, and Allen Miller, a former AFL player, served as general counsel for the group until January 1971, when he was asked to resign.

From their first meeting with the NFLPA, the owners refused to treat the players with any sense of equity. Mackey quickly withdrew and contacted a labor law firm, Lindquist and Vennum of Minneapolis. Ed Garvey was assigned by the firm to its new client. Following the legal advice, player reps agreed to seek certification from the National Labor Relations Board (NLRB). This was the first time the NLRB took jurisdiction over labor relations in professional sports.

Lines were being drawn on what was not an even playing field. Owners had the upper hand in public relations. Fans expressed little sympathy for what they saw as highly paid players threatening the smooth operations of professional football. Owners exploited the press, who shared the fans' view of the overpaid players, saw the owners as sportsmen serving the public interest, and treated Rozelle as a minor deity. The NFLPA had a small staff hampered by poor communication with its members, and lacked both the money and skill to respond to the NFL public relations juggernaut.[6]

The players sought increased pension benefits, a modification of the option clause, a larger share of product licensing revenue, and improvement in such fringe benefits as training camp, preseason, and severance pay. In 1970 the owners announced another lockout. When the Kansas City players announced they would report and play in the College All-Star Game of 1970 despite the lockout, the owners backed off. The NFLPA then called a strike, but the game was played.

An agreement was reached after twenty hours of negotiations, in which it was reported that Rozelle brokered the deal by locking the negotiating parties in a room. Ed Garvey, legal counsel to Mackey, called the claim of Rozelle's role "bullshit." It did, however, enhance the commissioner's reputation, yet again. Eventually the sides reached a four-year agreement, increasing minimum salaries to $12,500 for rookies and $13,000 for veterans. The pension was improved and dental benefits added. For the first time, players were given the right to have agents and afforded representation on the Retirement Board, and an independent arbitrator was appointed for injury disputes.

Of the agreement Mackey said there were no winners and no losers. Garvey was more candid, saying: "The owners gave us nothing." It took almost a year to get the final agreement on paper. As would become customary, the aftermath of the agreement included the release or trading of player reps by their teams, including Mackey, who was traded to San Diego, essentially ending his playing career.

At the heart of the owners' control was the so-called Rozelle Rule, which allowed the commissioner to award compensation for any free-agent signing. In early 1972 the practice began to attract media attention. Sportswriter Leonard Koppett found it strange that Rozelle seemed proud of the fact that since the merger in 1966, only nineteen players out of six thousand under contract had changed teams. At the time of the merger, the NFL had promised Congress that there would be freedom of movement within the league. In May 1972 eight players filed a class-action suit against the NFL charging that the option clause and Rozelle Rule constituted an anticompetitive device, and that the teams had agreed to boycott the free agent process.[7]

This case, *John Mackey et al. v. National Football League*, directly challenged the Rozelle Rule as a violation of the Sherman Anti-trust Act. David Harris calls the decision to file the Mackey case a preview of "the civil war to come," with the case as "the weapon of choice." From this point on, Ed Garvey was the focal point of hostility for the owners.[8] Rozelle characterized Garvey as "a prototypical early sixties radical, a militant ideologue who is unable to see any good, any justice, in any action of management." Wellington Mara detested him. Other owners believed that Garvey was an opportunist who had duped the players who seemed to follow him blindly.[9]

Ed Garvey and the Freedom Issues

After John Mackey retired in 1973, Houston Oilers' center Bill Curry became president of the NFLPA. Curry believed that the biggest problem between owners and players was that the owners didn't understand that grown men do not like being told how to dress and how to cut their hair.[10] Labor relations were further strained by the coming of the World Football League (WFL). It began signing NFL players who were free agents. They also signed NFL players to future contracts. The most sensational of these signings came in 1974 when John Bassett, millionaire owner of the Toronto franchise, signed the core of the Miami Dolphins offense—Larry Csonka, Jim Kiick, and Paul Warfield—for a collective total of $3.5 million.[11]

The collective bargaining agreement hammered out in 1970 was ending, and negotiations for a new agreement began amid a good deal of mistrust and anxiety on all sides. The players made "Freedom" the theme of their negotiating position. The first meeting in March 1974 began graciously, with Curry talking about the need for mutual trust and respect amid mutual interests. Wellington Mara, speaking for the owners, echoed these sentiments. Ed Garvey spoke next in "very frank and strident language," and presented a list of sixty-three (variously reported as fifty-eight, sixty-three, ninety, ninety-one, and ninety-three) demands, ranging from the highly significant to the trivial.

At the heart of the matter were the reserve list, the option clause, the waiver system, the authority of the clubs and the commissioner to levy fines, and the absolute power of the commissioner to settle disputes. Michael Oriard points out that the latter was spelled out "with thrilling redundancy," describing the commissioner's decisions as "final, complete, conclusive, binding, and unappealable." Garvey called for a union shop, a veto on trades of

Ed Garvey and Gene Upshaw, New York, September 18, 1982. AP Photo/Mario Suriani.

veteran players, a ban on all psychological testing, and an end to cutting or trading player reps without their consent. The "freedom issues" were not only anathema to ownership, but they were a public relations failure for the players. Sixty-three of anything was apparently too much for the public or press to handle, and the press ridiculed the size and the content of some items on the list.[12]

On July 1, 1974, the NFLPA called a strike, with the primary objective being to kill the Rozelle Rule. Ed Garvey was certain the veteran players would not report to camp, and that they would hold out until a new agreement was signed. Garvey's first big mistake was saying it was critical for rookies and free agents to be kept out of camp, because someone trying to make a team is not likely to stay away. The first picketing was in San Diego, where the players wore T-shirts with a clenched fist on it and the slogan "No Freedom, No Football," reminiscent of the civil rights and antiwar movements. One newspaper characterized the freedom issues as basically black issues, an idea confirmed when the majority of stars who turned against the union were white. The rookies and free agents crossed the line in San Diego, and that proved a preview of what was to happen across the league.[13]

To counter the pressure being brought by the WFL, the NFL developed a counterstrategy that was both effective and a violation of labor law. The NFL signed its players to long-term contracts that included large bonuses with clauses forfeiting the bonus money if they failed to report to training camp on time. These clauses may have affected close to sixty players. The union pointed out that these clauses were illegal yellow-dog contracts that punished players for union activity. Red Smith pointed this out in his *New York Times* column, but few others seemed interested. The NLRB ruled for the players two years after the fact.[14]

The player reps were under pressure from teammates, their teams, and the local press. Fans sent them hate mail and harassed them by telephone. More pressure on the players came when management unilaterally raised pay for exhibition games to 10 percent of the players' salary. This was another action by owners in violation of labor law, but again this would not be ruled on until 1976.

The NFL reported on July 21 that 108 players were in camp, eight days later the number rose to 248, and by August 7 it was placed at 360. On the other hand, the NFLPA reported that the teams had lost $1.8 million in ticket sales on exhibition games in the first week of the strike. Another major development came on August 1 when Roger Staubach reported to camp in Dallas. Ed Garvey told a reporter: "I'd hate to have been at Pearl Harbor with him." Staubach was an ex-Navy man and a Vietnam veteran, and the press and public blowback from the comment was strong. Staubach returned fire, calling Garvey belligerent, arrogant, and tactless.

In the end the strike could not be sustained. On August 10, the Management Council, smelling blood, told Garvey that they were terminating all negotiations unless the "freedom issues" were taken off the table. Garvey offered to comply with that demand, but they also wanted him to abandon the Mackey case, which he would not do. The owners continued to claim that team profits averaged only $472,000 and team revenue averaged $6.2 million. Later an NFLPA economist calculated the average profit figure for 1973 at $2.3 million.[15]

Few reporters questioned Management Council figures on profits or most other issues associated with the strike. The press generally accepted the notion that the "freedom issues" would produce anarchy and accepted the owners' financial figures, and few questioned the total disregard the league had for labor law. There were occasional isolated stories about the low pay of players, their lack of impartial arbitration, or their short careers, but these were seldom circulated nationally. A Brookings Institute study showing the huge invisible profits available to sports owners in public subsidies and tax write-offs was largely ignored.

Reporters tended to reinforce the notion that somehow the fans were "victims" in the strike, and that anything that the players gained from the strike would be paid for by the fans. Strikebreakers were seen as attending camp because of their love of the game, rather than fear, economic interest, distrust of unions, or self-interest. However, a Harris poll showed that 38 percent of fans supported the players, 22 percent the owners, and 40 percent as indifferent. Again, few in the media noticed. On the extreme among the critics was Wells Twombly of the *San Francisco Examiner,* who called the players "denim wearing Bolsheviks," or "sweaty tycoons" and called Ed Garvey the "Karl Marx of the shower stall." There were only a few sportswriters who supported the players, the most prominent being Red Smith of the *New York Times* and Ed Pope of the *Miami Herald.*[16]

It is often said that success has many fathers but failure is an orphan. The failure of the 1974 strike showed otherwise, as it was attributed not only to Garvey but also to Rozelle, the owners, the players, and the press. Most analysts, including historian Michael Lomax, placed the greatest share of blame on Ed Garvey. He couldn't control the players, failed the public relations challenge, and proved inept and inflexible in negotiations. In a sense Garvey would be vindicated when, in December 1974, federal district Judge William T. Sweigert ruled in the Joe Kapp suit that both the college draft and the Rozelle Rule were "patently unreasonable and illegal."

A year later the Mackey case concluded, with Judge Earl R. Larson ruling that the Rozelle Rule violated antitrust law. Then in July 1976 came the rulings from the National Labor Relations Board that the NFL was guilty of unfair labor practices. In September 1976 Judge William Bryant declared the college draft illegal in the Yazoo Smith case. A month later the Eighth Circuit Court in St. Louis upheld Judge Larson's ruling in the Mackey case. However, in all these cases, the courts took the view that the issues ultimately needed to be settled by collective bargaining and not by the courts.

More immediately, the end of the strike found the owners again ready to punish the striking players. Player reps were traded or cut, as were those on the bargaining team. In a wider view the Associated Press reported that 272 rookies made NFL rosters in 1974, compared with 168 the previous year. Many players emerged from the experience disillusioned. Divisions within teams and in the league itself did not heal easily. According to Michael Oriard, the most serious long-term casualty of the strike was the relationship between players and fans. "The love affair of fans with 'their' football heroes had always been built on illusions, of course, on a willed innocence that would never again be quite as easy to maintain."[17]

This strike ended, but the conflict was just beginning and would continue over the next two decades. In addition, as we have seen, this was a period of strife within ownership as well, as Pete Rozelle proved not only incapable of settling the labor strife but also unable to maintain his control over the owners. Eventually "freedom" did triumph. In the early 1980s Al Davis won his struggle with the NFL over moving the Raiders, and that led to freedom of movement for franchises. The struggle between the players and the NFL would be won by the players, but that would take until the early '90s, when again freedom led to movement. In neither case did freedom and movement bring anarchy, and indeed the NFL continued to prosper under freedom.[18]

The Mackey Case

In the mid-1970s freedom was in the distant future, and the fear of freedom within the NFL executive ranks was still quite strong. In the aftermath of the 1974 strike the owners no doubt felt that they were on their way to crushing the NFLPA, and that such a victory was only a matter of time. Pete Rozelle and the owners were never short on arrogance and hubris, and if they feared the Mackey case, they hid it well.

The NFLPA came out of the 1974 strike on shaky ground, and the events of 1975 seemed ominous. Again there was a strike. This time it was not really a strike of the NFLPA, but as Michael Lomax termed it, the action of twenty-six mini-unions. The first team to walk out was the New England Patriots. Only four other teams voted to strike, and player unity proved illusory. The question of whether there was a viable players union had been answered in the negative.

At the 1975 annual meeting Rozelle reported that things were going well. The NFLPA and the WFL were still problem areas, but he had confidence that they could be handled. Indeed the WFL was on the brink. As for the NFLPA, it too was struggling. Dues check off, in which the owners took union dues out of a player's paycheck as required in the old contract, was brought to an end because there was no contract. This made the proposition of trying to collect dues from disillusioned players a dicey one. Negotiations went nowhere, and the NFLPA as well as Ed Garvey were going into considerable debt. The trial of the Mackey case began on February 3, 1975, to be argued before a judge by mutual agreement.[19]

The Mackey decision came on December 29, 1975. A district court ruling held that the Rozelle Rule "constituted a concerted refusal to deal and a group boycott, and was therefore a per se violation of the Sherman Act." The court found that the NFL did not provide sufficient evidence to justify the claim that the Rozelle Rule was essential to the operations of the league, and that "the Rozelle Rule was invalid under the Rule of Reason standard." The court also "rejected the club's argument that the Rozelle Rule was immune under the Sherman Act because it had been the subject of a collective bargaining agreement . . ."[20]

By all accounts the ruling was a major victory for the NFLPA. Rozelle immediately announced that the NFL would appeal the decision, a process that started in June and ended in October when the Court of Appeals upheld the lower court. However, the court directed the parties to return to the bargaining table to resolve the Rozelle Rule.[21]

At the NFL annual meeting in March 1976 the negotiations took a different turn. Dolphins safety Dick Anderson, the new NFLPA president, spoke to league owners and talked of conciliation. He said that he wanted to take the focus off Ed Garvey and to discuss issues. On the owners' side, there was a growing feeling that Wellington Mara had gotten too emotionally involved, particularly on Garvey. So a decision was made to remove Mara as chairman of the management counsel's executive committee and replace him with Dan Rooney.

The Anderson-Rooney talks began in June, and an agreement was reached on a modified Rozelle Rule and a package of economic benefits. After the two men reached the agreement, they both had to sell it to their constituents and that was difficult on both sides, but it proved most difficult for Anderson. Ed Garvey rejected the new deal and his position carried the day.[22]

Five months later Garvey reached an accord on a new collective bargaining agreement with the NFL, and to the surprise of many it looked very much like the Anderson-Rooney agreements. Michael Oriard called it "a major turning point in the history of NFL labor relations, a decision by Ed Garvey for which he would still be vilified in 1987." Basically Garvey gave up the gains of the Mackey case in exchange for "a more powerful union." Throughout his tenure, claims Oriard, Garvey pushed for across-the-board benefits for the rank and file players, rather than great wealth via free agency for the stars. He wanted an organization strong enough to run the NFL with the owners, and what he achieved in the 1977 CBA was an opportunity to rebuild the strength of the union for the battles that lay ahead.

The 1977 agreement settled the Mackey case, increased benefits, created an arbitration panel for grievances, and ended arbitrary hair and dress codes. Also as a result, the college draft was shortened from seventeen to twelve rounds, and a player unhappy with the team that drafted him could play out his option in one year at a lower salary. The Rozelle Rule was modified with a right of first refusal and a modified compensation system. The player could play out his option at 110 percent of salary and then was free to negotiate with other teams. His club would have the right to match the offer, and if the player moved on his new team would have to pay compensation determined by the existing wage scale.

For many of the star players and their agents, the agreement looked like a disaster, but for the faithful rank and file (863 dues-paying members out of fourteen hundred total players) the new CBA was viewed with favor. Although only 593 players voted on the CBA, it was approved by 91 percent of those voters, although that constituted less than 39 percent of all the players. For Garvey the two most important elements in the CBA were "dues check-off" and an "agency shop." The NFLPA would again become solvent, and Garvey willingly sacrificed the "freedom issues" for this gain.[23]

On the ownership side there was considerable satisfaction. The commissioner reported to the annual meeting in March that the league's troubles were now in the past. All the numbers looked good. Average game attendance was up, television ratings were up, and the Super Bowl and *Monday Night Football* had their highest ratings ever. The greatest achievement was the signing of the CBA, and Rozelle predicted that the result would be "intelligent planning" and solidification "of franchises and the League."[24]

As seen previously, the optimism was unwarranted, as the league was about to go through a period of major contention complete with lawsuits and a successful challenge of the commissioner's power. Although the players had yet to gain their freedom, Al Davis was about to begin a process that brought freedom for the owners. As for Rozelle's optimism over the CBA, it was premature, because the labor struggle proved closer to its beginning than to its end.

The Conflict Grows

The decade of the eighties saw more trouble on the labor front and in several other areas off the field. Al Davis remained a thorn, other owners followed Davis into the nomadic life, and off-field conduct became an issue of increasing concern. Arrests and convictions for drugs became commonplace, and fans were less than impressed by players making good money and demanding free agency while blowing their lucre on cocaine. By the end of the decade nine teams had been sold or resold, and these new owners were increasingly concerned about the state of their very large investment. The NFL seemed to have no coherent labor strategy beyond trying to break the union, and there seemed to be no sense of what to do about controlling either salaries or drugs.[25]

The first major labor confrontation of the decade came in 1982 when the previous four-year CBA ended. Few doubted that a strike was in the offing. The NFLPA was still ill-prepared for such an eventuality. It had no strike fund and little player support for a work stoppage. On the management side, Jack Donlon, a former vice president for industrial relations at National Airlines noted for his hard-nosed style, was hired by the Management Council to head their negotiating team and bust the union. Garvey characterized Donlon as a hit man, thus setting the stage for negotiating in something less than good faith.[26]

Garvey, having abandoned the freedom issue, decided to pursue the money issue. There had been virtually no player movement in the league since 1977.

Looking at average salaries in the other major sports, the players knew they were grossly underpaid. At the time the average salary in professional baseball was $240,000 and in basketball $215,000, while in football it was less than half of either at $95,000. Team profits were greater than the average expenditure on player salaries. Garvey said that the average team in the NFL had no incentive to sign players because they had no real incentive to win. Revenue sharing meant that everyone got the same money regardless of performance.

It was a system of socialism for the owners, and Garvey wanted the same system for the players. To achieve this goal, he wanted player salaries set at 55 percent of NFL team revenues. (Garvey claimed the current rate was 31 percent, while Donlon said it was 44 percent.) This change in percentage of the gross would, claimed Garvey, increase the average NFL salary to $200,000 immediately. The money would be distributed by a formula based on seniority and overseen by the NFLPA. According to Michael Oriard this system would have rendered agents superfluous and made the NFLPA a full partner in running the NFL, something neither the owners nor agents could abide.

Negotiations began in Miami on February 16, 1982. Gene Upshaw and Ed Garvey both commented unfavorably on the absence of owners and announced that the NFLPA would need to look at the owners' books. Donlon responded that there would be no access to the books, no improvement in pensions, and a new player dress code would be instituted. A second meeting went about the same way.[27] It was clear that by this point Pete Rozelle was a figure of declining power, as he played no role in the negotiations. At one point he offered to serve as mediator, but Garvey and Upshaw rejected the idea out of hand. He had become, said Oriard, "a mere bystander," and David Harris termed Rozelle "a diminished figure in this time of crisis."[28]

The negotiations were on and off, with no progress and plenty of animosity. At times tempers flared and there were threats of physical violence. Both Donlon and Garvey were frustrated by one another. Pressure increased on the players when the owners made their "final offer," consisting of $1.313 billion for four years, along with immediate payments to players ranging from $10,000 to $60,000. What Garvey needed was recognition from the owners that the NFLPA had the right to negotiate wages. The owners refused and walked away on November 5, sending copies of this final offer directly to players. Within days several teams voted to accept the offer. Garvey's position was then untenable.

Garvey tried unsuccessfully to get the NLRB to end the strike, and that failed. Finally he turned to Dan Rooney to negotiate his surrender. On November 17 the strike was over. The approved contract was essentially what the owners had offered two weeks earlier. After fifty-seven days and the loss of eight games, the players gained almost nothing, while losing a half year of salary. The San Francisco 49ers, in voting for the contract, also voted for Garvey's resignation. Indeed Garvey was the big loser. There was an attempt to fire him in February 1983 that failed, but he resigned his position in June.

As for Rozelle, he played no role in the negotiations or the settlement, nor would he do so in 1987. He was a major loser in the entire affair, as *Sports Illustrated* pointed out. For all those who had come to see Rozelle as a savior, the Pope of Professional Sport, this strike exposed the myth of the infallible one. The owners claimed victory, but it was temporary. They failed, says Michael Oriard, to see how a partnership with the players could strengthen the league, as many business leaders had failed to see when dealing with unions over the course of modern labor history.

As for the players, they were down but would not give up. They turned once more to free agency as a goal. After another failed strike, six years of litigation, and a new farsighted commissioner, the players would achieve equity within the league. In the short run there was a legacy of ill-will, not only among the players but also the fans. Lower attendance and lower television ratings followed for the remainder of the season. The financial losses were great, as the fifteen hundred players lost $72 million in wages, stadium employees lost $4.5 million, concessionaires lost $17 million, business in NFL cities was down by $110 million, and local governments lost $11 million in taxes. The owners who came away feeling they won this strike lost $240 million in television and gate revenues.

In June, when Garvey finally resigned, he was succeeded as executive director by Gene Upshaw, who moved to distance himself from the Garvey regime. Ultimately it would be Upshaw's and Rozelle's successors who found a solution to the labor wars.[29]

More Problems and One More Strike

At the bargaining table in 1986 the owners wanted to reduce pay in the option year, set a rookie salary scale, expand the draft to fifteen rounds, roll back salaries, and offer nothing in increased benefits or free agency. As for the players, they were most concerned about free agency, as only one out of a potential five hundred players signed as a free agent under the 1982 CBA. This led to the third and final strike by the players in September 1987, following the second game of the season. The NFLPA believed that television money did not come to the owners until after the third week, but they were wrong. It came after the first week.[30]

This time the owners and Management Council were under the influence of hard-liners. Tex Schramm and Hugh Culverhouse were determined to offer the nation televised Sunday football. Indeed the league was ready with its scabs, or as the NFL called them, "replacement players." Only week three was lost. Television ratings and crowds were modest, but the players had no leverage. Oriard sees the owners' use of scabs as one more sign of the chaos that hit the game. It also exposed the owners' claim that they had a concern for the "integrity of the game" when they were willing to dump "a fraudulent version of NFL football on a gullible public."[31]

The use of scabs increased the bitterness of the negotiations and probably decreased the length of the strike. The players lost $75 million in salary. It cost the average player $15,000 per game, and the stars up to four times that figure. Players with million-dollar contracts paid a heavy price, and all were not willing to do so. Boomer Esiason, Jim Kelly, Warren Moon, John Elway, and Walter Payton remained on strike, while Joe Montana, Lawrence Taylor, Randy White, Tony Dorsett, Howie Long, Steve Largent, Ozzie Newsome, and others did not. When Montana, Dwight Clark, Roger Craig, and nine other 49ers returned to work on October 7, the handwriting was on the wall. A week later the strike ended, and the players returned to work without a contract. The twenty-eight NFL teams together lost about $80 million, and more than half the teams lost money. To pour a little salt on the wounds, the players were not allowed by the owners to return to work immediately, costing the players one more week of pay.

The press was particularly critical of the use of strike breakers. George Vecsey of the *New York Times* said that players crossing the line deserved the contempt of fellow players and fans for the rest of their career. On the other hand, Tex Schramm of the Cowboys waxed eloquent on the Walter Mitty character of the scabs and the opportunities they were being given. In San Francisco Bill Walsh encouraged his players to stay out on strike, and Glenn Dickey, a San Francisco writer, reported that Montana's teammates were bitter about his defection. Dave Kindred called Montana "a jerk in love with his checkbook." Most writers outside the South were hostile toward the owners, with such lines appearing like this one from Joan Ryan of the *San Francisco Chronicle,* who wrote of the scabs: "You can drape chiffon on a chimpanzee and you still don't have a debutante."

The strike of 1987 further illuminated the relationship between the NFL and television. The mutual support was displayed in many ways. Television news and sports, unlike much of the print media, was uncritical of the owners and much kinder to the scabs. Indeed the willingness of the networks to continue to pay for such an inferior product and to present it as "the NFL" worked for the owners. The public continued to watch the games, as ratings dropped only 1 to 5 percent. Some sponsors pulled out of the telecasts, but others were brought in on discounted advertising rates. In turn the NFL, in its appreciation of this collaboration by the networks, gave rebates on their fee payments.

Oriard called the 1987 strike "unwinnable but necessary." The owners would never allow free agency, but demanding it was the only leverage the NFLPA had. Money did not come under the purview of antitrust law, but free agency did. Having given away free agency, the union had to bring it back to the bargaining table and hope the owners would not bargain in good faith, and this would allow them to go back to the courts. This was Upshaw's Plan B. Given the subsequent history, it is difficult to argue with Oriard's judgment.

The day after the strike collapsed, the union filed *Powell v. NFL* in the Minneapolis court that was the site of earlier victories. In 1988 Judge Doty ruled for the NFLPA in *Powell,* agreeing that reaching impasse in bargaining meant that antitrust protection no longer applied. The Management Council, against Rozelle's wishes, appealed and won on November 1, 1989 in the Eighth Circuit Court. It ruled that the players could not sue over issues bargained and that impasse did not remove the application of labor law, giving antitrust exemption to the terms of the bargaining agreement. The NFLPA then moved to decertify themselves as the collective bargaining agent for the players, freeing the players to return to court where, as Oriard put it, "they could not lose."[32]

This is where matters stood on March 22, 1989, when Pete Rozelle shocked the owners by announcing his retirement. He was weary of the battles, most of which he seemed to be losing. His announcement was met by stunned silence and followed by a standing ovation. As he went out the door, ending twenty-nine remarkable years as commissioner, Rozelle was embraced by Al Davis, who wished him the best of luck. It was the start of a changing of the guard. Bill Walsh had retired following his third Super Bowl win, and Tex Schramm was preparing to end his thirty years at the helm of the Dallas Cowboys and, some would say, as assistant commissioner of the NFL.

At the press conference following the announcement, Rozelle broke down. Paul Zimmerman, the dean of football writers, said Rozelle's legacy was "solvency, parity, public awareness, and his own decency." Zimmerman felt that the new commissioner would be faced with three major problems: keeping the league solvent, resolving the labor impasse, and restoring owner unity. Wellington Mara, who was chosen to head the search committee for the new commissioner, said they would be looking for a replacement for an "irreplaceable man."[33]

III

The New NFL

10

A New Era

Choosing a successor for Pete Rozelle was not an easy task. From a public relations perspective Rozelle still had a lot of luster left on his reputation, and as with many major public figures he seemed irreplaceable. Many, however, were relieved to see his departure and regarded it as an opportunity to end the intractable problems that he had allowed to develop and fester.

The selection process was a long one. Fifty hours of committee debate, four meetings at various sites across the country, and eleven ballots finally led to an announcement on October 26, 1990, that Paul Tagliabue was the choice. In the NFL's age of litigation, Tagliabue had been the NFL's top legal adviser for two decades. He understood the current issues facing the league better than anyone.[1] It was an inspired choice.

The Labor Issues

Rick Telander described Tagliabue as "The Face of Sweeping Change," and his first major change and achievement came on the labor front. Al Davis told the new commissioner that the Management Council and Jack Donlan had become a major obstacle to any labor settlement by showing total disrespect for Gene Upshaw and the Players Association. The commissioner had a personal friendship and good working relationship with Upshaw, but nothing would be resolved until the pending legal cases were settled.[2] First the NFL lost the Freeman McNeil case on September 9, 1992, when Plan B free agency was declared an antitrust violation. Then in December Judge Doty pressured the two sides into a settlement of the Reggie White case challenging restrictions on free agency. Approval of a new CBA followed.

The new agreement reached in early 1993 included free agency after four years in the league, a guarantee of 56 percent of the gross, and a salary cap.

There was an incentive to renew the contract before it expired by making the final year of a contract a year with no cap. It made the players partners with the owners and gave them both freedom and football. The NFL Players Association was recertified and a significant period of labor peace was on the horizon.[3]

The CBA was renewed in 1996, 1998, 2000, 2002, and 2006, bringing a period of stability and prosperity to the NFL for nearly two decades. It was a period in which two-thirds of the NFL teams appeared in the Super Bowl, a result of free agency and very good management decisions. Achieving football excellence was difficult, as the salary cap forced player movement, making dynasties less likely. On the other hand construction and reconstruction of teams by organizations was easier. General managers, capologists (experts on the salary cap), and coaches became key figures, while every owner grew rich whatever the level of performance by his team.[4] It was the best of times and it was the best of times.

The 2006 collective bargaining process seemed in greatest danger of failing over the issue of revenue sharing. The players took the position that revenue sharing was being undermined by a growing gap between the rich and the poor. A number of owners worked on the agreement as it went through several stages of development. In the end only Mike Brown of the Bengals and Ralph Wilson of the Bills voted against it. Some described the 2006 CBA as a triumph for Paul Tagliabue in this his final negotiations before retirement. Mark Yost predicted that it would be seen as "one of the defining moments in the history of a very successful NFL commissioner." There was a three-year reopener in the agreement that turned out to be significant as misgivings mounted among owners, who felt the players were getting too big a share of the growing wealth.[5]

In his first year Tagliabue strengthened the league's drug program by increasing the frequency of tests for steroids and initiated testing for league executives and game officials. The new commissioner approved the formation of developmental squads. He extended the season by one week, playing sixteen games in seventeen weeks, with twelve of the games in-conference matchups. The league created another round of playoffs by adding another wild card team in each conference.

Television

The labor settlement set the stage for television contract negotiations that in 1990 produced the richest deal in league history. The four-year contract was worth nearly $3.8 billion, with approximately $33 million per team per year.

Turner Network Television (TNT) picked up the first eight weeks of the season on Sunday night, becoming the newest cable outlet for the NFL.

FOX entered the mix in 1994, accelerating the rates despite all the discussion of losses. CBS decided that it could no longer afford to play, while FOX was willing to spend like a drunken sailor to get what they felt would be a fabulous property. This development put the new network on the map and made it a true player in the prime-time market. The "FOX Factor" propelled the 1994 contract to $1.1 billion for each of the four years, or approximately $36 million per team per year. Another Rupert Murdock media property, DirecTV, signed with the NFL to offer "NFL Sunday Ticket," a service bringing all NFL games to subscribing fans.

By 1998 CBS was suffering from NFL withdrawal and got back into the bidding on the NBC portion of the contract. NBC walked away from the madness, an action it soon regretted. The 1998 contract was for eight years at the gaudy fee of $17.6 billion, or double the annual rate of the previous contract, going from $1.1 billion to $2.2 billion per year. This came to $73.3 million per team per year. CBS bid $500 million to drive out NBC, FOX put in $550 million, ABC did the same with *Monday Night Football* to prevent NBC from taking it, and ESPN paid $550 million for the full Sunday night package. As Sean McManus, president of CBS Sports said, the NFL understood the basics of supply and demand. "And at this time there is supply of three and demand of four."[6]

All of this wild spending came at a time when ratings were flat and the networks claimed they were losing money. But were they? In the world of sports television, profit was in the eye of the beholder rather than the calculations of the accountants. For FOX the benefits were clear and came quickly. The one-time marginal network increased its prime-time viewers by 7 percent, as NFL football served as an advertising and promotional venue for FOX programming across the prime-time platform.

The flip side of the calculus hit CBS when they left the NFL. CBS lost eight affiliates to FOX, a loss of eleven million prime-time viewers over the next two years, producing a drop of morale at the network. *60 Minutes* dropped out of the top ten shows without the NFL lead-in on Sunday night. There was much discussion of the intangibles in the NFL contracts, and as Michael Oriard put it, the "relative importance of the intangibles was itself an intangible." Similar analyses were made of the state of NBC after CBS took the AFC, which coincided with the departure of *Seinfeld* from NBC. The result was a 26 percent drop in male viewers for the network.

Over at ABC, ratings for *MNF* continued to fall, but that loss was offset by the fact that *MNF* was the highest-rated prime-time show for eighteen to forty-nine-year-old males, and it had a large and growing female audience. "By the 'new math of TV sport,' the networks collectively were projected to lose $100 million a year on football contracts, yet this was possibly the best of investments."[7]

With the DirecTV Sunday Ticket contract in place and the NFL Network operating by 2005, the NFL had strengthened its hand prior to negotiating its next television contract. The *Wall Street Journal* reported that the networks were looking for a modest increase in television fees of 3 to 7 percent. The NFL, for its part, was thinking in terms of a minimum of 7 percent. What they got was another bonanza. CBS and Fox extended their contracts through 2011 at a fee increase of 25 to 30 percent. The cost to CBS was $3.7 billion and to FOX $4.3 million. DirecTV increased their payment from $2 billion to $3.5 billion over the next five years. Then, a few months later came the announcement that ABC was dropping *Monday Night Football* and that ESPN would pick it up at $8.8 billion for eight years, which was double the ABC fee. NBC then took *Sunday Night Football* for $600 million for six years. "At this point the NFL looked forward to more than $3.7 billion per year, or $117 million per club, up from $2.8 billion in the last year of the expiring agreements and nearly 70 percent higher than the $2.2 billion average over the life of the old contracts." While some questioned the wisdom of the networks, few questioned the good fortune of the NFL.[8]

Franchise values quickly reflected the revenue bonanza. *Forbes* reported that there were now five franchises worth more than one billion dollars. At the top were the Washington Redskins, the first to crack the billion-dollar barrier, valued in 2006 at $1.423 billion. Second and third were the Patriots, $1.176 billion, and the Cowboys, $1.173 billion. The Houston Texans, $1.043 billion, and the Philadelphia Eagles, $1.024 billion, rounded out the NFL billionaire club. At the bottom of the list was Minnesota, valued at $720 million, up from the purchase price of $600 million the previous year. It is also significant that the New York Yankees were the only Major League Baseball franchise worth more than the Vikings.[9]

Expansion and Relocation

Pete Rozelle had dangled expansion franchises in front of cities and Congress for various purposes over the years, but there had been no expansion since the mid-70s. In March 1990, the Committee on Expansion and Realignment was appointed. This set off a tidal wave of political lobbying and maneuvering that offered further proof of just how much the NFL dominated the American sports scene.

Baltimore was seen as a front-runner with the promise of a $165 million stadium from the Maryland Stadium Authority. In St. Louis, the original ownership group headed by Fran Murray collapsed, while both Memphis and Jacksonville offered solid bids. In May 1992, league owners accepted the committee's report naming Baltimore, Charlotte, Jacksonville, St. Louis, and Memphis as the five finalists for the new franchises. On October 16, Charlotte was awarded one of the franchises, with former Baltimore Colts player Jerry Richardson, a food service and fast food millionaire, as the owner. On November 30, the second expansion franchise was awarded to Jacksonville and owner Wayne Weaver, who made his fortune with Shoe Carnival and Nine West.

Baltimore was outraged when it was passed over. Jacksonville, regarded as a long shot, was the major surprise. The St. Louis group felt that they had a strong bid, even though the first potential ownership group collapsed. The two cities began pursuing potential relocation franchises and both ultimately succeeded.[10] Both St. Louis and Baltimore were former NFL cities.

When expansion came to Tampa Bay and Seattle in the mid-70s, the sale price per franchise was $16 million. In Charlotte and Jacksonville the price stood at $140 million. In part this was a reflection of the television contracts that now brought each franchise $32 million per year. It also illustrated the new revenue being generated by stadiums. In 1994 the new high values were reflected in the sale price of the Miami Dolphins for $160 million and the Philadelphia Eagles for $173 million, and in 1995 the Tampa Bay Buccaneers sold for $192 million.

The expansion and relocations of the '90s resulted in massive giveaways of tax dollars, revenues, and any number of inducements to owners motivated by greed and need. Cities and states lusted after that elusive perk of being known as "a major league city" or, even better, an "NFL destination." For owners, not moving became as lucrative as moving, because threatening to move could extort their current city for a new stadium with more perks and increased revenue opportunities.

In the mid-'90s St. Louis offered the Rams a new domed stadium, a state of the art practice facility in the team complex, 100 percent of concession revenue, and other perks. The league owners rejected the move 23-1 on the grounds that the Rams situation did not meet the "need test." When the State of Missouri threatened to sue, the NFL reconsidered. This left the Raiders alone in Los Angeles, trapped in a crumbling Coliseum. Al Davis announced on June 23, 1995, that the Raiders would return "home" to Oakland.

Also in 1995, when it became clear that Art Modell would not get a new stadium, he shocked Cleveland and much of the NFL universe when he announced the Browns were moving to Baltimore. The city felt betrayed and threatened a lawsuit. The commissioner responded by promising Cleveland a new team by 1999, and that the name "Browns" would stay in Cleveland, as would the team colors and heritage. For Baltimore the game had come full circle. Having denounced Robert Irsay for betraying their city, Baltimore boosters now facilitated Art Modell's betrayal of Cleveland.[11] Shortly thereafter Bud Adams announced that the Houston Oilers would move to Nashville in 1998. In an attempt to calm the waters, Commissioner Tagliabue announced the NFL would oppose any attempt to move a team to Los Angeles.

As promised, in 1998 the commissioner announced that Al Lerner would be the owner of the new Cleveland Browns at a mind-numbing cost of $503 million. This left the NFL with an unbalanced number of thirty-one franchises. Unable to get back into Los Angeles, the NFL in early 1999 awarded its thirty-second franchise to Houston and Robert McNair for a further mind-numbing $700 million.

Much of the relocation and threatened relocation of franchises centered on stadium issues. In 1999 Tagliabue proposed the G-3 Program, which changed the stadium financing landscape. The new program offered 50 percent of the financing for new stadium construction or renovation from a fund derived from television revenues. Each team would provide $1 million from their share of television money to create the G-3 Fund. During Tagliabue's tenure as commissioner, seventeen new stadiums were built and several others, including Green Bay's Lambeau Field, were renovated.

G-3 was created not to relieve communities of their roles as chief subsidizers of the NFL, but rather to deal with those teams that could not successfully extort their community. This applied primarily to larger communities with multiple sports franchises or major entertainment alternatives to the NFL. Smaller communities without competing franchises were the most vulnerable to threats and therefore most willing to offer the largest subsidies to retain their NFL franchise.[12]

Leadership and Public Issues

Early in his tenure, Commissioner Tagliabue indicated that he was not shy when it came to public issues. When Head Coach Sam Wyche refused to conform to league policy and allow a female reporter into the Cincinnati Bengals' locker room, the new commissioner docked him a week's pay. Also that year, twelve members of the New England Patriots exposed themselves to *Boston Herald* reporter Lisa Olsen in the locker room following a game. Victor Kiam, the Pat's owner, reportedly called Olsen a "classic bitch" (Kiam denied the charge in full-page ads in Boston and New York papers). The commissioner ordered an investigation and later fined Zeke Mowatt and two other players over the incident. On another major issue Tagliabue acted with conviction and firmness. When the State of Arizona voted not to recognize a Martin Luther King Jr. holiday, Tagliabue recommended that the 1993 Super Bowl be moved to another location, and it was.

His first public test of leadership arrived in January 1991 when Operation Desert Storm in Iraq began just before the conference championship games. Tagliabue made an unflinching decision to go forward with the games and with the Super Bowl that followed. He then turned these events into opportunities for public expressions of patriotism on a grand scale. The 1991 Super Bowl set new standards for excessive patriotic display, matching the excess that had come to mark all activities associated with the new midwinter national holiday. Whitney Houston's singing of the national anthem is widely considered one of the best ever, and one of the most emotional as well. Shortly thereafter, Tagliabue was named the most powerful man in sports by *The Sporting News,* and the *Sports Business Journal* named him sports executive of the year.[13]

Tagliabue faced a similar but more serious decision following the September 11, 2001, terrorist attacks. The attack came on Tuesday; on Wednesday the New York Giants players told their general manager they would not play on Sunday, and on Thursday morning the commissioner wrote a statement and sent it to the owners for approval. By late morning he was able to announce that the NFL would not play games on the coming Sunday. Other sports teams and leagues followed suit. Also, the NFL and its players worked in relief efforts and donated generously to them. Tom Boswell wrote that by its actions, the NFL "established itself as a caring and community-oriented entity."[14]

To Share or Not to Share

One of the major challenges to the commissioner was the growing intrusion of non-league–controlled advertising into the NFL. In 2000 all of the league's ancillary interests were grouped together under NFL Business Ventures. The high cost of teams led to increased pressure for new revenue sources. Related to need for revenue growth, a battle developed over revenue sharing. The league divided its revenues into "shared" and "unshared" categories, and in the '90s "unshared" revenue grew at the fastest rate. Stadium revenue led the way, as the percentage of "unshared" revenue expanded from 12 percent in 1994 to 21 percent in 2003.[15] Building new stadiums and renovating old ones provided owners with new ways of growing their unshared revenues. The first bonanzas resulting from the new stadium game were luxury boxes and seat licenses. Stadium renovations also increased local revenue in Green Bay, Chicago, and six other cities.

The NFL gold standard was set in Washington, where there was no public financing. FedEx Field offered an array of seating options that defined personal football and power status while enriching the Redskins. The 205 Dream Seats brought in $5.2 million, Touchdown Club seats $2.25 million, Tailgate Club initiation fees $3.9 million, Tailgate Club season fees $1.5 million, loge seats $9.7 million, and club seats $48.8 million. Regular seats, regular suites, and owners' suites were also available. The furnishings, appointments, and emoluments available at each level were scaled progressively upward on the cost meter and culminated at levels of decadence for which the term "luxury" seemed grossly inadequate.[16] The surge in unshared revenues meant that television revenue in the NFL dropped below 50 percent of total revenue for the first time since 1977.[17]

Cowboys' owner Jerry Jones was the most adept at turning stadiums into revenue. In 1989 the oil millionaire bought the Dallas Cowboys at a record purchase price. Jones put up $90 million in cash and borrowed the rest of the money against his assets. By 1991 Jones estimated he was losing about $40,000 a day on interest payments. Faced with this drain, he needed to find ways to generate revenue and cut expenses. He managed to do both quite effectively.

The Cowboys had gone 3-13 in the previous season, lost $9.5 million, but took in revenues of $41 million. Jones moved his practice facility to save $1 million, found sponsorship for the Dallas Cowboy cheerleaders, and convinced the Irving city council to approve beer sales at the stadium. He also filled the ninety-nine empty luxury boxes at Texas Stadium and then added sixty-eight more, bringing the total to a league-leading 360 luxury boxes. By 1994 the luxury boxes were generating $30 million per year. According to *Sports Illustrated,* in 1990 Dallas broke even, in 1991 the team turned a $10 million profit, and in 1992 they showed a $20.6 million profit.

On the field the team was also doing well, with two Super Bowl victories in Jones's first six seasons as owner. Revenues kept climbing, and *Financial*

World ranked Dallas the most valuable professional sport franchise, as the team's worth tripled during Jones's tenure. By 1994 Jones was looking to literally raise the roof on Texas Stadium and thereby add forty thousand seats to the venue, putting capacity at 104,000. He wanted to add a retractable roof with air conditioning and return to a grass field. By 2000 Jones hoped to have a theme park adjacent to the stadium. The price of the project would reach $200 million, and he looked to the City of Irving for joint financing.[18]

In his quest for new revenue sources, Jerry Jones had an endless stream of plans, some of which did not sit well with fellow owners, who thought Jones was out to destroy the shared revenue model that had served the NFL so well. Jones's first major move was signing a $2.5 million-per-year, ten-year contract with Pepsi. This raised the revenue sharing issue as well as conflicted with Coca Cola's exclusive contract as the official soft drink of the NFL. Jones concluded a similar seven-year deal with Nike giving the company exclusive rights to outfit Cowboys' sideline personnel and to build a theme park at Texas Stadium. A large Nike swoosh would be painted on the stadium.

The NFL felt this was a violation of league rules, and the result was a $300 million lawsuit filed in September 1995 by NFL Properties (NFLP) against Jones and his companies. Jones filed a countersuit against the NFL and NFL Properties for $750 million. He called NFL Properties an illegal cartel and announced his countersuit on the *Monday Night Football* telecast. Jones argued that the stadium deals were outside the purview of NFLP, which controlled only league contracts.

Tagliabue called Jones's actions a clear attack on NFL marketing operations that undermined league partnership, revenue sharing, and competitiveness. The commissioner charged that Jones's actions were a threat to free agency, parity, the salary cap, and were simply intolerable. Jones signed additional stadium deals with American Express, Pizza Hut, KFC, Taco Bell, and AT&T. On December 13, 1996, both sides dropped their suits and reached a settlement that allowed Jones to keep all current sponsors and sign new ones.[19]

Some league owners saw Jones as a threat to the NFL. First, he was a threat to revenue sharing, which in turn impacted parity and the ability of the smaller franchises to compete. Second, increases in revenue resulted in growth of the salary cap. If the salary cap moved too high, owners feared that Jones and a handful of other owners would be the only ones that could compete financially and hold sufficient wealth to spend at the cap level.[20]

One could argue that the most significant result of the *Jones v. NFL* dustup was an increased awareness of the significance of merchandise sales, marketing, and the need to reinvigorate NFL Properties. By the "ringing of the cash register in the night," Jones moved the NFL toward a brand identity rather than a mere football one. By the end of the '90s, as Michael Oriard has so persuasively demonstrated in his book *Brand NFL,* the NFL was no longer a mere football league. The NFL was a brand.

Expanding the Market

In the league's early years there was NFL Enterprises, a division of Roy Rodgers Enterprises, selling NFL logo glassware to be given away at Standard Oil gas stations. By the beginning of the twenty-first century, NFL logos had become ubiquitous in the consumer marketplace. In the early 1980s the free market on the streets realized that there was money to be made from NFL merchandise. Free market vendors hawked unlicensed NFL merchandise wherever they saw a market. In 1983 the league sought a restraining order against those operating without a license.[21]

In the early '90s selling was at the heart of NFL Properties. You could get almost anything with a team logo on it, including bowling balls, Christmas tree ornaments, watches, inflatable helmets, dog collars, pacifiers, bumper stickers, and bathroom accessories of varied description and use. Team clothing of all kinds, starting with Pro Line jerseys and warm-up jackets, spread into every imaginable clothing line and then multiplied itself with throwback gear. In 1991 NFLP added the Spirit Line for women and "quality" became a goal, pushing up the price ceiling. National Football League Properties was becoming a huge milking machine.

The big change at NFLP came on July 12, 1994, when Sara Levinson, once co-president at MTV, was hired as president of NFL Properties. Levinson produced a subtle shift in marketing strategy in which the NFL itself was marketed and extended into new markets. The NFL no longer endorsed products. It was the product itself. In Oriard's words, "Her hiring confirmed something more fundamental: that the NFL now openly regarded itself as a 'brand' and pro football as a 'product' to be marketed."[22]

Under Levinson's leadership the NFL placed an emphasis on exclusive sponsorships rather than the number of sponsors. The role of the NFL Web site expanded. The "Punt, Pass, and Kick" competition was tied in with children's channel Nickelodeon. There would be a new focus on the international market, as an annual regular-season game was taken overseas. There was outreach to the Hispanic population with a Latin-themed NFL float in Macy's Thanksgiving Day Parade. The college draft, already the most overhyped non-sporting event in the history of sport, was given even greater marketing attention. Looking to profit from every available space, the league sold game-day sponsorships for replay, the first-down line, and the red zone. Commercials came to the stadium, where something was needed to fill the increasing amount of dead time during television timeouts.

During Levinson's six years at NFLP, revenues increased 40 percent and the NFL was clearly a brand within the world of sports and entertainment. Both Paul Tagliabue and Gene Upshaw saw it as such. The commissioner told John Seabrook of the *New Yorker* in 1997 that ESPN and FOX had introduced a "more youthful" and "more iconoclastic" attitude toward sports. *Business Week* expressed the view that the hiring of Levinson was just what the NFL, "that 75-year-old temple of testosterone," needed to connect with the new generation while still holding its core in the "Joe Sixpack Crowd." In marketing the NFL, Levinson had no peer. She found something for everyone as she developed an in-house consumer research unit. Levinson didn't miss a single demographic with her genius, and *Advertising Age* named her "Promotional Marketer of the Year" in 1996.

When in 2000 Levinson's dynamic run ended, the NFL consolidated its business operations and turned them over to Roger Goodell. He moved back to more traditional marketing objectives like building the audience, increasing the reach of NFL.com, growing merchandise sales, building player image, and increasing youth interest. Then, the following year, the league hired an outside agency and charged it with emphasizing the "social currency" of the NFL, showing how it brings people together for outdoor barbeques and to watch games.[23]

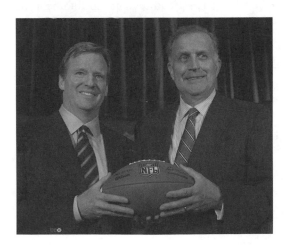

NFL Commissioners Roger Goodell and Paul Tagliabue passing the torch, August 8, 2008, Northbrook, Illinois. AP Photo/M. Spencer Green.

The major item in the hard goods category was the Madden NFL video game featuring the voice of John Madden, which sold $1.5 billion worth of product in the first sixteen years of its existence. EA Sports paid the NFL and the NFLPA more than $400 million to license the game. Its release each season became a major media event. Beyond video the NFL became the first of the major sports leagues to embrace the fantasy game, and fantasy football quickly became the largest and most popular of the fantasy sports games.[24]

NFL Europe offered another opportunity for merchandise sales, as did international television distribution. This opened up Japan, continental Europe, Canada, and the United Kingdom and led to games played in London. In 2005 the NFL provided 190,000 hours of programming to 234 countries in thirty-one languages across twenty-four time zones.[25]

The search for new revenues was a perpetual quest. In 2003 Business Week reported that the NFL planned to sell its rich archives of video through a video-on-demand outlet, that ESPN was working on a deal to develop two movies, and that the NFL and Time Inc. were about to announce a deal to publish an NFL magazine. It was only a beginning.

The money flow made it difficult to remember that the NFL was, after all, about football. Team values rose rapidly. In 2000 Dan Snyder paid $800 million for the Redskins and their stadium. Jack Kent Cooke had paid $300,000 for a 25 percent stake in the team in the early '60s. Within a few years Snyder's Redskins were the first NFL franchise to reach a value of one billion dollars. In 1965 Rankin Smith paid $8.5 million for the Atlanta Falcons, while in 2002 Arthur Blank paid $545 million for the franchise, which at the time drew the second-lowest attendance in the league. By 2005 Forbes valued the Falcons at $690 million and by 2007 at $796 million, and this for the club with the second-lowest value in the NFL in both those years.[26]

Michael Oriard calls Tagliabue the best commissioner in NFL history. He dealt deftly with every major problem he faced. This began with the labor situation, which Tagliabue built into a league partnership, and ended with revenue sharing, the extension of the labor agreement, and a new television agreement before he retired in 2006. His sixteen-year tenure resulted in a frenzy of stadium construction and renovation, which helped to fuel the NFL's expanding revenues.

By 2001 there were 493 millionaires playing in the NFL, an average of fifteen millionaires per team earning an average of $2.86 million per year. In 2005 the average salary across the NFL had risen to $1.4 million and the median stood at $596,000. Signing bonuses made up for lack of guaranteed salaries.[27]

For *Forbes* analysts the bottom line was the bottom line on Tagliabue. They called his greatest achievement the creation of a tremendous amount of wealth for his bosses. The television deals were massive and franchise values jumped. The inauguration of the NFL network, although producing little initial revenue, kept the broadcast networks on edge and increased their bids for broadcast rights.[28]

Race

Race had long been an issue in the NFL. The African American quarterback was the most publicly discussed aspect of the race issue in football in the 1960s. After the initial appearance of Marvin Briscoe with the Denver Broncos in 1968, further change was slow. In 1969 James Harris in Buffalo was the first black quarterback to open a season as the starter, and Joe Gilliam started a few games for the Pittsburgh Steelers in the mid-'70s.

Doug Williams joined the Tampa Bay Bucs in 1978 and led them to the first playoff appearance in their history. After the 1982 season Williams left Tampa for Oklahoma of the United States Football League (USFL). When that league folded in 1986, Williams joined the Washington Redskins, where he served as backup. When the playoffs began, coaches named him the starting quarterback. In Super Bowl XXII Williams led the Redskins to a rout of the Denver Broncos, throwing four touchdown passes. Voters named him the game's Most Valuable Player.

Some regard Williams's success as a key in growing acceptance of the black quarterback in the NFL. Jim Brown did not agree. "The story of the game wasn't Doug William's blackness," rather it was the persistence of this man, whose career was nearly over, and his great comeback. "I don't buy its profundity for other black people. They need equal rights. What Doug Williams did in the Super Bowl won't do shit for a cat who can't throw a football." Brown's views were not echoed across the NFL.[29]

In 1991 *Sports Illustrated* revisited the race question and included a survey of black professional athletes. As with most surveys on race in America, the perceptions differed widely across the black and white communities. For example, 63 percent of black players felt they were treated worse than white ones, while only 2 percent of whites believed this to be the case. Seventy-one percent of blacks believed that they had to be better than whites to make a team, while no whites shared that view. Sixty-nine percent of blacks believed that whites got special preference when certain key positions were involved, while only 8 percent of whites agreed with that point of view. A majority of black players believed that white players enjoyed better contract terms and higher salaries than black ones, and thought that they were much less likely to become part of team management upon retirement.[30]

At the end of the 1990 season there were eight black quarterbacks among the eighty-two signal callers in the league, and two of them started in the Pro Bowl. In 1991 there were no black owners, no black general managers, and one black head coach. The one head coach was the only change since 1968. Data gathered in the '90s by the Institute for Diversity and Ethics in Sports at the University of Central Florida illustrated the glacial pace of change. Art Shell was the first African American to serve as a head coach in the NFL in the postsegregation era, coaching the Raiders from 1989 to 1994. In 1992 the number of head coaches doubled when the Minnesota Vikings hired Dennis Green. The number increased to three from 1996 through 1998 when Ray Rhodes was in Philadelphia and Tony Dungy was in Tampa. In 2000 the number fell back to two and then went back up to three the following season, when the Jets hired Herm Edwards.

With little progress occurring, and in the shadow cast by the firing of Tony Dungy and Dennis Green in 2002, Johnnie Cochran Jr. and Cyrus Mehri issued a report titled, "Black Coaches in the National Football League." The study showed that over the previous fifteen years black coaches averaged 1.1 more wins per season than white coaches. The black coaches led their teams to the playoffs 67 percent of the time, compared with 39 percent for white coaches, and they won 2.7 more games on average than white coaches in their first season. The report called for change.

In response Tagliabue announced the formation of a Diversity Committee in October 2002. The following year, the NFL adopted the Rooney Rule, which required that minority candidates be interviewed for all openings at head coach or any senior football position. By the end of the 2004 season and Super Bowl, the number of African American head coaches stood at six, twice the total prior to the Rooney Rule. There were seven African American head coaches in 2006 and six in 2007, 2008, and 2009.

The league reached a notable milestone in Super Bowl XLI when two African American head coaches faced each other: Tony Dungy of the Colts and Lovie Smith of the Bears. Then, at Super Bowl XLIII, Mike Tomlin of the Steelers became the second African American head coach in three years to win the Super Bowl. These changes are generally attributed to the efforts of Tagliabue, the Rooney Rule, and groups advocating diversity, such as the Fritz Pollard Alliance.

At the level of assistant coach, there also was change. In 2003 there were 169 African American assistant coaches and twelve offensive or defensive co-ordinators. The next year there were fourteen African American coordinators. By 2009 there were nine African Americans holding the position of assistant head coach, an increasingly significant title as it was becoming a clear stepping stone up the coaching ladder.

The NFL has never had an African American principal owner. Between 2002 and 2008 the numbers of vice presidents and general managers rose, with twelve VPs and five GMs in 2008. In 2003 49 percent of the support staff in the league office were people of color, with 25 percent of these African American. At the management level in NFL headquarters 14 percent were African American in 2003.

Another major concern historically was the issue of "stacking" in the NFL. This refers to a tendency toward overrepresentation of race by position. The UCF Diversity Institute studies of "stacking" found that positions involving speed and agility generally were overwhelmingly held by African Americans, whereas whites have occupied those positions described as "central" and "involving thinking." The changes at the quarterback position have been substantial, but white dominance remained at the 80 percent level five years into the new century. African Americans continued to be overrepresented at running back and wide receiver, with percentages running from the upper 80s to low 90s. Tight end, offensive tackle, and guard positions were split evenly, while white players were overrepresented at center. The historical trends of high African American percentages at cornerback and safety continued.[31] The changes on the "stacking" issue came slowly and often painfully. Pressures on those who broke the color line were considerable and reinforced by large quantities of hate mail. Black coaches often felt similar pressures.[32]

In the area of race, Paul Tagliabue's time as commissioner was one of considerable change. Richard Lapchick, the director of the UCF Institute for Diversity and Ethics in Sports, offered a generally favorable assessment of Tagliabue's tenure. The NFL showed considerable improvements in racial diversity in the areas of head coach, general manager, and assistant coach over the final five years Tagliabue was commissioner.[33]

Another Era Ends

As the Tagliabue era closed, there remained a number of outstanding problems with potential for disruption of the NFL's euphoric ride. Owners remained edgy about revenue sharing and the amount of money ending up in the players' bank accounts. The drug issues, both performance enhancers and recreational drugs, remained a concern. Player conduct, especially off the field, was a growing concern, as were the soft television ratings.

On March 20, 2006, Paul Tagliabue announced his retirement after seventeen years as commissioner. The analysts found much to admire. New accords on revenue sharing and a collective bargaining agreement running through 2011, huge television contracts, and the G-3 stadium-building program headed the list. Often cited as his major strength was Tagliabue's ability to function effectively in a much more complex media and sports world than the one confronted by previous commissioners. *Forbes* counted his greatest achievement as guaranteeing a tremendous amount of wealth to his bosses, while for Michael Oriard and others Tagliabue's greatest achievement was labor peace, which was a prerequisite to all else.[34]

Defending the Shield

Roger Goodell seemed to have been born for the position of NFL commissioner, and he trained for the role most of his adult life. When Dan Rooney, the co-chair of the Commissioner Search Committee, knocked at Goodell's hotel room door, Roger was delighted, overwhelmed with emotion, but hardly surprised. When he graduated from Washington and Jefferson College in 1981, Goodell wrote a letter to his father, the former senator from New York, telling him that he wanted to accomplish two things in life: become commissioner of the NFL and make his father proud of him.[1]

Armed with little more than an undergraduate degree in economics, Goodell joined the league office as an unpaid intern in 1982 during the reign of Pete Rozelle. Goodell landed this position after an extensive letter writing campaign to league and team offices. In 1983 he moved on to a paid position with the Jets, and then returned to the league office the following year as a public relations assistant. In 1987 Rozelle appointed Goodell as assistant to Lamar Hunt, president of the AFC. Three years later he went to work for Commissioner Paul Tagliabue where, over the next decade, Goodell served in nearly every capacity of league operations. In December 2001 Tagliabue appointed him NFL executive vice president and chief operating officer. Goodell once said that his work with Rozelle and Tagliabue were his MBA equivalent. No doubt that was true, and with a very well-connected placement department. Goodell was one of five finalists for commissioner and he never trailed in the voting through the five ballots it took to make the decision. He assumed his duties on September 1, 2006.[2]

From the start Goodell faced numerous problems, issues, and public relations disasters. Some of them were serious and had the potential to inflict damage on the NFL, while others were minor challenges for a leader with well-honed public relations skills. Goodell styled himself as protector of the brand, or even more pretentiously, protector of the shield. He displayed a combination of great skill, woodenness of personality, and an imperious pairing of hubris and arrogance.

In his first year as commissioner Goodell dealt with several public relations issues. "Spygate" produced charges that the hooded genius, Patriots Head Coach Bill Belichick, was using video equipment to spy on opponents. Much more serious was the firestorm of media and public protest over Falcons quarterback Michael Vick's involvement in a dog-fighting ring. These were followed by an array of serious issues, including player conduct, concussions, the bounty scandal, and the maintenance of labor peace.

Discipline

Spying on practices, stealing signs, or seeking insider information is nearly as old as team sport. In the NFL it was assumed that teams used espionage, but the rule was, "Don't get caught." For nearly a year the charges of spying and a cover-up swirled around Bill Belichick and the New England Patriots. The opportunity to attack an elite team and elite coach fueled a media frenzy that seemed in retrospect worth no more than a few days or a few weeks of national attention. In the end, little was found of significance beyond the perfunctory taping, which violated Article 9 of the NFL constitution and by-laws. To avoid the appearance of favoritism or being soft, Goodell fined the New England Patriots $250,000 and Coach Belichick $500,000 and took away one first-round draft pick.[3]

High on the list of issues facing the commissioner in his first year was player conduct, especially off-field. During Goodell's first year, in the neighborhood of three dozen players were arrested. In response the commissioner moved to strengthen the league conduct policy to allow him to discipline teams, league and team personnel, and players. He consulted many people, including Gene Upshaw of the NFLPA. Goodell emphasized that to be found not guilty was not sufficient for exoneration. NFL personnel would be held to a higher standard.[4]

The case of Michael Vick, the talented and charismatic quarterback of the Atlanta Falcons, was the first test of the new policy. Cruelty to animals in any form in America is seen as a horrific crime. In July 2007, following an investigation of a dog-fighting ring, a federal grand jury in Richmond, Virginia, indicted Vick and his associates on charges of crossing state lines to

Goodell as Patsy for Owners. TANK MCNAMARA©2009 Miller/Hinds. Reprinted with permission of UNIVERSAL UCLICK. All Rights Reserved.

conduct competitive dog fighting, betting on these fights, and participating in the execution of dogs that did not perform well or were seriously injured in the fights. The NFL quickly issued a statement indicating that any final decisions on actions against Vick under the league conduct policy would follow the legal proceedings. The statement also condemned the activities as "cruel, degrading and illegal."[5] Vick pleaded guilty to both federal and state charges and served eighteen months of his sentence, while losing millions in salary and endorsements. After his release, Vick sought reinstatement into the NFL and Goodell, despite considerable pressure, conditionally reinstated the Falcon quarterback.[6]

At both ends of the Vick case Goodell moved with care, disciplining Vick in a carefully measured manner, and then accepting Vick's pleas when the player came out of prison. It was a difficult tightrope to walk, as the commissioner needed to heed the public outcry, to be seen as fair and just, and yet not cross any legal lines surrounding the court proceedings, his powers as commissioner, or his relationship with the NFLPA. Goodell seemed to have succeeded in this difficult and delicate task.

The conduct policy got another test from his handling of frequent charges of sexual misconduct brought against players. The high-profile case of Ben Roethlisberger, the Steelers' star quarterback, was a major challenge to Goodell's skills and the NFL conduct policy. In early 2010 Roethlisberger was charged with the sexual assault of a twenty-year-old female college student in Milledgeville, Georgia. This was the second time within a year that Roethlisberger was charged with sexual assault. It was a seedy and sordid affair.

During the investigation by Georgia and Milledgeville authorities, Goodell maintained a very low profile and came under fire for his near silence. He was accused by at least one prominent writer, Jemele Hill of ESPN.com, of racism, as she compared Goodell's actions in this case with those involving a number of African American players over the previous few years. Hill noted that punishment in many of those cases did not await the outcome of criminal investigations, as in the Roethlisberger case.[7]

Goodell's first major action in the case was a memo to the league CEOs, presidents, GMs, and head coaches. In it he noted that there had been several cases in recent weeks involving alcohol, weapons, and violence against women. He reiterated that conduct by anyone associated with the NFL reflected on the league and its values. Failure to conduct oneself properly, he said, "undermines the respect for our league by our fans, lessens the confidence of our business partners and threatens the continued success of our brand."

The Georgia district attorney announced at a press conference that all charges against Roethlisberger were being dropped because he did not have enough evidence to prosecute. The D.A. then went on to offer lurid details of Roethlisberger's unsavory conduct. Goodell met with the quarterback the next day and then appeared on talk radio to announce that Roethlisberger had violated the league conduct policy and was suspended for the first six games of the next season. Roethlisberger was required to undergo a "comprehensive behavioral evaluation by professionals."[8]

In another public relations challenge, the commissioner was quick to speak. When a story circulated that the right-wing radio demagogue Rush Limbaugh was interested in buying a minority share in the St. Louis Rams, Goodell was quoted as saying that "divisive comments are not what the N.F.L. is all about." The commissioner referred specifically to Limbaugh's racist comments about Eagles quarterback Donovan McNabb, which Goodell characterized as "polarizing." The NFLPA joined those in opposition to Limbaugh's ambitions. Selena Roberts of *Sports Illustrated* noted that few players, seven by her count, had spoken out on the issue, and no players from the Rams had anything public to say about Limbaugh. She claimed that the players had been "cowed by Goodell," and that the league conduct policy gave Goodell the power of judge, jury, and censor over the players.[9]

If there were doubts about Goodell's leadership, these were not reflected in a 2009 poll of 296 players taken by *Sports Illustrated* and CNN. Players gave the commissioner high marks on job performance, and the younger players rated him even higher. Two months later, in February 2010, the owners expressed their views by extending Goodell's contract by five years. The extension was prompted in part by the need for stability of leadership heading into the coming CBA battle with the players, but the owners recognized Goodell's "already significant list of accomplishments" and supported "his strategic vision for the future of our league." Goodell was compensated just under ten million dollars in 2009.[10]

Having learned the art of running the NFL at the feet of Pete Rozelle, Goodell understood the importance of public relations. The new conduct policy with a tougher face was paired with a new public relations campaign with a softer face. There was little surprise at seeing Matt Hasselbeck of the Seattle Seahawks reading to his daughters, or Willie McGinest of the Cleveland Browns calling his mother to tell her he loved her. Rather than directly confronting the issues of bad conduct, the NFL chose to focus on the positives and devoted 25 percent of its advertising during the 2007 season to positive messages. Lisa Baird, senior vice president for marketing at the NFL in New York, said the marketing people we're doing "everything necessary to protect the strength of our brand."[11]

In September 2007 Roger Goodell was not only protecting the NFL brand but was establishing one of his own. In late September *Business Week* anointed him a member of its "Power 100" and the "most powerful man in sports."[12]

New Media

At the time of Goodell's second State of the League address in early 2008, there was much to feel good about. Record attendance was on a five-year streak, with 90 percent of stadium capacity filled in 2007. Television ratings were up, with FOX reaching its largest audience in more than a decade at 17.1 million per game, and CBS's audience was up nearly 9 percent. The conference championship games television audience increased 10 percent that year. Although *Monday Night Football* was down, it remained atop the cable numbers. As the world of new media continued to evolve, Goodell moved to control it. He ended the outsourcing of NFL.com to CBS SportsLine and brought it back in-house. To further increase NFL control of video highlights, Goodell created a new Digital Media Committee in the owners group, headed by Paul Allen, cofounder of Microsoft.[13]

The future of the NFL Network remained cloudy. Its growth was slow and its war with the cable operators appeared counterproductive. The assumption that showing eight regular-season games on the network would create pressure on cable providers to offer the NFL Network proved erroneous. In fact the league was under great pressure to make NFL Network games available to local fans even if they didn't have the NFL Network on their cable system.[14] Political pressure arrived in a letter from thirteen U.S. senators, led by Arlen Specter of Pennsylvania. It expressed displeasure over the limited access to games shown on the NFL Network, and reminded the commissioner that much of the NFL media success was based on the antitrust exemption congress granted the league.

On May 18, 2009, the NFL Network and Comcast finally came to a settlement as Comcast agreed to carry the NFL Network. For its part the NFL reduced the subscriber fee, and in turn Comcast agreed to make the channel available on its basic tier of service, adding 10.8 million potential viewers to the NFL Network. Comcast also agreed to carry the Red Zone Channel. The agreement was for nine years and opened the likelihood that the NFL Network could move to a similar agreement with Time Warner, Cablevision, and Charter. At the same time, FOX and CBS agreed to allow the Red Zone Channel to go to Comcast, and agreed to a two-year contract extension with the NFL to 2013, with a 1 to 2 percent increase in annual fees.[15]

It's Always about the Money

For some franchises, additional revenue streams grew from stadium sponsorship and advertising. The league estimated that Dallas, Houston, New England, Philadelphia, and Washington generated more than $20 million each. Sponsors invested $1 billion into media and marketing efforts with NFL themes and promotions. It was no wonder then that franchise values continued to rise. In 2006 five franchises were valued at more than one billion dollars each: Redskins ($1.4 billion), Patriots ($1.18 billion), Cowboys ($1.17 billion), Texans ($1.04 billion), and Eagles ($1.02 billion).[16]

Once again, when it came to generating revenue for individual franchises, Jerry Jones led the way. In 2009 Jones was destined to take franchise revenues to a new level with the opening of the new Dallas Cowboys Stadium, known in some quarters as "The House that Jerry Built." According to *Forbes,* the billion-dollar stadium housed two hundred suites leased for more than $350,000 per year and $50 million in stadium sponsorships, none of which was part of shared revenue. The stadium was designed to host major non-football events, and Glorypark—an office, retail, and housing complex built in the shadow of the new stadium—would generate even more revenue.[17]

Even before the new facility opened, it was inspiring off-the-charts prose, much of which was not hyperbolic. Articles were written, tours were offered on site, and best of all was the tour being offered online with the man himself, Jerry Jones, serving as tour guide. Prior to the gala opening, the networks, both sports and news, presented their video tributes to the man and his monument. This may have been the most genuinely American moment in the history of the NFL's pretentious claims as national symbol.

The numbers alone impressed. Covering seventy-three acres and containing three million square feet, the stadium accommodated approximately 110,000 fans for football, with thirty thousand in standing-room-only areas. The opening game of the NFL season produced an NFL regular-season record crowd of 105,121, topping the 103,467 that saw a game in Mexico City in 2005. The cost of the facility was in the neighborhood of $1.15 billion, with the City of Arlington chipping in a modest $300 million and Jones raising the remainder in the credit markets. Jones noted that he could have built the stadium for $800 million, but "we wanted to have all the bells and whistles. We wanted this stadium to have a 'wow factor.'" It did, and then some.

Jones's Pigskin Mausoleum rests on a flat landscape and dominates the horizon in a manner similar to Mont Saint-Michel in northern France. Two steel trusses run the length of stadium for a quarter-mile. The end zone area has retractable glass walls, creating open-air plazas and allowing for events other than football. In one sense it is a stadium located inside a multipurpose building. Ticket prices produced more "wows." Seat licenses were best described by season ticket holder Len Allen as reaching the "you have more money than you should" level. Allen and four other families paid $2 million for the next twenty years for their suite holding twenty-one people. Catering is an extra, at $1,000 per suite, per game. The interior of the stadium is decorated by works of art, has spacious walkways flanked by club rooms and suites, and contains areas for exhibitions where, among other things, vendors can display their wares.

Either missing the point entirely, or revealing the unspoken truth about the NFL, Roger Goodell called the stadium "awesome" and "terrific," as in: "It's such a great thing for the fans. That's what so remarkable. It's adding a whole new dimension for our fans to be able to experience NFL football." Jones suggested otherwise, showing more insight than one might expect, when he said "Only a small percent of our fans will ever be here. They'll live vicariously through this."[18] Wow, indeed!

As Jones suggested, most fans found their way to the new Dallas Stadium and all other NFL venues via television. During the 2009 season the television picture looked better than ever, literally and figuratively. Super Bowl XLIV, featuring New Orleans and Indianapolis, was the "most watched event in the history of television." This capped a year of very strong television ratings for

NFL football and demonstrated that the league was still the "monster of the media" available on flat screens, in HD, and in 3-D.[19]

The NFL remained a very valuable sports commodity with the expectation that it would continue in that position. When the U.S. housing bubble burst and the banking and finance system was put in jeopardy, and the American economy went into a tailspin, expectations changed. At the beginning of the 2009 season *Forbes* reported a drop in franchise values for eight of the thirty-two NFL teams. There were a number of mixed signals. The year 2008 was the third most profitable in league history, as player costs rose 4 percent while operating income jumped 31 percent. Some teams saw their season ticket waiting list shrink while demand for seat licenses was soft. On the upside, of the top thirty-three sports franchises in value in the United States, thirty-two were from the NFL, with only the New York Yankees breaking through at number sixteen. *Forbes* also reported that at least three owners—Jerry Jones, Robert Kraft, and Jeffrey Lurie—had become billionaires in just fifteen years, as the rate of return on their investment in the NFL outpaced the S&P 500. The keys to such recession-proof prosperity lay in lucrative television contracts and advertising deals, as well as the massive cash flow from high-priced luxury boxes, many of which were in new stadiums.[20]

The flagging economy provided support for other issues of interest to the commissioner. In the spring of 2009 Goodell floated the idea of expanding the schedule to seventeen or eighteen games within a twenty-week season, with a reduction of exhibition games. Such changes were subject to the collective bargaining process, agreements with the television networks, and of course the consent of the owners. Also on the financial front, Goodell raised the issue of excessive rookie salaries. This issue too would be put on the table in discussions over the new CBA.[21]

In the end, a new CBA without a disastrous lockout or strike was the most important thing on Goodell's plate. The issues were familiar. Some owners felt that the player share of revenues was getting much too high, while small-market owners felt that the coming of new stadiums in Dallas and New York/New Jersey would drive up the salary cap and put increased financial pressure on them. Other owners seemed to have a renewed interest in breaking the power of the NFLPA and returning to the good old days of total owner dominance. A new CBA became necessary when on May 20, 2008, NFL owners voted unanimously to opt out of the existing agreement.

In August 2008 the labor situation became more difficult with the death of Gene Upshaw, longtime NFLPA executive director. After forty years in pro football, Upshaw's legacy was vast, but two things stand out: the achievement of free agency, and the labor peace that he forged with Paul Tagliabue. The latter brought a level of stability and prosperity to the league never before achieved. Whether Upshaw and Goodell would have developed such a relationship was doubtful.[22] Before his death Upshaw had made it clear that the major financial issues lay within the NFL, not the wider economy, and could only be rectified when the differences between small-market and large-market teams over revenue sharing were resolved. He reminded everyone involved that under the existing CBA, all parties were doing well, and everyone was making money.

Nearly seven months passed before DeMaurice Smith was named Upshaw's successor. Smith was a Washington lawyer with limited experience in labor law and sports. The new executive director made it clear that neither he nor the players were impressed by the notion that the owners were hurting or the players were taking away too large a share of league revenue. Smith faced the task of uniting a divided union that turned to him as executive director in part because he was an outsider unburdened by identification with any of the factions within the organization.[23]

The first major consequence of the CBA opt-out was the coming of the uncapped season of 2010, to be followed by a possible lockout for the 2011 season. In theory the absence of a salary cap would result in greater spending by teams seeking free agents and larger contracts for rookies. Many teams did save money by not setting a minimum level of spending, but the price of starting players continued to rise. Under the competitive pressure to win, payrolls rose 6 percent for the average team without the cap.[24]

As the lockout date approached, both sides loaded their war chests for the struggle ahead. The NFLPA was said to have a strike fund of $210 million, while the NFL had a contingency fund exceeding a billion dollars. In its television contract extensions with CBS, FOX, and DirecTV, the NFL was guaranteed the $5 billion for 2011 even if there were no games. The NFLPA successfully challenged this contract provision in court, but final disposition of the case, including damages and the status of the television money, was not resolved before the end of the lockout.

Goodell strongly supported the need for concessions by the players. On Super Bowl Sunday 2010, he appeared on CBS's *Face the Nation,* arguing that the owners needed more money to cover the costs of "international ventures and infrastructure projects such as new stadiums." Goodell said that player share of revenues must come down from the current 59 percent to 41 percent.

He claimed that of the $3.6 million in new revenues since 2006, the players walked off with $2.6 million.[25]

The lockout began at midnight on March 11, 2011, after negotiations on a new CBA failed. The owners blamed the players, the players blamed the owners, and both sides headed to court. The players opened with a decertification of the NFLPA, which enabled individual players to go to court and challenge the NFL for violations of antitrust law and have the lockout declared illegal. In late April the courts ruled the lockout illegal, but a U.S. court of appeals reversed the lower court ruling in early July.

The NFL went to the National Labor Relations Board (NLRB) to challenge the NFLPA's right to decertify, with little chance of success. The commissioner announced that he would take only one dollar as his salary during the lockout, and he sent a letter to the players asking them to encourage the union to return to the bargaining table. NFLPA executives were not pleased by Goodell's blatant attempt to undermine player unity.[26] The sports media went into panic mode, certain that the sky was falling and the next season was now in jeopardy. On sports talk radio, home of NFL obsessive-compulsive fans, it sometimes sounded as if the cancellation of games was imminent, even though it was mid-March and no regular-season games were scheduled until September.

In the end the settlement came under the pressure of the calendar and the move by Roger Goodell and DeMaurice Smith to press for a settlement away from the limelight. The end came on July 25, four and one-half months after it began. The new CBA was a ten-year agreement essentially containing several compromises over the distribution of the growing pot of money in the NFL. Some claimed the winners were the owners, some said the players, and most agreed it was the lawyers. More specifically, the owners and players agreed to a new split on revenues, with 52 percent going to the owners. However, this imbalance toward the owners was offset by a $120 million salary cap, additional benefits, and a guarantee that teams will spend up to an average of 90 million of the salary cap. Players received 55 percent of revenues from national media, and 45 percent of NFL Ventures revenue. Player health and safety concerns were addressed, including health care after retirement.

The losers were the first-round draft picks and their agents. The draft was increased to seven rounds, and drafted players were required to sign four-year contracts at approximately half of the 2010 market rate. The agent compensation rate was reduced to 2 percent. Savings from this change on rookie salaries were put into a veteran player compensation pool and into retired player benefits.

The other winners coming out of the settlement were Goodell and Smith. In the end they were able to approximate the relationship between Tagliabue and Upshaw and achieve a continuation of labor peace over the long run. Both offered leadership in achieving the settlement and both proved able leaders of their constituencies. What most commentators termed a total lack of trust as a prime cause of the lockout was clearly replaced by considerable trust at the end of the lockout.[27] Lest anyone get the impression that all was now settled between the NFLPA and the NFL owners, it should be noted that the issues and lawsuits surrounding concussions were still active. In addition the NFLPA filed a lawsuit charging collusion by the NFL owners to create a salary cap during the uncapped 2010 year.[28]

Drugs, Concussions, and General Health

During his first State of the League address, the new commissioner indicated that drug testing was high on his list of concerns and that he would push for blood tests for human growth hormone (hGH). Goodell expressed concern over the concussion issue that was raised when former Patriots linebacker Ted Johnson told the *New York Times* that Coach Bill Belichick had pressured him to play too soon following a concussion.[29]

Drug issues continually surfaced, and the NFL faced legal obstacles to enforcement of their drug-testing policy. Defensive linemen Pat and Kevin Williams of the Minnesota Vikings both tested positive and were suspended four games for a banned substance, Bumetanide, an over-the-counter weight-loss supplement. In December 2008 a U.S. district court judge in Minnesota blocked the suspension, saying he needed more time to make a ruling. The two players and the NFLPA argued that the league did not warn players about using this particular supplement, and it carried no listing of the banned diuretic on its label. Once the NFLPA joined the suit on behalf of the players, the case moved into federal court. The following September a federal appeals court ruled that the Williamses could continue to play, which they did right on through the 2009 season. The NFL sought relief from Congress but got nowhere.[30]

More significant was a growing concern over head injuries, concussions, and the overall health of former NFL players. The health issue first surfaced in early 2006 when the Scripps-Howard News Service conducted a study of 3,850 football players who had died in the twentieth century. The majority of the 130 deceased players born since 1955 were among the heaviest athletes in sports history. Twenty percent had died of heart disease and were statistically twice as likely as others to die before they were fifty years old. Prior to 1985 it was rare to find players who weighed more than three hundred pounds, but in 2006 greater than five hundred NFL players attending summer training camps exceeded 300 pounds. A study in 2004 by the National Institute for Occupational Safety and Health reported that both offensive and defensive linemen had a 52 percent greater risk of dying from heart disease than the general population. In 2006 56 percent of all NFL players were classified as obese. Between 1985 and 2005 the average weight in the NFL increased by 10 percent, while the average offensive lineman expanded from 281 to 318 pounds.

Commissioner Tagliabue offered no comment on the study, but NFL spokesman Greg Aiello said that obesity as an issue was beyond sports and affected all of society, and added that the Scripps-Howard survey "contributes nothing." The NFL also criticized an article in the *Journal of the American Medical Association* reporting on a study by a North Carolina endocrinologist that found 56 percent of all NFL players were clinically obese. The NFL called the study misleading because the body-mass index used did not account for players' muscles.[31]

These attitudes foreshadowed the reaction when the issue of concussions became a leading media topic. In early 2007, Patriot Ted Johnson also told the *New York Times* that he believed his severe depression and addiction to amphetamines were the result of concussions in his playing days. Johnson's neurologist told him that at age thirty-four, he displayed early signs of Alzheimer's disease. Johnson charged that Coach Belichick of the Patriots sent him into a high-impact drill four days after his concussion, even though the Patriots trainer recommended that Johnson be protected in practice.

Commissioner Goodell responded that the NFL had a committee working on the concussion problem: the Mild Traumatic Brian Injury Committee

Head Injuries—A Major Concern? Joe Heller's Football Cartoon, "The Other NFL Draft" ©HELLER SYNDICATION. All Rights Reserved.

(MTBI), formed by Commissioner Tagliabue under pressure in 1994. Dr. Elliot Pellman, a rheumatologist, served as chair, and there were no neurologists on the committee. At times its primary function seemed to be to deny any connection between football and concussions. Under the committee's guidance, players who sustained a concussion were allowed to return to the field if they appeared to have recovered, a policy that ran counter to most medical guidelines. When asked if the NFL would consider taking action against a coach on the concussion issue, Goodell ducked the question.[32]

Indeed, the NFL had been made aware of growing scientific studies pointing to a connection between concussions and football. The first of these came from an autopsy and study of the brain of Mike Webster, a former Pittsburgh Steeler who died at age fifty, homeless on the streets of the city, by Bennett Omalu, a neuropathologist employed in the coroner's office. What he found inside Webster's brain was tau, a substance that strangles the brain and produces results usually associated with Alzheimer's and other brain diseases, although not in the same patterns as in those cases. Omalu took his results to a prominent neuropathologist and an Alzheimer's expert, who confirmed the finding. Then a second case of a former Steeler came to Omalu, and then others followed.

Omalu, Dr. Robert Hamilton, and Dr. Steve DeKosky submitted a paper to the Journal *Neurosurgery*, published by the MTBI, that had been publishing studies showing no connection between football and long-term brain damage. They published the paper in early 2005. The NFL demanded a retraction, which it did not get, and then an assault began on the character and work of Bennett Omalu. Meanwhile, the number of researchers coming to similar conclusions was growing. The NFL insisted there was no connection even after the NFL Retirement Board awarded disability payments to Webster and several others on the grounds that their problems had been caused by football. In 2007 Goodell conveyed a Concussion Summit, at which the league's medical experts attacked the research and researchers connecting football with brain damage. But more players died and more CTE was found.[33]

In June 2007 the House Judiciary Subcommittee on Commercial and Administrative Law held hearings that featured moving testimony by former NFL players about their medical conditions, while the NFL basically denied any connection between dementia and football. A number of players testified that professional football had left them with "broken bodies, brain damage, and empty bank accounts." The lawyer for Mike Webster, former Pittsburgh Steelers Hall of Fame center, told the committee of Webster's mental illness and how he died homeless in 2002.[34]

At the NFL meetings in March 2009, the League took action related to the head injury issue, as four new rules were adopted to increase player safety. Blockers were to be protected from helmet-to-helmet blindside hits, and receivers from hits to the head when in a defenseless position.[35]

In the fall of 2009 the University of Michigan Institute for Social Research reported the results of a study it had conducted on behalf of the NFL. In a phone interview, they asked 1,063 retired players of various ages whether they had received a diagnosis of "dementia, Alzheimer's disease, or other memory-related disease." About 6 percent, or five times the national average, reported they had. Those aged thirty to forty-nine had a rate of 1.9 percent, or nineteen times the national average for men that age. Neither the NFL spokesman nor the NFLPA spokesman would comment on the study although, and perhaps because, it had clear implications for NFL disability payments.

Reacting to the Michigan Study, U.S. Congresswoman Linda Sanchez of California, who had conducted the 2007 hearings, said that the study created a "degree of urgency" in the matter of disability eligibility. Congressman John Conyers of Michigan, also a participant in the hearings, said it was clearly time for the NFL to step up and provide full coverage for its players. Eleanor Perfetto, whose husband Ralph Wenzel, a seven-year lineman for the Steelers and Chargers, was institutionalized for dementia, said it was time for the eligibility window to be changed. The fifteen-year limit made no sense, as dementia usually did not appear until after that time limit had passed.[36]

When full congressional hearings opened in October 2009, one of the key witnesses was Gay Culverhouse, a former president of the Tampa Bay Bucs. She was there along with former Bucs who suffered from an assortment of problems stemming from head injuries. Culverhouse was particularly critical of team doctors, whose primary function seemed to be to get players back on the field.

Another subject of contention at the hearings was the NFL's study of brain injuries. Its committee of doctors at the MBTI discredited all evidence of a link between football and brain diseases. Roger Goodell insisted that the NFL had been studying the issue for fifteen years, and that its committee of doctors were independent of the NFL and consisted of scientists and medical professionals. None of the primary authors of the NFL study were present at the hearing. During the hearings Congresswoman Sanchez told Goodell that the attitude of the NFL reminded her of the tobacco companies when they kept saying, "Oh, there's no link between smoking and damage to your health."[37]

Following the congressional hearings, public criticism mounted. Television coverage was affected, with announcers downplaying the use of terms like "warrior" and "toughness," and more frequently used terms like "injury" and "dementia." NBC removed the bone-crunching sounds from its NFL promos, and at FOX former Giant defensive lineman Michael Strahan talked about ex-teammates in their forties who were dealing with Alzheimer's, and former Steelers quarterback Terry Bradshaw denounced the NFL for its policies. Under increased public scrutiny, Goodell finally began to address this issue. In November 2009 he issued a directive that any player sustaining a concussion was required to seek advice from "independent" neurologists. In addition the codirectors of the NFL study committee resigned, and the committee suspended its activities. This ended a long history of ignoring and/or denying the issue within the NFL.[38]

On December 20, 2009, the NFL announced a donation of $1 million to the Center for the Study of Traumatic Encephalopathy at Boston University that had emerged as the focal point of brain research and was headed by Chris Nowinski, Dr. Ann McKee, and Dr. Robert Cantu. The Center studied brain damage in former NFL players of a type commonly associated with boxers. In a dramatic reversal of position, NFL spokesman Greg Aiello without fanfare said that the NFL would encourage players and former players to donate their brains to Boston University for research, thus acknowledging the connection they had long denied. The NFLPA joined in that effort. After determining there would be no strings attached by the NFL and no conflict of interest, the Boston University Center announced its acceptance of the financial donation.[39]

The NFL was now ready to concede some connection between the consequences of head trauma and football. Nor was the league alone in arriving late at the recognition of this connection. In an op-ed piece in the *New York Times* in early February 2010, Dr. Deborah Blum of the University of Wisconsin cited an article from the *Journal of the American Medical Association* warning that in football, there was a "very definite brain injury due to single or repeated blows to the head or jaw which cause multiple concussion hemorrhages. . . . The condition can no longer be ignored by the medical profession or the public." The article had appeared in 1928, and had been frequently cited through the years, and just as frequently ignored. Somehow it had never been applied to the contemporary discussions of head injuries in football.[40] Try as it might, the league seemed unable to get out front on the concussion issue, as Commissioner Goodell found himself, more often than not, reacting to developments that at times seemed to come in waves. In 2010 former players like Bears quarterback Jim McMahon publicly discussed their severe memory loss and multiple concussions of their playing days. The NFL reacted with rules changes barring helmet-to-helmet hits, and prior to the 2010 season the protocols for handling head injuries were changed.[41]

For several years the NFL had moved slowly to alter its presentation of violence. NFL Films moved away from the bone-crunching hits, at least the illegal ones, in its highlight presentations. Promotional material from the league and the networks stressing violent collisions was toned down. This was a delicate process because it was clear that violence was a major attraction of the game.

In February 2011 former Chicago Bears linebacker Dave Duerson committed suicide. At his request the Boston University Center conducted a study that showed he suffered from the brain disease CTE (chronic traumatic encephalopathy) associated with repeated concussions. Duerson was one of at least twenty players studied at the Center who suffered from CTE Other suicides by former players were linked to their problems stemming from head trauma. Former Chargers linebacker Junior Seau's suicide in early 2012 may be the most shocking of all. It provoked a renewed debate over violence in football and led some to suggest that children should not be allowed to play the game.[42]

As the number of reported cases mounted and the studies of concussions multiplied, it was no surprise that this issue would move to the courts. Between 2011 and 2012 the number of players suing the NFL was rising rapidly, and in mid-2012 these had been consolidated into one class-action suit ultimately involving a reported forty-five hundred players. The case was assigned to Judge Anita Brody of the United States District for the Eastern District of Pennsylvania. After a number of hearings and preliminary rulings, Judge Brody appointed Federal District Judge Layn Phillips as mediator between the two sides in the spring of 2013. In August the sides reached a settlement involving a $765 million payment to the parties by the NFL without requiring the NFL to acknowledge any wrongdoing. It also closed the books on the case, which meant that the NFL would not have to disclose any information on the issue, and could again deny any connections between football and brain disease.[43]

In the midst of trying to appear proactive on the issue of head trauma and violence, Roger Goodell found himself in the middle of a two-year investigation on the use of a "bounty system" in the NFL centered on the New Orleans Saints. The Saints' defensive coordinator, Gregg Williams, created the system involving between twenty and twenty-seven players and payouts of $1,000 to $1,500 for "taking out" an opposing player. Quarterbacks were a favorite target.

Given the developments on violence, head trauma, and the attempt to respond while facing increasing numbers of lawsuits over head trauma, the NFL and Goodell handed out severe punishments. Saints Head Coach Sean Payton was suspended without pay for a year, Gregg Williams faced indefinite suspension, Saints General Manager Mickey Loomis was out for eight regular-season games, and Assistant Head Coach Joe Vitt was out for six games. In addition, the Saints were fined $500,000 and lost their second-round draft picks in 2012 and 2013. Four Saints defensive players were also suspended: Jonathan Vilma for the 2012 season, Anthony Hargrove for eight games, Will Smith for four games, and Scott Fujita for three games.[44]

Roger Goodell also handled the "bounty scandal" with a heavy hand. A rash of arbitration appeals and lawsuits followed, and this issue came to a conclusion with arbitrator Paul Tagliabue giving a sharp reprimand to his chosen successor. The former commissioner lifted the suspensions on the four players involved in the Saints' bounty program, but at the same time ruled that the commissioner was within his authority in punishing the players. Although the NFL claimed Tagliabue's ruling was a victory, in the court of public opinion it was seen as a slap on the wrist of Goodell. In either case, Goodell's leadership proved to fall well short of expectations set by his handling of the lockout of players in 2011 and the new television contract.[45]

Television

Clearly Roger Goodell was dealing with and/or reacting to a remarkable number of issues and changes. One of these, about falling television ratings and declining interest in the NFL, was all but gone by 2009. The record Super Bowl rating in 2010, for a game between the Saints and the Colts, was an 8 percent increase over Super Bowl XLI of 2007, making it the most-watched television program in history. It capped a season of high ratings and one in which an NFL regular-season game outdrew a World Series game. The notion that the World Series could not beat an NFL regular season game in the ratings, whatever the explanation, was one more sign of the status of the NFL in American sport.

At the end of the decade, while most of television continued to struggle with fragmented markets, the NFL audience was growing. "Of the 13 television programs that drew over 30 million viewers over the past year (2010), 11, or 85%, were sports related," according to a report by Horizon Media. Why this was happening was a matter of speculation. Factors such as new interest generated by the Internet, social networking by players and NFL insiders, the spread of mobile devices, and the growing distribution of HD television all seemed to play some role. Couple that with the high price of tickets to events and the declining economy, and it was nearly a perfect storm for television success.[46]

During the 2011–2012 regular season, twenty-three of the top twenty-five highest-rated television programs were NFL contests. Games on the major networks averaged twenty million viewers, while prime-time programming on the networks averaged 8.2 million viewers. NFL ratings were 144 percent higher than those for regular prime-time programming. Five years earlier that gap was 61 percent. Super Bowl XLV of 2011 was watched by 111 million people in the United States, the highest total ever, and 4.5 million viewers higher than the previous year, yet another all-time record. The encore at Super Bowl XLVI in 2012 was more of the same. For the third consecutive year the Super Bowl had a record television audience, this one at 111.3 million viewers, surpassing the previous year by 300,000.[47]

For those who thought the new NFL television contract signed in mid-December 2011 was out of hand, these Super Bowl and regular-season ratings answered the doubters and validated the mind-numbing numbers. Over the nine years of the new contract, CBS, NBC, and FOX agreed to pay about $3 billion per year, or about 50 percent higher than the existing contract. DirecTV's payment of $1 billion per year added to the bonanza. ESPN paid $1.9 billion annually for its eight-year contract. Cumulatively this worked out to an average of nearly $184.4 million per team per year. What would Al Davis think now?

There was a realization among television executives that the NFL was an absolutely essential piece of programming. David Hill of FOX said, "The N.F.L. transcends everything, as it has soared to astronomical heights." Sean McManus of CBS concurred, saying "The product is so important, and it's such a foundation for CBS." For his part, Goodell acknowledged that the deal would not have been possible without the ten-year CBA signed with the NFLPA. Goodell said, "the players deserve great credit. Long-term labor peace is allowing the NFL to continue to grow, and the biggest beneficiaries are the players and fans."[48]

In 2005 the first regular-season game outside the United States was played in Mexico City between the Arizona Cardinals and the San Francisco 49ers. A crowd of 103,467 filled Estadio Azteca and saw the Cardinals win, 31-14. Under Goodell the NFL renewed its efforts to expand its fan base across the Atlantic. The first regular-season game in Britain was played in October 2007 when the Dolphins and the Giants met at London's Wembley Stadium. It became an annual affair, and speculation increased that the NFL would eventually place a team in London.

With the first decade of the twenty-first century coming to a close, there was much uncertainty leaguewide, but Roger Goodell was able to navigate some very troubled waters in 2011. The ten-year CBA and new television contract were impressive achievements. Fortunately for the NFL, the economic downturn beginning in 2008 had only short-term effects, as did the brief downturn in television ratings. The game proved to have its most popular years ever in 2011 and 2012.

Out of it all, there momentarily emerged a new rock of stability. Rodger Goodell was regarded by many as a strong and fair leader who had a firm grip on the league and its owners. He guided the NFL through troubled times, and many were confident that this strong and effective leadership would continue.

Then came the debacle with the lockout of the NFL referees and the use of scab referees at the opening of the 2012 season, once again throwing Goodell's leadership into serious question. Clearly avoidable, this issue once again put the spotlight on a combination of ownership pique and the commissioner's tendency to arrogance. The issue of replacement referees came from the owners' desire to reassert their control over someone, anyone. The lockout of the referees union looked like an easy target. Then, the use of scabs to break the union backfired when the incompetence of the scabs led to ridicule and criticism of Goodell and the NFL owners. Worse, Goodell's insistence that nothing was amiss in all this blew-up in his face with the

The Replacement Refs. Joe Heller's Football Cartoon, "NFL Refs" ©HELLER SYNDICATION. All Rights Reserved.

Keystone Cop ending to the Seattle–Green Bay game on *Monday Night Football*. The public outcry seemed to bring at least some back to their senses, and the confrontation with referees was quickly brought to settlement.

A few months later, and nearly simultaneously with the conclusion of the bounty issue, the concussion issue came roaring back with the most damaging revelations yet seen. In mid-November PBS's *Frontline* reported that despite all the denials over the years, the NFL knew all along that concussions in several cases were directly related to football.

In the late 1990s and early 2000s the NFL Retirement Board awarded disability payments to several former players. The board concluded that the brain injuries were linked to their football careers. The awards exceeded $2 million dollars. These payments were made while simultaneously the league's medical experts were claiming there was no such link. The NFL spokesman, Greg Aiello, pointed out that the Retirement Board was an independent panel, implying that this was not an NFL decision. The panel consisted of three representatives of the owners, three of the players, and a nonvoting representative of the commissioner. Until December 2009 the NFL insisted that there was no evidence to make the link between concussions and dementia or other brain disorders. But the PBS production offered documentary evidence that indeed the NFL had knowledge of this link and had paid out disability benefits as a result, while denying that it had any knowledge of any kind. The program was heavily based upon Mark Fainaru-Wada and Steve Fainaru's book *League of Denial*.[49]

These revelations may impact the lawsuits faced by the NFL over concussions. Even if they do not affect the court cases, it is clear that once again the NFL's dissembling had caught up to them. Commissioner Goodell found himself in the midst of yet another public relations disaster, one that even Pete Rozelle, the public relations master, would find it nearly impossible to allay.

12

Super Sunday

Excess is a relative term. Many would agree that you know it when you see it. Even at a glance, it is clear that excess defines the Super Bowl.

Mary Riddell, *The Observer*'s superb columnist, once noted that sports heroes reflect and amplify "the fixations" of their society. It is who they are and what they do. It is also what sports cultures do. Both offer a distorted or exaggerated version of social reality and social values, and this happens whether one sees positive or negative images emanating from sport.[1]

For even the most casual observer of contemporary American culture, it is apparent that Super Sunday has grown exponentially and has become a bloated monster. Over the past four decades, Super Sunday illustrates the ability of a sporting event to offer a distorted and exaggerated version of social reality and social values. The Super Bowl has done so on a grand, glorious, and obscene scale.

Becoming Super

When exactly the Super Bowl reached larger-than-life proportions is difficult to pinpoint, but certainly it achieved that standard by the end of the 1970s. At Super Bowl XV in 1981 the *New York Times* headline proclaimed that seventy thousand fans made "New Orleans Throb with Super Bowl Mania." Gerald Eskenazi's account described a "gridlock" of people in the French Quarter, and an influx of "tens of millions" of dollars into the New Orleans economy.[2] The extravagances of the fans and everyone associated with the game had achieved extraordinary proportions.

By 1980 only the vocabulary created by Thorstein Veblen was capable of fully capturing the Super Bowl scene. Veblen's *The Theory of the Leisure Class* coined those wonderful phrases "conspicuous consumption," "conspicuous leisure," and "conspicuous waste" to describe the habits of the rich in late-nineteenth-century America. Along with "predatory barbarism," "pecuniary emulation," "vicarious consumption," and "conspicuous waste," Veblen's colorful vocabulary is ideally suited for describing this distinctive American midwinter holiday. The difference is that the habits of the rich in the late nineteenth century have trickled down the social order to those riding the wave of corporate wealth and consumption in the second half of the twentieth century. As a consequence the Super Bowl has become an ideal television production, an event so totally devoted to consumption that the television commercials have become a centerpiece of its appeal.

One quantifiable indicator of the growth of excess was the skyrocketing price of commercial television time. At the first Super Bowl in 1967, before it was known by that name, a thirty-second commercial on CBS sold for $37,500 ($245,000 in current dollars). By the early '80s the price for thirty seconds reached $400,000 ($956,000), and by the end of the decade it was a whopping $800,000 ($1.41 million). Thirty seconds of advertising reached the $1 million ($1.43 million) mark in 1995, climbing to $2.1 million ($2.66 million) in 2000. In 2007 the price tag was $2.6 million ($2.8 million) and by 2010 it reached $3 million for a thirty-second spot.[3]

This, and so much more, is on display on Super Sunday and during the excesses of Super Bowl week. The levels of conspicuous consumption and conspicuous waste reach new and dizzying heights with each succeeding Super Bowl.

Three aspects of Super Sunday offer a sense of the scale of the game: the technical presentation, the creation of a festival atmosphere, and the development of a massive midwinter bacchanalia indulged in by a considerable portion of the nation. Beyond the event itself, its real significance is revealed in the way in which the nation has come to measure and compare the festivities, and delight in its apparently limitless growth.

In the second year of the Super Bowl, while paying a $2.5 million rights fee, CBS used twelve cameras, including one in the Goodyear Blimp, along with four video machines for isolated replays and highlights, including stop-action and slow motion in color. This was up from the two-camera coverage that both networks used at the first game.[4] In 1989 NBC deployed twenty-three cameras and twelve replay machines, while NFL Films used fourteen photographers and twenty-six miles of film. Two years later in Tampa, ABC utilized twenty-two cameras operating around the stadium, on the ground, and in the air. In 1995 ABC employed twenty-seven cameras, and in 2001 CBS used thirty-four cameras and introduced freeze-frame technology. That same year, NFL Films was up to twenty-two cameras and shot the game in both 16mm and 35mm formats. In 2006 NFL used thirty-six cameras and deployed ninety miles of cable.[5] And on and on it goes.

The first claims of a Super Bowl economic impact were made for Miami at the second Super Bowl. For the first time ever, hotels were booked solid in mid-January, normally a quiet season following the holidays. Eastern Airlines reported brisk business into Miami as it took part in package tours being offered for the Super Bowl. The best restaurants had waiting lists, while the vendors at the game expected record sales from the sellout crowd.[6] Super Bowl III was expected to bring $50 million into the Miami economy over a ten-day period. One-third of all the spectators were from the New York area, and package tours to the game sold out. Hotels were at a premium and restaurants heavily booked. Twenty-five years later the Super Bowl brought $150 million into Miami.

Back in New York City at Charley O's Restaurant, where Jet fans gathered for Super Bowl III, Marshall McLuhan called the Super Bowl "world theater." According to McLuhan, "The world is a happening. In the speed-up of the electronic age we want things to happen. This offers us a mosaic that the fans love—everything is in action at once." And the replay added to the experience, offering "another means of audience participation."[7]

In 1967 the league issued only six hundred press credentials, and the newspapers in some NFL cities did not bother to send a reporter to cover the game. In 1997 press credentials reached the league-mandated ceiling of twenty-five hundred.

Roman Numerals in the Imperial Age

After Super Bowl III, the league made the decision to move the game from city to city. Super Bowl IV was awarded to New Orleans. Other than the willingness to spend freely to stage the game, warm weather seemed to be the only requirement for the host city. New Orleans produced the first major stadium spectacular. There were three thousand pigeons and one turtle dove released during pregame ceremonies, and a tableau of the Battle of New Orleans and a Mardi Gras parade. Actor Pat O'Brien read the words to the national anthem, backed by a chorus and band from Southern University and the trumpet playing of Doc Severinsen. It was called the second-largest bash in America, second only to Mardi Gras. Halftime pageantry included many acts, from the *Ed Sullivan Show* to the opera singer Marguerite Piazza offering her rendition of "Basin Street Blues." Astronauts, baseball stars, government figures, and show-business types were all there to be seen as part of this growing NFL exercise in self-promotion.

Super Bowl V in Miami was the first game officially designated by roman numerals, and they were displayed prominently on the tickets. However, the official logo of the Super Bowl displayed the roman numerals for Super Bowl II. Clark Haptonstall from the Sports Management Department of Rice University claims that the commissioner chose roman numerals because the NFL season crosses two calendar years, and more important: "He thought if you could use Roman numerals, it kind of gave that gladiator feel and was something that made the game special."[8] As for those who find the use of roman numerals a bit pretentious, it is clear they didn't understand the importance of this event, the historical origins of Super Sunday, and its association with the sacred and profane in American culture.

First, the Super Bowl was the creation of the first great emperor of the NFL in America's imperial age, the Caesar Augustus of professional football, Pete Rozelle. Over the years, Rozelle managed to consolidate his imperial power, and in fact with the help of Brent Musburger and those at CBS turned himself into a minor deity. One of the high points of each Super Bowl telecast was the three minutes in which Rozelle consented to be interviewed by Musburger. It was as if some mere mortal were interviewing God.

Second, it must be remembered that the Super Bowl was adopted by American middle-class males, and assorted other folks, as a midwinter ritual of pleasure in the midst of frozen bleakness. The bonding of middle-level executive types has never had a more perfect setting.

Third, it has become an event that no average football fan or even most season ticket holders could afford to attend. The NFL boasted several years ago that 25 percent of those who attended the game owned their own businesses. Nearly all the tickets go to NFL executives, sponsors' executives, high-level government officials, and their clients and sycophants. It is an occasion for display and decadence, and a week in which local prostitutes, pimps, and bookies experience a gold rush. Roman numerals seem not only appropriate but required.

The commissioner's party in this imperial age became one of the biggest and most opulent events, as well as the most sought-after party invitation of the festival. After a modest beginning, it quickly outgrew the capacity of any mere hotel ballroom. This led to some magnificent venues for the much-anticipated annual bash. At Super Bowl VII in Los Angeles, the commissioner played host aboard the *Queen Mary*. At Super Bowl VIII in Houston, the party occupied the expanse of the Astrodome. A giant barbecue, with pigs roasting on spits, dotted the floor of the facility. Commissioner's parties in Miami were held at Hialeah Racetrack and at Miami Airport's new International Terminal just prior to its opening. For that venue the NFL hired six hundred musicians from fourteen Caribbean nations to entertain.[9]

The cost of the 1978 commissioner's party hit $75,000, a figure that drew some critical comment. Commissioner Rozelle responded to those critics and unintentionally proved their point by noting that it may be fashionable to knock money and the Super Bowl, but "you think about money all the time with the Super Bowl, more than any other sports event. That's because it's a one-shot event." An Oakland Raider executive was closer to the mark: "the measurement of what it means is this: It's the victory. It's the cult of Number Oneism."[10] Among the two thousand invited guests were the media, the commissioner's immediate family, including the league office staff, league management, executives from each team, television executives, and sponsors. Players and their wives were not invited. Wives of the elite were.[11]

Corporate Collaboration

The corporate world found the Super Bowl venue congenial to their purposes. The Ford Motor Company used the Super Bowl as an incentive for its salespeople, spending $1 million to bring in dealers to Super Bowl XIX, where Gladys Knight and Neal Sedaka entertained. Nissan spent $2 million at Super Bowl XVIII in Tampa on a five-day Caribbean cruise, while eight hundred private jets were cleared for landing in the Tampa Bay area that weekend. In San Diego for Super Bowl XXII two thousand limos were in use, and many headed for the party that featured Frank Sinatra and Liza Minnelli in concert.[12]

As early as 1971 there were reports of the excesses and successes of the Super Bowl. The two weeks of preparation and the building pressures on the teams produced a game heavy with turnovers and errors. Tickets were becoming a problem as demand exceeded supply, and Rozelle said he made as many enemies as friends because of this. An estimated $20 million in business came to Miami, but many citizens were outraged by the television blackout in the city. Ellis Rubin, a local attorney, tried to force the NFL to open local television through the courts, but failed. Rozelle became angry with Rubin, and the Commish stayed in the Bahamas an extra two days to avoid being served with subpoena papers. Despite the sellout, Rozelle resisted any lifting of the blackout for fear it might then lead to attacks on the blackout rule for all games.[13]

By Super Bowl VI in New Orleans in 1972, there were reports that the game itself could be hazardous to your health, with doctors warning of "television angina," a form of angina pectoris that strikes while watching professional football. This was a problem at all sporting events and was first seen in connection with televised sport during the early days of televised wrestling. In 1970 it was estimated that two hundred deaths from angina occurred annually at college games. One doctor warned that the Super Bowl produces Super stress, which presumably could produce a Super Heart Attack. One Dallas fan with a history of angina said that if he had tickets to the game he would not go, and that he would not watch the game on television.[14]

After Super Bowl IV in 1970 President Richard Nixon called Len Dawson, the Kansas City Chiefs quarterback, to congratulate him on the victory over the Vikings. Earlier in the season Nixon had suggested an end-around play to George Allen of the Redskins, which produced a thirteen-yard loss. Then for Super Bowl VII, Nixon offered the first presidential play in Super Bowl history to Miami Head Coach Don Shula. It was the "down and in" pass play to Paul Warfield, which the Dolphins were likely to run several times in the game even without presidential prompting. Nixon was the logical president to inaugurate presidential intervention in the Super Bowl, as he once told Roone Arledge in a very excited tone that he, the president of the United States, "knew" Frank Gifford.[15]

Super Bowl VII in Los Angeles offered the first major signs of the growing synergy between business and the Super Bowl. Salesmen were there as rewards for their prowess in what the *New York Times* called "the perfect marriage of sports and commerce that the National Football League's Championship game has become." Among those rewarded were a Taster's Choice salesman, a Dodge dealer, and 267 Chrysler dealers. Ford flew in 650 of its best people from their national convention in Las Vegas. "Commercial ties to the league—television contracts, promotional schemes, sales incentive contests, and football competitions for boys" occupied ten thousand of the ninety thousand seats in the Los Angeles Coliseum. NBC paid $2.75 million in rights fees for the Super Bowl, and RCA Chairman Robert Sarnoff joined Pete Rozelle in the commissioner's luxury box, along with executives of Chrysler and Ford, two of the game's major sponsors. Chrysler bought twenty minutes of commercial time on the telecast.[16]

In a similar fashion, "Sears has product lie ino much as sweaters and pajamas, youth-room products such as bed spreads, pennants and posters. Shell offers tumblers with team logos, Sunoco offers NFL Action Player Stamps. Tickets also go to public figures, politicians, and other VIP's. Well known gambler and odds maker Jimmy the Greek had 100 tickets to the big game. He was not yet at CBS but was in his $475 a day six room suite at the Beverly Wilshire Hotel."[17]

A Proliferation of Fun and Excess

Within a decade the Super Bowl was important enough to be the subject of a *Time* cover story. The game was described in vintage *Time* style:

> [T]he Great American Time Out, a three-hour pause on a Sunday afternoon in January that is—as sheer, unadorned spectacle—an interval unique. For 70 million Americans, life compresses to the diagonally measured size of a cathode ray tube. Work goes undone, play ceases too; telephones stop ringing, crime disappears, romance is delayed and, in all the land, there is just one traffic jam worthy of the title—on highways leading to the Super Bowl site. If it is not literally McLuhan's global village, the Super Bowl certainly is the national town, and all the inhabitants have gone to watch a game on the community screen. . . . The Super Bowl spectacle pivots around a grand, but parochial American passion. It was born a mere decade ago, the child of technology, a unique combination of slick and schlock with no history at all save a profound connection to a taproot of the human psyche.[18]

At the public level, excess is always a part of the scene. For Super Bowl XXII in San Diego, a Super Salad was tossed just across the border in Tijuana, Mexico. It was a fourteen-foot-long, eight-foot wide, and eighteen-inch-deep Caesar salad made from 840 heads of romaine lettuce, 1,400 ounces of garlic oil, 175 lemons, 350 cups of croutons, 980 ounces of parmesan cheese, and 840 eggs. To ask why this happened would be obtuse.

Arriving in Minneapolis for Super Bowl XXVI, visitors to the Twin Cities were greeted at the airport by pianists playing on four grand pianos. What this had to do with football has yet to be established. In downtown Minneapolis, twenty-five tons of heated sand was dumped in the International Market Square to accommodate five hundred people for a beach party. Veblen would have savored this example of the reversal of nature. A sister party was hosted that year by former Washington Redskin running back John Riggins in Cancun, Mexico. Not to be outdone, the St. Paul Hotel, where the Buffalo Bills were staying, stocked 750 pounds of buffalo (bison) meat, which some unidentified hotel staffer apparently thought measured up to the standards of conspicuous consumption. Veblen would no doubt have seen it all as a perfect example of predation, display, and conspicuous waste.[19]

Corporate America followed suit with its parties and tents. In 1985 at Super Bowl XIX in Palo Alto, California, twenty-six of the nation's largest corporations set up tents for pre- and postgame parties costing from $250 to $350 per person. For Super Bowl XXX some two hundred corporations took part in the triple-X celebration. Large corporations flew in hundreds of employees and spent up to $5 million. Smaller companies wined and dined clients at five-figure costs. There were thirty-five corporate tents set up in Miami near the stadium for Super Bowl XXX. When this practice began in 1984 there were twelve tents in Tampa. Bigger is better, and better will never be big enough.

In 2001 in Tampa the largest tents, 100 × 360 feet, accommodated more than 1,500 people. The carpeted, climate-controlled structures contained everything from big-screen TVs to a giant ship's mast. In addition the 800,000-square-foot corporate hospitality area was transformed into a pseudo-beach. Ten-foot-tall macaw statues, twenty-five-foot-tall lifeguard chairs, and a sand castle dotted the phony atmosphere.

By 2001 if you didn't arrive by private jet for the Super Bowl, it might be asked, why did you bother to come at all? It is estimated that more than one thousand private jets landed at the several airports in the Tampa Bay area beginning as early as Super Thursday. This represented a doubling of the number of private and corporate jets that arrived for college basketball's Final Four in 1999. If private planes and helicopters seemed too plebeian, then "Silent Wings II" offered an alternative. This modest 104-foot yacht featured a staff of four, including a gourmet chef. The accommodations offered a jacuzzi, along with "his" and "her" bathrooms in the largest of the suites. This package came with six luxury suite tickets to the big game and a chauffeured Rolls-Royce. The cost? A modest $100,000. The Super Bowl was consistently the priciest event in the sports world, and of course worth every tax-deductible dollar of it.

Sex and the Super Bowl were another important pairing offering a full range of delights to the corporate elite. The high-priced hookers loved this scene, as successful executives on corporate expense accounts enthusiastically displayed their macho and their cash to grateful clients. The term "half-time show" took on new meaning. New Orleans may be the best Super Bowl city in this respect, but places like Scottsdale, Arizona, offered twenty-five escort services, and in Minneapolis the escort services offered a 10 percent discount for the Super Bowl, along with a warning to beware of the Rolex girls, a particular classification of hooker who rolled clients and relieved them of their high-priced time pieces.

A former prostitute claimed that "Pimps see the Super Bowl as a money-making opportunity sent by God." Indeed, members of the world's oldest profession have found the Super Bowl an extremely active venue. From special service in the private suites to the "halftime quickie," the demand side of the economic equation was highly active, even before Viagra.[20]

Partying can take many forms and extravagance can take place at many levels. In 1995 *USA Today* reported that five men from Chicago were preparing to attend their twelfth straight Super Bowl party in Las Vegas. Each year they went to the same hotel and stayed in the same rooms. One year they booked a catered bus that took them to the airport at 6 A.M. with a waitress preparing eggs Benedict. Then there were the Morrisons of Fairfield, Ohio, who hosted one hundred guests each year. They put TVs in every room, including the bathrooms, taped the carpets to look like yard lines, installed football-shaped door knockers, and attached two seven-foot helmet cutouts to the house, painted in team colors. Mr. Morrison started the preparations at Thanksgiving when he created the first of a freezer full of football-shaped ice cubes.

An Emerging National Holiday

Indeed parties take place all across the nation and the world as Americans gather together on this special day.[21] Super Bowl parties are not confined to the United States. Across the globe, wherever there is a critical mass of Americans, a Super Bowl party is likely in this age of global television and laptop streaming video. This is a phenomenon that started in the first decade of Super Sunday. In London, Frankfurt, and Paris, Americans and Europeans, infected by Super Bowl fever, gathered in the wee hours to watch the game and to party. In Asia, where the Super Bowl takes place on Monday (no doubt, Super Monday), elaborate breakfast gatherings take place.

For Super Bowl XLIII, friends from Florida gathered with their children, grandchildren, and a crowd of two hundred others at the Bourbon Street Inn. This was not in New Orleans but rather on a dusty side street in Bangkok, nine thousand miles from Tampa. The party began at 5:30 A.M., necessitating a 4:30 wake-up call. The establishment run by a Louisiana native was decked out in the colors of the Pittsburgh Steelers and Arizona Cardinals, and the patrons arrived dressed in the colors of their favorite. The black and gold of the Steelers dominated, as it did in the game itself.

Richard Turkiewicz described it this way: "There we had a choice of New Orleans style breakfast price fixe or an alternative breakfast price fixe which included all the beer or 'Bloody Mary's' you wished to accompany your breakfast. All the meats for the breakfast are flown in from New Orleans and you think you are actually in New Orleans. The restaurant has that much flavor. The main difference is that all the waiters and servers are Thai." Turkiewicz said there was a real void produced by the lack of commercials, which were sorely missed by the Americans in attendance.[22]

Television coverage grew and changed over the years. Pregame and halftime shows became the bane of the Super Bowl. The 1976 halftime show featured a bicentennial theme featuring "Up With People." Robert Wussler, chief of CBS Sports, decided its telecast should feature entertainment over football, with more glamour injected into the telecast. Production techniques produced a sequence of play, replay, and celebrity crowd shots, all in short order. *New York Times* television critic John J. O'Connor described the CBS style as "belligerently restless . . . a kind of rhythmic quality that was nearly hypnotic," with musical breakaways for commercials. CBS devoted seven hours to the Super Bowl that weekend, including a ninety-minute entertainment special on Saturday night hosted by Jackie Gleason. The pregame show offered a ninety-minute review of previous games, and just before kickoff Phyllis George and Irv Cross made their way to the stadium via a yacht and helicopter, with stops along the way for interviews and plugs for the Fontainebleau Hotel. There were plenty of celebrity sightings along the way, including Phyllis George enticing Joe Namath to predict the outcome of the game.[23]

By 1978 social analysts were examining the rituals of the Super Bowl. Warren Farrell, author of *The Liberated Man*, a study of masculinity in America, found much of interest in the Super Bowl. Males in America would watch, analyze, and critique the game and be ready on Monday to display their expertise in the office. Farrell pointed out a linkage within "a closed circuit effect" that ties "televised professional football, masculinity, anxiety, sexism, patriotism, religion and war." To question any element in the circuit was to risk having your masculinity questioned. A "mini-all-male club" was created where women served as water-boys bringing in the beer and chips.[24]

In times of national crisis, patriotism was put on excessive display. There is nothing else quite like a supersized American flag covering an entire football field while jet fighters or stealth bombers buzz the stadium at the conclusion of the national anthem. Additionally, celebrities were always an important ingredient. One of the greatest pregame and halftime combinations occurred in 1993 in Pasadena, California, when former star running back O. J. Simpson handled the coin toss and Michael Jackson was the featured halftime entertainment. Who knew then what a marvelous and historic daily double this would become?[25]

By the time of Super Bowl XL the pregame coverage reached beyond extra large, to super proportions. The ABC pregame show began at 2:30 for the 6:20 kickoff. ESPN offered *NFL Sunday Countdown* from 11 A.M. to 5 P.M., ESPN2 presented all the Super Bowls in thirty-minute highlight films airing from 7 A.M. to 6:30 P.M. ESPN Classic offered Super Bowl programming from 10:00 until 6:00, and the NFL Network was in the mix for five hours of coverage. Even Animal Planet Television got in on the action with Puppy Bowl I, which quickly became a Super Sunday tradition, as part of their pregame programming. And just in case you didn't have enough coverage, ESPN Cell Phone offered seventy-five Super Bowl video reports.[26]

Another indicator of big numbers and high interest is found in the gambling statistics. Legal Super Bowl betting in Nevada was in the neighborhood of $50 million in 1989, while worldwide estimates were that in excess of $2.5 billion was wagered both legally and illegally. More than half the American adult population bets on the Super Bowl. By 2006 it was reported that the worldwide handle had grown to $7 billion. The variety of specialty bets or "prop bets" were nearly unlimited in Las Vegas, and those included bets on first team to call a timeout, team to score last in first half, or total field goals.[27]

At Super Bowl XL attention was called to the Super numbers for the event described by some as an "annual paean to capitalism." The players' winning share reached $32,000. CBS paid $4.5 million for rights while selling advertising at $325,000 per minute. The Louisiana Superdome grossed $2.3 million, and the only other bigger live gate ever recorded was the Dempsey-Tunney fight at Chicago's Soldier Field in 1927, which took in $2.6 million at the gate. Each team received $170,000 in expenses for ten days in New Orleans, the equivalent of eighty first-class airline tickets from the home city, and a ring allowance ($42,000 for winners). The Raiders estimated they spent in excess of $250,000 in expenses at the 1977 Super Bowl.

This Super Bowl has been described as "a national social spectacle" and an "annual electronic communion." The Super Bowl brunch became a suburban institution with its scrambled eggs and bloody marys. The nation moved indoors to living rooms, hotel rooms, and bars. Other events were cancelled or postponed. Telephone calls dropped off sharply, except at halftime. Airline passenger numbers were down. Attendance at such attractions as Disney World dropped off. Crime took a holiday. Golf courses were nearly empty. X-rated movie houses did almost no business. Some have questioned these sorts of claims as Super Bowl myths. Some were.

NFL officials did not appreciate the social analysis being done, and did not refer to this day as Super Sunday, as they tried to claim it was just the last game of a long season. Michael Novak, author of *The Joy of Sports*, described spectacles such as this as "therapeutic rituals, perhaps a religion, of modern high-speed society." Large societies tied together by mass communications move from spectacle to spectacle, claimed Novak. The Super Bowl had "detailed planning and brute strength" qualities that Americans admired. Players acted out resentment and anger with nondestructive violence, and that was very satisfying to many Americans. "The liturgy of the game may not be pleasant," wrote Novak, "but it's true to life."[28]

Commercially and Virtually Super

As Super Sunday grew it become an occasion for the advertising industry to unveil its new television commercials for appreciative clients. Pepsi, Coke, Burger King, Nike, and Apple Computer used the Super Bowl to launch major advertising campaigns with extremely high-priced commercials starring, in one case, Michael Jackson and, in another, Michael Jordan.

It was at Super Bowl XXIII in 1989 that the "Bud Bowl" was created as an advertising gimmick, and it became an advertising centerpiece for the Anheuser-Busch Corporation for several years. It featured a "football game" matching bottles of Bud and Bud Lite. The company spent $5 million to produce Bud Bowl I, and by the next year the Vegas odds-makers were quoting a point spread on the faux game.

Between 1967 and 1985 the total U.S. television audience for the Super Bowl went from 23.3 million households to 41.5 million. In addition, the demographics of the Super Bowl audience were such that they were especially appealing to advertisers looking for an adult audience with large disposable income.

Super Bowl XXX (1996) produced the first major sojourn into cyberspace. Advertisers found that sponsorship of Web sites was the new hot spot to make their pitch, both audio and visual, to the upscale consumer. The cost for promotion of a home page was $150,000. Advertising space sold at the rate of four cents per view. One estimate was that 2.5 million people would visit the official Internet site of the Super Bowl, which was sponsored by NBC and Microsoft.

When you arrived at the Virtual Super Bowl, the first thing you noticed was that this world too was heavily sponsored. The lead site sponsor was Miller Lite. REAL was the Official Streaming Media of Superbowl.com; at WebMD you could learn more about injuries; VISA offered your official NFL credit card. Also there was RCA's Direct Satellite System; UPS; Mel Gibson's new movie; E*Trade Knowledge Center; and Hotjobs.com. All were sponsors of Superbowl.com, and links transported the viewer to their Web sites. There was only one danger. If you ventured out into link land, it was wise to put a time limit on your travels and leave virtual droppings along the way so you could find your way back.

Beyond the advertising, there was an amazing assortment of information packages, featuring the history of the game, the statistical records of the game, the results of the previous games, interviews with thousands of people (a number of whom even had some knowledge of the game of football), all sorts of directions to the restaurants and hotels in the host city, and the tourist attractions of the region complete with maps. House and condo rentals complete with photos were listed. One-bedroom condos went for $300 per night, while the rent for the home was not listed.[29]

The Funfacts Web site offered the curious or bored some interesting and little-known bits of information. No president had ever attended a Super Bowl, while two vice presidents had: Bush and Gore. Only one game was not a sellout: the first. Only one player had played in the Super Bowl in three different decades: Gene Upshaw. Eighteen starting quarterbacks had worn the number twelve. Al Hirt played the national anthem at the first game. Crime rates drop significantly during the game, while water usage goes up significantly at timeouts and halftime. Approximately 750 million people in more than 170 countries see the game on television. You could even find a recipe for Super Bowl dip.

In 2000 there were diaries by players and the wives of players, each offering a variety of "insights" on the weekend. A link at ESPN.com connected to Dan Patrick, who was accumulating celebrity sightings, certainly a major public service. However, the highlights of Superbowl.com were Tips for Throwing a Super Bowl Party, animated Super Bowl greeting cards, an electric football game, NFL for Her, and the Miller Lite Beer Pager. The first Web casts using streaming video were produced at Superbowl.com for Super Bowl XXXV, with interactive action available every night of Super Bowl week.

One of the most interesting Web sites was www.gospelcom.net. At this location it was revealed why Dr. Norman Vincent Peale said at Super Bowl X: "If Jesus were alive today, he would be at the Super Bowl." At this Web site Jesus is there, virtually. At gospelcom.net you could order your Super Bowl outreach kit for hosting a Christian Super Bowl party in your own home. The kit came with a twelve-minute video (ideal for the halftime show) hosted by CNN's Fred Hickman and featuring All-Pros Brent Jones and Steve Wallace of the Super Bowl Champion 49ers. Jones and Wallace discussed their close friendship and mutual faith in Jesus Christ. Other players offered testimonies on such subjects as racial harmony and salvation.

Included in the kit were ten Sports Spectrum Magazines, and the sixteen-page "More Than Winning Booklet." Both were recommended as ideal door prizes at your party, and both provided additional testimonies and messages of salvation delivered with the appropriate sports metaphors. All of this was available from the Reggie White Christian Super Bowl Web page, and came with pregame, halftime, and postgame prayer service suggestions. White's godly site was not updated after 1997, but then how much do Super Bowl prayers change each year anyway? A Reggie White video was credited with "saving" thirty young people in Melbourne, Florida, while a reported forty-two hundred Reggie White Super Bowl parties led to twenty-five hundred decisions for Christ. Each year thereafter the religious involvement seemed to be one of the largest growth areas of the Super Bowl extravaganza.

The use of Web sites turned out to be only the beginning of the movement of the Super Bowl into the digital world. The advent of Facebook and Twitter brought new outlets for Super Bowl nonsense and advertising, while the more recent editions of the Super Bowl brought the app to the forefront of marketing, making the multifaceted phone the latest vehicle to host the Super Bowl universe. Virtual reality may be the only reality that matters.

Meanwhile, scalpers and ticket brokers were getting anywhere from $1,000 to $4,000 per ticket for the actual game, while no doubt praising the Lord with a vigor unmatched at any Reggie White Party. Is it any wonder that Deion Sanders once said that sport and religion go together like peanut butter and jelly?

Beyond Super

As to the question of the future growth of the Super Bowl, one only need look at the trends of four decades. What started in Los Angeles as a rather modest event had become a national spectacle and midwinter holiday. Tickets were given mainly to insiders, while ordinary fans had to turn to the free market, where tickets in 2007 were bringing anywhere from $1,500 to $10,000 dollars each.

The corporate parties, once few in number, became a weeklong staple of the Super Bowl scene. Early in the new century the hot tickets in this category were for the *Playboy, Penthouse,* and *Maxim* parties. Tickets to one *Playboy* event held at the American Airlines Arena in Miami went for $2,500, roughly the price of an end-zone seat for the game. For those with smaller budgets, the *Penthouse* party cost a mere $1,000 per ticket. Among other preferred venues in this category were the NFLPA party, the ESPN party, and the CBS party.[30]

Super Bowl XL in Phoenix was chronicled by Allen St. John in his excellent book, *The Billion Dollar Game.* He describes Super Bowl Sunday as the "most significant secular holiday," in the American calendar. "And there's a much different feel to it—while many other holidays feel like an obligation, Super Bowl Sunday still seems like a pure celebration." In the previous year 36 percent of the people surveyed said they would be attending a Super Bowl party. The average party had eighteen people in attendance. Half of those surveyed said they would rather go to a Super Bowl party than a New Year's Eve party.

St. John reported that more than 2 million TV sets were sold in the week before the Super Bowl, five times more than in a normal week. Super Bowl Sunday was the second-largest food consumption day of the year, behind only Thanksgiving, and generated a 20 percent boost in antacid sales on Monday. In the host city there was an average of one hundred parties per night in the week leading up to the game. They ranged from small to large, open and free, open for cash, and by invitation only.[31]

Over the years the commercials continued growing in cost and interest. For those who cared only about the commercials, numerous Web sites offered them in advance of the game and then for weeks following. While the cost of running a Super Bowl commercial had jumped to $3 million for a thirty-second spot, the networks had little difficulty selling the time slots. Production costs for most commercials added an additional $1 million to the total costs for those seeking visibility for their product on this huge national stage.

St. John calls the Super Bowl the "world's largest festival of short films," as the commercials have become increasingly important. There is a clear consensus that the 1984 Apple Computer commercial is the all-time greatest of these small films. It had a 1984 Orwellian theme. "While it never showed the keyboard or the monitor, it communicated a compelling idea that the Apple Macintosh computer represented *possibilities*. It was also stirring television, done by Ridley Scott, who'd brought a similarly bleak vision of the future to life in the seminal *Blade Runner* only a couple of years earlier." (This video is still available at multiple Internet locations.) The commercial had tested badly and people were questioning Steve Jobs's judgment. Within minutes after airing, it was proclaimed as pure genius. It aired over and over again on news programs, $4.6 million worth of computers were sold within six hours of the broadcast, and seventy-two thousand Macs sold in the first one hundred days, which represented a 50 percent increase over the most optimistic predications of sales.[32]

Over the years, Anheuser-Busch has done more advertising on the Super Bowl than any other single company. To measure the success of their Super Bowl ads, they used Ad Meter, a morning-after poll conducted by *USA Today*. In the nine years prior to Super Bowl XLII, their commercials were number one in Ad Meter voting. Robert Lachky, Anheuser-Bush's executive vice president for creative development, told St. John: "It's about having the greatest performance on Super Bowl Sunday so that the consumer, the people who sell your product, and the distributors all feel you're the market leader and that nobody can top you. It's very important to look like a winner that day."[33] Another excellent example of Number Oneism.

Even a significant economic downturn had little impact on the revelers. At Super Bowl XLIII in Tampa in 2009, there were reports of some unsold hotel rooms, fewer corporate jets, and some cancelled parties, but in the end this Super Bowl didn't look all that different from the others. NBC sold all of its advertising at the average rate of $3 million for a thirty-second spot, reaching a record total of $206 million in advertising sales. Celebrities from the world of sport and show business, if that is a distinction that still needs to be made, were appearing nearly everywhere, pushing products and causes throughout Super Bowl week. In the end, according to Steve Rushin of *Sports Illustrated,* Tampa lived up to its reputation as being a "nexus of night life and professional sport" with its plethora of casinos and strippers.[34]

A year later at Super Bowl XLIV in Miami, any slight sign of economic impact there may have been at XLIII was long gone. The excess was in full flight, as the biggest event of the week was the competition between *Playboy* and *Maxim* to give the most opulent, outrageous, and ultimately decadent party. According to Darren Rovell's account, *Maxim* bested the bunny franchise in nearly every category. Most importantly it was in the man/woman ratio that *Maxim* outshined *Playboy*. "Everywhere you looked, there were beautiful women chatting it up. 'It takes a lot to figure out how to execute that ratio, but luckily most who know how to do it work at *Maxim*,' said *Maxim* publisher Ben Madden."[35] The opulence had returned in full bloom, as one would have expected of the Super Bowl in its natural habitat on South Beach.

Can the Super Bowl and all that surrounds it get any bigger? Of course it can. And if it can get bigger, it must get bigger, and it will get bigger because in the words of Harriet Lake, "Too much is never enough." There are only two things that can stop it: a massive economic collapse or a hysterical wave of sanity sweeping the country. Given the remote possibility of either of these happening, the hype will roll onward and ever upward, finally turning back on itself. Mike Tanner of the *New York Times* considers the Super Bowl Pete Rozelle's "greatest marketing achievement," as the hype has become a story transcending the story. "The news media does not just cover the Super Bowl, it covers itself covering the Super Bowl, self-referentially glorifying in the excess while gorging on television hours and column inches," so that after over forty years, "the hype has become metahype: excessive analysis of excess itself. We can only marvel at how long we have marveled at the spectacle. Rozelle would be proud."[36]

Without a doubt the Super Bowl is now a national holiday that excessively celebrates excess.

Postscript

The history of the National Football League is a remarkable story. The geographic origins of the league in the older Midwest were the product of the growing popularity of football generally, and the desire for those not attached to the college game to have access to football both as participants and spectators. It was the product of the entrepreneurial vision and skills of those men who came together to try to bring order out of the chaos in the semipro game, and with some luck and skill, to turn a profit.

The obstacles faced in the formation of the league, both internally and externally, were many, but by the end of the Great Depression the future National Football League was showing clear signs of success. Coming out of World War II, the league and its rivals were able to ride the wave of the growing prosperity of a consumer culture and simultaneously tie themselves to the growing power of the new technology of television.

The game itself was ideal for the new urban consumer society characterized in David Riesman's *The Lonely Crowd*. Football had a powerful appeal to the sedentary urban culture, bringing with it a vivid physicality and the visceral appeal of violence. Americans periodically develop anxiety about the softness and feminization of their society, and football offered a vicarious antidote for that anxiety. More than any other mass spectator sport, football was ideally suited to the small screens that were filling the homes of America in the postwar world.

At this critical point, the world of professional football was blessed with leadership of a very high quality in the persons of Bert Bell, Pete Rozelle, Lamar Hunt, and many others who joined with and built upon the foundations laid by George Halas, the Mara family, and the Rooneys. NFL leadership mastered the world of television, dominated governments at federal, state, and local levels, and created a cartel behind a facade of devotion to the free enterprise system.

Coming out of the AFL and NFL conflict of the sixties, the new NFL was positioned for success, which it quickly achieved with the major exception of labor-management relations. Success brought with it new issues and problems, many of which were internal and centered on league governance, driven in no small part by greed and ego. This led to considerable conflict and litigation and produced a power shift in the NFL that opened a new era of movement and expansion.

With the advent of cable television and the subsequent electronic explosion over the past three decades, the NFL has once again proven itself adept at accommodating and exploiting the opportunities of the communications revolution. By the end of the century, the league was riding a new wave of wealth, and with new leadership it was able to solve its serious labor problems. In all these areas Paul Tagliabue and Roger Goodell showed the way. This is not to say that as the NFL completed the first decade of the twenty-first century, all was well. Concerns over drug use, the growing controversy over the use of "Redskins" by the Washington franchise, player conduct on and off the field, and the health of players and former players all present very serious challenges.

Concussions and their potential aftermath for early dementia was the most serious of these issues. For a game like football that has violence as one of its key ingredients, any attempt to diminish the violence is a very tricky proposition. On the other hand, when the consequences of violence are shown to be extremely serious, it is clear the league must take corrective action. When players and former players are questioning the existence of youth football, and saying they are not inclined to allow their children to play the game, the NFL and the game of football have serious problems.

Commissioner Roger Goodell has shown considerable skill in navigating the labor issues and as a negotiator with the television networks. On the issue of the scab referees, he proved to be a tool of ownership that desperately wanted a victory over some union, any union. Most difficult of all has been the concussion issue, which the NFL and Goodell handled very poorly on the public relations front. However, the settlement of the class-action suit has been important to the league, and may have been a major victory over the players, although that remains to be seen. It certainly was a victory for the NFL, as it has avoided full disclosure of its policies on concussions and has, in the view of some, settled at a bargain price. However, at this writing, the presiding judge has not accepted the terms of the settlement and there is now some doubt that she will accept them.

Looking back to those first meetings at the Hupmobile showroom in the early 1920s, it may be difficult to grasp that the NFL of 2014 has been the result. But then much the same can be said of any business success over such an extended period of time. As with all stories of human endeavor and success, this one has its many heroes and villains, its turning points and crucial decisions, and its highs and lows.

It is my hope that this overview of the league's history has rendered its critical elements in a fashion that is entertaining and informative, and provides a sense of the complex motives of human behavior that make studying history worth our time and effort.

NFL Franchises

Listed by year of founding, with franchise movement and name changes indicated by indentation, and current teams indicated in bold. The names and dates for the early franchises are sometimes in dispute. Basically I have followed the names and dates found in Craig Coenen's *From Sandlots to the Super Bowl,* Appendix A, with modifications suggested by *Total Football II: The Official Encyclopedia of the National Football League* and *The ESPN Pro Football Encyclopedia* (second edition).

1920

Akron Pros (1920–1925)
   Akron Indians (1926)
Buffalo All-Americans (1920–1923)
Canton Bulldogs (1920–1923)
   Cleveland Bulldogs (1924)
Chicago Cardinals (1920–1959) also Racine Cardinals (1920)
   St. Louis Cardinals (1960–1987)
   Phoenix Cardinals (1988–1993)
   Arizona Cardinals (1994–)
Chicago Tigers (1920)
Cleveland Tigers (1920)
   Cleveland Indians (1921)
Columbus Panhandlers (1920–1922)
   Columbus Tigers (1923–1926)
Dayton Triangles (1920–1929)
Decatur Staleys (1920)
   Chicago Staleys (1921)
   Chicago Bears (1922–)

Detroit Heralds (1920)
  Detroit Tigers (1921)
Hammond Pros (1920–1926)
Muncie Flyers (1920–1921)
Rochester Jeffersons (1920–1925)
Rock Island Independents (1920–1925)

1921

Cincinnati Celts (1921)
Evansville Crimson Giants (1921–1922)
Green Bay Packers (1921–)
Louisville Brecks (1921–1923)
Minneapolis Marines (1921–1924)
  Minneapolis Red Jackets (1929–1930)
New York Brickley Giants (1921)
Tonawanda Kardex (1921)
Washington Senators (1921)

1922

Milwaukee Badgers (1922–1925)
Ourang Indians (1922–1923)
Racine Legion (1922–1924)
Toledo Maroons (1922–1923)
  Kenosha Maroons (1924)

1923

Cleveland Indians (1923)
  Cleveland Bulldogs (1924–1925)
Duluth Kelleys (1923–1925)
  Duluth Eskimos (1926–1927)
St. Louis All-Stars (1923)

1924

Buffalo Bison (1924–1925)
Frankford Yellowjackets (1924–1931)
Kansas City Blues (1924)

1925

Canton Bulldogs (1925–1926)

Cleveland Bulldogs (1925)
Detroit Panthers (1925–1926)
Kansas City Cowboys (1925–1926)
New York Giants (1925–)
Pottsville Maroons (1925–1928)
   Boston Bulldogs (1929)
Providence Steam Roller (1925–1931)

1926

Brooklyn Lions (1926)
Buffalo Rangers (1926)
Hartford Blues (1926)
Los Angeles Buccaneers (1926)
Louisville Colonels (1926)
Milwaukee Badgers (1926)
Racine Tornadoes (1926)

1927

Buffalo Bison (1927)
Cleveland Bulldogs (1927)
New York Yankees (1927–1928)

1928

Detroit Wolverines (1928)

1929

Buffalo Bison (1929)
Orange Golden Tornadoes (1929)
   Newark Tornadoes (1930)
Staten Island Stapletons (1929–1932)

1930

Brooklyn Dodgers (1930–1943)
   Brooklyn Tigers (1944)
Portsmouth Spartans (1930–1933)
   Detroit Lions (1934–)

1931

Cleveland Indians (1931)

1932

Boston Braves (1932)
   Boston Redskins (1933–1936)
   Washington Redskins (1937–)

1933

Cincinnati Reds (1933–1934)
   St. Louis Gunners (1934)
Philadelphia Eagles (1933–)
Pittsburgh Pirates (1933–1939)
   Pittsburgh Steelers (1940–)

1937

Cleveland Rams (1937–1942 and 1944–1945)
   Los Angeles Rams (1946–1994)
   St. Louis Rams (1995–)

1944

Boston Yanks (1944–1949)
   New York Bulldogs (1949)
   New York Yanks (1950–1951)
   Dallas Texans (1952)
   Baltimore Colts (1953–1983)
   Indianapolis Colts (1984–)

1946

Cleveland Browns (AAFC, 1946–1949; NFL, 1950–1995 and 1999–)
Miami Seahawks (AAFC, 1946)
   Baltimore Colts (AAFC, 1947–1949; NFL, 1950)
San Francisco 49ers (AAFC, 1946–1949; NFL, 1950–)

1960

Dallas Cowboys (1960–)
Boston Patriots (AFL, 1960–1969; NFL, 1970)
   New England Patriots (1971–)
Buffalo Bills (AFL, 1960–1969; NFL, 1970–)
Dallas Texans (AFL, 1960–1962)
   Kansas City Chiefs (AFL, 1963–1969; NFL, 1970–)

Denver Broncos (AFL, 1960–1969; NFL, 1970–)
Houston Oilers (AFL, 1960–1969; NFL, 1970–1996)
  Tennessee Oilers (1997–1998)
  Tennessee Titans (1999–)
Los Angeles Chargers (AFL, 1960)
  San Diego Chargers (AFL, 1961–1969; NFL, 1970–)
New York Titans (AFL, 1960–1962)
  New York Jets (AFL, 1963–1969; NFL, 1970–)
Oakland Raiders (AFL, 1960–1969; NFL, 1970–1981)
  Los Angeles Raiders (1982–1994)
  Oakland Raiders (1995–)

1961

Minnesota Vikings (1961–)

1966

Atlanta Falcons (1966–)
Miami Dolphins (AFL, 1966–1969; NFL, 1970–)

1967

New Orleans Saints (1967–)

1968

Cincinnati Bengals (AFL, 1968–1969; NFL, 1970–)

1976

Seattle Seahawks (1976–)
Tampa Bay Buccaneers (1976–)

1995

Carolina Panthers (1995–)
Jacksonville Jaguars (1995–)

1996

Baltimore Ravens (1996–)

2002

Houston Texans (2002–)

Notes

Chapter 1. The First Pros

1. PFRA Research, "Forward into Invisibility 1920," www.profootballresearchers. org; Marc Maltby, *The Origins and Early Development of Professional Football* (New York: Garland Publishers, 1997), 199.

2. Robert W. Peterson, *Pigskin: The Early Years of Pro Football* (New York: Oxford University Press, 1997), 16–17; and Keith McCellan, *The Sunday Game: At the Dawn of Professional Football* (Akron, Ohio: University of Akron Press, 1998), 23–27.

3. PFRA Research, "Out in the Boondocks Westmoreland County Leads the Pros: 1897," www.profootballresearchers.org.

4. PFRA Research, "Five Hundred Reasons Football's First Pro: 1892," www.profootball researchers.org.

5. PFRA Research, "Ohio Tiger Trap Ohio's First Football Ringers: 1903," by Bob Carroll, www.profootballresearchers.org, and Bob Carroll, Michael Gershman, David Neft, and John Thorn, eds., *Total Football II: The Official Encyclopedia of the National Football League* (New York: Harper and Collins Publishers, 1999), 8–9; Mark Maltby, *Origins and Early Development,* 108–9 and 125.

6. PFRA Research, "Blondy Wallace and the Biggest Football Scandal Ever: 1906," and "Shelby Who? 1910," www.profootballreseachers.org; Carroll et al., *Total Football II,* 9–11.

7. PFRA Research, "Out in the Boondocks," www.profootballresearchers.org.

8. McCellan, *Sunday Game,* 3–15.

9. Ibid., 15.

10. Ibid., 16–31.

11. Ibid., 18–23.

12. Ibid., 24–27.

13. PFRA, "Twilight, 1919."

14. Carroll et al., *Total Football II,* 14: Will McDonough et al., *75 Seasons: The Complete Story of the National Football League, 1920–1995* (Atlanta: Turner Publishing and National Football League Properties, 1994), 23–24.

15. Joe Horrigan, "National Football League Franchise Transactions," *The Coffin Corner* 4 (1982): 1–2.

16. PFRA, "Forward into Invisibility 1920"; Maltby, *Origins and Early Development,* 199.

17. Robert W. Peterson, *Pigskin: The Early Years of Pro Football* (New York: Oxford University Press, 1997), 70–74.

18. PFRA, "Once More, With Feeling 1921"; McDonough et al., *75 Seasons,* 25–28; Jeff Davis, *Papa Bear: The Life and Legacy of George Halas* (New York: McGraw Hill, 2005), 50, 53, 57, 62–63.

19. Ernest L. Cuneo, "Present at the Creation: Professional Football in the Twenties," *American Scholar* 56 (Autumn 1987): 488; Bill Gates, "Papa Bear," *Los Angeles Times,* August 13, 1976, C1.

20. McDonough et al., *75 Seasons,* 28–29.

21. Cuneo, "Present at the Creation," 491; John Carroll, *Red Grange and the Rise of Modern Football* (Urbana and Chicago: University of Illinois Press, 1999), vii–viii, 1–9, and 40–41.

22. Carroll, *Red Grange,* 92–97, direct quotes from 97.

23. Ibid., 102.

24. Michael Oriard. *King Football: Sport and Spectacle in the Golden Age of Radio & Newsreels, Movies & Magazines, The Weekly & The Daily Press* (Chapel Hill: University of North Carolina Press, 2001), 104–5.

25. Carroll, *Red Grange,* 107–10.

26. Ibid., 111–13.

27. Ibid., 113–26; Bob Carroll, "Red Equals Green 1925," PFRA.

28. Carroll, *Red Grange,* 126–27, 132.

29. Ibid., 133–39; Bob Carroll, "The Grange War 1926," PFRA; Horrigan, "National Football League Franchise Transactions," 6–8.

30. Carroll, *Red Grange,* 141–44; Hensley, "NFL Competitors"; Horrigan, "National Football League," 8–9; Don Smith, "Here's Your Hat 1927," PFRA.

31. Smith, "Here's Your Hat 1927"; Bob Carroll, "Giants on the Gridiron," PFRA; Oriard, *King Football,* 105; Carroll, *Red Grange,* 125–26; Craig Coenen, *From Sandlots to the Super Bowl: The National Football League, 1920–1967* (Knoxville: University of Tennessee Press, 2005), 62–69.

32. Bob Carroll, "Giants on the Gridiron."

33. Bob Carroll and John Hogrogian, "Steamrollered 1928," *Coffin Corner* 31, no.1 (2009): 7–11; Coenen, *From Sandlots,* 51.

34. Chuck Frederick, *Leatherheads of the North: The True Story of Ernie Nevers and the Duluth Eskimos,* (Duluth, Minn.: X-Communication, 2007), 2–4.

35. Ibid., 11–25 and 35–55.

36. Ibid., 58–60.

37. Ibid., 104–8.

38. Ibid., 62–66; Coenen, *From Sandlots,* 12–14.

39. Frederick, 116–20.

Chapter 2. Depression and War

1. Joe Horrigan, "National Football League Transactions," PFRA, *The Coffin Corner* 4 (1982): 9–14; McDonough et al., *75 Seasons,* 60.

2. Stephen Hensley, "NFL Competitors· 1926–1975," PFRA, *The Coffin Corner* 3, no. 9 (1981): 1–2.

3. C. Robert Barnett, "Playing for the Pack in the 30s: An Interview with Clarke Hinkle," PFRA, *The Coffin Corner* 4, no. 5(1982).

4. Coenen, *From Sandlots,* 44–49.

5. Kevin Britz, "Of Football and Frontiers: The Meaning of Bronko Nagurski," *Journal of Sport History* 20, no.2 (Summer 1993): 101–26, closing quotes from 117 and 125.

6. Coenen, *From Sandlots,* 75–85.

7. Charles K. Ross. *Outside the Lines: African Americans and the Integration of the National Football League* (New York: New York University Press, 1999), 10–13; Alan H. Levy, *Tackling Jim Crow: Racial Segregation in Professional Football* (Jefferson, N.C.: McFarland, 2003), 11–12; Maltby, *Origins and Early Development,* 86.

8. John Carroll, *Fritz Pollard: Pioneer in Racial Advancement* (Urbana and Chicago: University of Illinois Press, 1992), 128–32, 134–37; Levy, *Tackling Jim Crow,* 30; Levy, *Tackling Jim Crow,* 26.

9. Levy, *Tackling Jim Crow,* 29.

10. Carroll, *Fritz Pollard,* 151–56, 171–76, 178–79; Levy, *Tackling Jim Crow,* 30–34.

11. Carroll, *Fritz Pollard,* 177–78; Levy, *Tackling Jim Crow,* 38–58; Oriard, *King Football,* 6; Timothy Smith, "Outside the Pale: The Exclusion of Blacks from the National Football League, 1934–1936," *Journal of Sport History* 15, no.3 (Winter 1988): 255–59; Andrew O'Toole, *Smiling Irish Eyes* (Haworth, N.J.: St. Johann Press, 2004), 57.

12. Bob Carroll, "1932 National Football League: The 60-Yard Circus," PFRA, 1932; Coenen, *From Sandlots,* 85–91; McDonough et al., *75 Seasons,* 48–49 and 54; "1933 NFL Championship Game," www.profootballhof.com/history.

13. McDonough et al., *75 Seasons,* 46; Coenen, *From Sandlots.* 98–99.

14. Coenen, *From Sandlots,* 93–94.

15. Ibid. 98–104; McDonough et al., *75 Seasons,* 50; Oriard, *King Football,* 49, 200–209.

16. Coenen, *From Sandlots,* 95–98.

17. Oriard, *King Football,* 208–9; McDonough et al., *75 Seasons,* 55–56.

18. George Preston Marshall, "Pro Football is Better," *Saturday Evening Post* 121, no. 21 (November 19, 1938): 21.

19. Coenen, *From Sandlots,* 108–10.

20. Bob Carroll, "Triumph of the T," PFRA (1940), 1–4; McDonough et al., *75 Seasons,* 68; Peterson, *Pigskin,* 12–13; *Total Football II,* 20–21.

21. Peterson, *Pigskin,* 136; McDonough et al., *75 Seasons,* 67.

22. Carroll, "Triumph of the T," 1; McDonough et al., *75 Seasons,* 67; Carroll et al., *Total* Football II, 19–20 and 90.

23. "Sunday, Dec. 7, 1941," *New York Times,* December 7, 1980.

24. McDonough et al., *75 Seasons,* 71.

25. Joe Horrigan, "& Iron Words," *The Coffin Corner* 2, no. 9 (1980); Peterson, *Pigskin,* 138.

26. McDonough et al., *75 Seasons,* 62–63; Joshua Robinson, "Steelers Shared Resources With 2 Teams During World War II," *New York Times,* January 15, 2009;

O'Toole, *Smiling Irish Eyes,* 127–34; http://www.profootballhof.com/history/decades/1940s/1942.jsp.

27. Peterson, *Pigskin,* 147.

Chapter 3. The NFL Comes of Age

1. Coenen, *From Sandlots,* 116–17.

2. Stan Grosshandler, "All-America Football Conference," Professional Football Researchers Association (PFRA), http://www.profootballresearchers.org/AAFC.htm, 1.

3. Coenen, *From Sandlots,* 117; Grosshandler, "All-America Football Conference," 1

4. McDonough et al., *75 Seasons,* 72; Grosshandler, "All-America Football Conference," 1 Coenen, *From Sandlots,* 118–20.

5. Michael MacCambridge, *America's Game: The Epic Story of How Pro Football Captured a Nation* (New York: Random House, Anchor Books), 14–15.

6. Ibid., 15–16; Coenen, *From Sandlots,* 125–30.

7. Grosshandler, "All-America Football Conference," 2; MacCambridge, *America's Game,* 51; Coenen, *From Sandlots,* 131–34.

8. Carroll et al., *Total Football II,* 24–25; McDonough et al., *75 Seasons,* 108–16; Dan Daley and Bob O'Donnell, *The Pro Football Chronicle* (New York: Macmillan: 1990), 133.

9. Andy Plascik, *The Best Show in Football: The 1946–1955 Cleveland Browns, Pro Football's Greatest Dynasty* (New York: Taylor Trade Publishing, 2007), 15–26; George Cantor, *Paul Brown: The Man Who Invented Modern Football* (Chicago: Triumph Books, 2008), 80–83; MacCambridge, *America's Game,* 23–27.

10. Cantor, *Paul Brown,* 3–4.

11. Andrew O'Toole, *Paul Brown: The Rise and Fall and Rise Again of Football's Most Innovative Coach* (Cincinnati: Clerist Press, 2008), 117, 136, 155; Cantor, *Paul Brown,* 93–94; MacCambridge, *America's Game,* 29–35.

12. Plascik, *Best Show,* 32–39; O'Toole, *Paul Brown,* 125; MacCambridge, *America's Game,* 29–30. Dan Daly and Bob O'Donnell, *The Pro Football Chronicle* (New York: Macmillan, 1990), 118.

13. Ross, *Outside the Lines,* 99–105, 114; MacCambridge, *America's Game,* 55–58; Coenen, *From Sandlots,* 123.

14. O'Toole, *Paul Brown,* 125–27; Cantor, *Paul Brown,* 111–12; Plascik, *Best Show,* 49–51, 158–60.

15. MacCambridge, *America's Game,* 52, 62–71; Piasick, *Best Show,* 162–84; Carroll et al., *Total Football II,* 1659.

16. William Nack, "The Ballad of Big Daddy," *Sports Illustrated,* January 11, 1999; Michael Oriard, *Brand NFL* (Chapel Hill: University of North Carolina Press, 2007), 42 and 122; "Les Bingaman" and "Gene Lipscomb," www.pro-football-reference.com/players.

17. Coenen, *From Sandlots,* 136; Plascik, *Best Show,* 170–71.

18. McDonough et al., *75 Seasons,* 103–4; MacCambridge, *America's Game,* 80–81; Oriard, *King Football,* 98–99.

19. Coenen, *From Sandlots*, 147 for Melvin Adelman and Andrew Linden, "The Business of Professional Football: The Profitability of National Football League Clubs in 1951 and 1952," Paper presented at 38th Annual Convention of the North American Society for Sport History, May 28–31, 2010.

20. "The 1950s and the King," www.profootballhof.com/history: Adelman and Linden, NASSH Paper.

21. MacCambridge, *America's Game,* 73, 103–4; Peterson, *Pigskin,* 196–99; Ron Powers, *Supertube: The Rise of Television Sports* (New York: Coward-McCann), 80–81; Mark Yost, *Tailgating, Sacks, and Salary Caps: How the NFL Became the Most Successful Sports League in History* (Chicago: Kaplan Publishing, 2006), 66–69.

22. Yost, *Tailgating,* 68; Powers, *Supertube,* 17, 80–81.

23. MacCambridge, *America's Game,* ix–xiii, 114; Peterson, *Pigskin,* 201; Tex Maule, "The Best Football Game Ever Played," *Sports Illustrated,* January 5, 1959, 10–13.

24. MacCambridge, *America's Game,* 114; Peterson, *Pigskin,* 199; "List of National Football League Records (individual)," Wikipedia, http://en.wikipedia.org.

25. Powers, *Supertube,* 81; MacCambridge, *America's Game,* 105–7; Robert S. Lyons, *On Any Given Sunday: A Life of Bert Bell* (Philadelphia: Temple University Press, 2010), 276–77; Benjamin G. Rader, *In Its Own Image: How Television Transformed Sports* (New York: The Free Press, 1984), 85.

26. "A Pride of Lions," *Time,* November 29, 1954.

27. Ibid.

28. Ibid.; MacCambridge, *America's Game,* 85–86; Oriard, *King Football,* 214–15; McDonough et al., *75 Seasons,* 109; "Jim Brown" and "Paul Hornung," www.Pro-Football-reference.com/players.

29. MacCambridge, *America's Game,* 117; Carroll et al., *Total Football II,* 186–89.

Chapter 4. Moving to Center Stage

1. Oriard, *King Football,* 220–21; "A Man's Game," *Time* (cover story), November 30, 1959; Bob Carter, "The Violent World," ESPN.com, September 7, 2005.

2. Coenen, *From Sandlots,* 175; *Time,* November 30, 1959.

3. Coenen, *From Sandlots,* 195; MacCambridge, *America's Game,* 135–50; Tex Maule, "The Infighting Was Vicious," *Sports Illustrated,* February 8, 1960; Jeff Davis, *Rozelle: Czar of the NFL* (New York: McGraw-Hill, 2007), 1–19.

4. Coenen, *From Sandlots,* 186–88; MacCambridge, *America's Game,* 116–21.

5. Coenen, *From Sandlots,* 192–97; MacCambridge, *America's Game,* 123–29; David Harris, *The League: The Rise and Decline of the NFL* (New York: Bantam Books, 1986), 102–5.

6. MacCambridge, *America's Game,* 128, 146–47; Coenen, *From Sandlots,* 198; McDonough et al., *75 Seasons,* 185–86.

7. Coenen, *From Sandlots,* 199; MacCambridge, *America's Game,* 130–33.

8. MacCambridge, *America's Game,* 129, 162; Coenen, *From Sandlots,* 199–200, 203–6.

9. McDonough et al., *75 Seasons,* 190–200; Paul Zimmerman, "The Team of the 90s?" *Sports Illustrated,* September 7, 1992: "Hornung's 176 Points," www.profootballhof.com/history.

10. Greg Thomas, "The AFL: A League Too Often Misremembered" PFRA, *The Coffin Corner* 13, no.1 (1991); "70 Points in Half AFL 1963," NFL History and Stats, www .profootballhof.com; McDonough et al., *75 Seasons,* 190; MacCambridge, *America's Game,* 194–96.

11. Oriard, *Brand NFL,* 211–13; Larry Felser, *The Birth of the New NFL* (Guilford, Conn.: The Lyons Press, 2008), 100; MacCambridge, *America's Game,* 249–50; Levy, *Tackling Jim Crow,* 138–49; Jason Whitlock, "Hunt Helped Open the Door," *Kansas City Star,* December 15, 2006, www.kansascity.com.

12. Thomas G. Smith, "Civil Rights on the Gridiron: The Kennedy Administration and the Desegregation of the Washington Redskins," *Journal of Sport History* 14, no. 2 (Summer 1987): 189–208; Michael Lomax, "The African American Experience in Professional Football," *Journal of Social History* 33, no.1 (Autumn 1999): 166–70.

13. Coenen, *From Sandlots,* 221–22; MacCambridge, *America's Game,* 206–9; Oriard, *Brand NFL,* 20.

14. Coenen, *From Sandlots,* 221–22; MacCambridge, *America's Game,* 209–16.

15. John Fortunato, *Commissioner: The Legacy of Pete Rozelle* (Lanham, Md.: Taylor Trade Publishing, 2006), 67–74; McDonough et al., *75 Seasons,* 201–2; MacCambridge, *America's Game,* 217–28; Felser, *Birth of the New NFL,* 41–45, 50–59, 70.

16. Fortunato, *Commissioner,* 75–76; McDonough et al., *75 Seasons,* 202–3; MacCambridge, *America's Game,* 229–30.

17. O'Toole, *Paul Brown,* 266–79; "New Orleans Saints," www.profootballhof.com/ history/teams.jsp.

18. MacCambridge, *America's Game,* 236–40; Don Weiss with Chuck Day, *The Making of the Super Bowl: The Inside Story of the World's Greatest Sporting Event* (Chicago: Contemporary Books, 2003), 62–69, 95–98.

19. MacCambridge, *America's Game,* 253–54; Felser, *Birth of the New NFL,* 184–85.

20. Fortunato, *Commissioner,* 61, 76–84; MacCambridge, *America's Game,* 268–72.

21. Weiss, *Making of the Super Bowl,* 75–90; MacCambridge, *America's Game,* 256–68.

Chapter 5. A Troubled Decade

1. David Zang, *SportsWars* (Fayetteville: University of Arkansas Press, 2001), chapter 1.

2. Michael Lomax, "Detrimental to the League: Gambling and the Governance of Professional Football," *Journal of Sport History* 29, no. 2 (Summer 2002): 289–311; Oriard, *Brand NFL,* 13–14; McDonough et al., *75 Seasons,* 193; MacCambridge, *America's Game,* 176–78; Kenneth Rudeen, "Sportsman of the Year." *Sports Illustrated,* January 6, 1964; Bernie Parrish, *They Call It a Game* (New York: The Dial Press, 1971), 184–88, 199–206; Powers, *Supertube,* 176.

3. Powers, *Supertube,* 174–75; Harris, *The League,* 16–17.

4. Fortunato, *The Commissioner,* 54; MacCambridge, *America's Game,* 185–89; Rudeen, Sportsman of the Year," January 6, 1964.

5. Oriard, *Brand NFL,* 14–18; MacCambridge, *America's Game,* 181–85.

6. McDonough et al., *75 Seasons,* 195–96.

7. Mike Freeman, *Jim Brown: The Fierce Life of an American Hero* (New York: Harper Collins, 2007), 32–44, 124–28, 133–36, 151–53.

8. Jim Brown, *Out of Bounds* (New York: Zebra Books, 1989), 49–58, 104–5; "Pro Football: Look At Me, Man!" *Time,* November 26, 1965: Freeman, *Jim Brown,* 37–39, 44, 127–53; Alex Haley, "Playboy Interview: Jim Brown," *Playboy,* February 1968.

9. Oriard, *Brand NFL,* 210–12; Levy, *Tackling Jim Crow,* 114–18.

10. Jack Olsen, "In the Back of the Bus," *Sports Illustrated,* July 22, 1968.

11. Martin Kane, "An Assessment of 'Black Is Best,'" *Sports Illustrated,* January 18, 1971; Harry Edwards, "The Sources of the Black Athlete's Superiority," *Black Scholar,* November 1971.

12. Oriard, *Brand NFL,* 41–44; Dan Jenkins, "The Sweet Life of Swinging Joe," *Sports Illustrated,* October 17, 1966; Tex Maule, "Say It's So Joe," *Sports Illustrated,* January 20, 1969; MacCambridge, *America's Game,* 251–52, 259–60.

13. Oriard, *Brand NFL,* 41–50; John D. Bloom, "Joe Namath and Super Bowl III: An Interpretation of Style," *Journal of Sport History* 15, no. 1 (Spring 1988): 66–74.

14. "Vinnie, Vidi, Vici," *Time* (cover story), December 21, 1962.

15. Oriard, *Brand NFL,* pp. 30–36; Vinnie, Vidi, Vici," *Time,* December 21, 1962; Leonard Shecter, "The Toughest Man in Pro Football," *Esquire,* January 1968.

16. David Maraniss, *When Pride Still Mattered: A Life of Vince Lombardi* (New York: Simon and Schuster, 1999), 62–65, 137–46, 216–25, 240–41, 270–94, 386–89, 397–406, 452, 476–77, 484; MacCambridge, *America's Game,* 261–63; William Phillips, "A Season in the Stands," *Commentary,* July 1969.

17. Oriard, *Brand NFL,* pp. 28–30.

Chapter 6. The Perfect Television Game

1. Robert S. Lyons, *On Any Given Sunday: A Life of Bert Bell* (Philadelphia: Temple University Press, 2010), 196–97, 245–48; Oriard, *Brand NFL,* 12; Joan Chandler, *Television and National Sport: The United States and Britain* (Urbana and Chicago: University of Illinois Press, 1988), 58–59; Powers, *Supertube,* 172–73; MacCambridge, *America's Game,* 130–32; George Halas, Gwen Morgan, and Arthur Veysey, *Halas on Halas: The Autobiography of George Halas* (New York: McGraw-Hill, 1979), 250; Harris, *The League,* 14–15.

2. Oriard, *Brand NFL,* 12; Coenen, *From Sandlots,* 200–204; Mark Yost, *Tailgating, Sacks, and Salary Caps: How the NFL Became the Most Successful Sports League in History* (Chicago: Kaplan Publishing, 2006), 72–74; Powers, *Supertube,* 173.

3. Powers, *Supertube,* 176–77; MacCambridge, *America's Game,* 156–59.

4. Chandler, *Television and National Sport,* 60; Ben Rader, *In Its Own Image: How Television Transformed Sports* (New York: The Free Press, 1984), 4–5.

5. Powers, *Supertube,* 178–79; MacCambridge, *America's Game,* 190–92; William Johnson, "After TV Accepted the Call Sunday Was Never the Same," *Sports Illustrated,* January 5, 1970, 22–29; Yost, *Tailgating,* 85–86.

6. Yost, *Tailgating,* 80; William Johnson, "After TV," 85–86.

7. Oriard, *Brand NFL,* 25–28, 175; Don Weiss, *The Making of the Super Bowl* (Chicago: Contemporary Books, 2003), 283–88; MacCambridge, *America's Game,* 275–80; Yost,

Tailgating, 84–85; Powers, *Supertube*, 18; Richard Sandomir, "One Night in 1970, the Revolution Was Televised," *New York Times*, November 23, 2005; Richard C. Crepeau, "Monday Night Football Left the Field a Long Time Ago," *PopPolitics.com*, December 28, 2005.

8. Fortunato, *Commissioner*, 116; Yost, *Tailgating*, 77–80; Robert V. Bellamy Jr., "The Evolving Sports Television Marketplace," in *MediaSport*, edited by Lawrence A. Wenner (London and New York: Routledge Publishers, 1998), 73–87; Mark Hyman, "How the NFL Loses Fans and Gets Richer," *Business Week*, January 26, 1998.

9. Weiss, *Making of the Super Bowl*, 291–99; MacCambridge, *America's Game*, 282–83, 302; recent revelations from the Nixon tapes suggest he would have been satisfied with the lifting of the blackout for playoff games only.

10. McDonough et al., *75 Seasons*, 253–59, 279; MacCambridge, *America's Game*, 339–40; Adrian Havill, *The Last Mogul: The Unauthorized Biography of Jack Kent Cooke* (New York: St. Martin's Press, 1992), 6–7.

11. Terry O'Neil, *The Game Behind the Game: High Stakes, High Pressure in Television Sports* (New York: Harper & Row, 1989), 114–15, 185–90; Adam Bryant, "The Nation: Out of Bounds; Beyond the Bottom Line: The New Math of TV Sports," *New York Times*, January 18, 1998.

12. Richard C. Crepeau, "Punt or Bunt: A Note on Sport in American Culture," *Journal of Sport History* 3, no. 3 (1976): 205–12; Oriard, *Brand NFL*, 188–89, 209.

13. McDonough et al., *75 Seasons*, 266–69; MacCambridge, *America's Game*, 341; Harris, *The League*, 548–52, 618, 643–44; Oriard, *Brand NFL*, 187–88; Jerry Gorman, Kirk Calhoun, and Skip Rosen, *The Name of the Game: The Business of Sports* (New York: John Wiley & Sons, 1994), 70–71.

14. Fortunato, *Commissioner*, 95–96; Jeff Davis, *Rozelle: Csar of the NFL* (New York: McGraw-Hill, 2008), 454–56; Richard Sandomir, "Nighttime Draft is Attracting More Viewers—The Fifth Down Blog," *New York Times*, April 24, 2010; Sigmund Bloom, "A Twitter Guide to the N.F.L. Draft—The Fifth Down Blog," *New York Times*, April 13, 2010.

15. Oriard, *Brand NFL*, 167–74; Mark Hyman, "How the NFL Loses Fans and Gets Richer," *Business Week*, January 26, 1998; Kurt Badenhausen, Michael K. Ozanian, and Maya Roney, "The Business of Football: The Tape on Tagliabue," Forbes.com, September 1, 2006.

16. Yost, *Tailgating*, 102–12; Oriard, *Brand NFL*, 172–73.

17. Tom Lowry, "The NFL Machine," *Business Week*, January 27, 2003; Richard Sandomir, "A Humbling Lesson in Cable Reality," *New York Times*, December 28, 2007, and "A Game of Smashmouth Cable Football," *New York Times*, November 6, 2008; Greg Bishop and Lynn Zinser, "Senators Criticize N.F.L. for Favoring League's Cable Network," *New York Times*, October 30, 2008.

18. Michael K. Ozanian, "The Business of Football: 'How 'Bout Them Cowboys?' " Forbes.com, September 13, 2007.

19. Oriard, *Brand NFL*, 250–57; Rader, *In Its Own Image*, 4–5.

Chapter 7. The Cartel

1. James Quirk and Rodney Fort, *Hard Ball* (Princeton, N.J.: Princeton University Press, 1999), 117–19.

2. Harris, *The League*.

3. Quirk and Fort, 112–13; Oriard, *Brand NFL*, 5; Hyman, "How the NFL Loses Fans,"; ESPN.com and Associated Press, "Forbes: Five NFL Franchises Worth Over $1 Billion Each," August 31, 2006.

4. Oriard, *Brand NFL*, 152–53.

5. Quick and Fort, *Hard Ball*, 117–19, 154–56; Yost, *Tailgating*, 174–77.

6. Harris, *The League*, 31–32; McDonough et al., *75 Seasons*, 221; Gorman, Calhoun, and Rozin, *Name of the Game*, 107.

7. Harris, *The League*, 25, 289–90; Yost, *Tailgating*, 168–73.

8. Harris, *The League*, 288, 608–11, and 84–85, 292–93.

9. Joe Marshall, "The NFL's Expansion Plan is Zero Population Growth," *Sports Illustrated*, October 31, 1972; Harris, *The League*, 147–63, 174–79, 190–96.

10. MacCambridge, *America's Game*, 344–45, 350; Harris, *The League*, 232–34, 253–54, 263–72, 306–12, 326–41, 372–87, 389–91.

11. Harris, *The League*, 342–43 with full letter on 343, 357–62, 533; MacCambridge, *America's Game*, .212; John Evers, "Davis, Allen Al," *Biographical Dictionary of American Sport: Football*, edited by David L. Porter (New York: Greenwood Press, 1987), 127–28.

12. Harris, *The League*, 406–15, 424–48.

13. Ibid., 449–72.

14. Oriard, *Brand NFL*, 99; Harris, *The League*, 481–97.

15. Harris, *The League*, 507–16, 533–34.

16. Kenneth Shropshire, *The Sports Franchise Game* (Philadelphia: University of Pennsylvania Press, 1995), 38–39; Harris, *The League*, 535–38, 552–55, 574–80, 636–40.

17. MacCambridge, *America's Game*, 296–97; Harris, *The League*, 291.

18. Harris, *The League*, 396–403.

19. MacCambridge, *America's Game*, 353; Harris, *The League*, 603–7.

20. Harris, *The League*, 90–100.

21. Ibid., 344–48.

22. Ibid., 318–23, 448–55.

23. Ibid., 313–15, 331–34, 455–58.

24. Ibid., 621–26.

25. Ibid., 563–69, 633–36; *Gries Sports Enterprises, Inc. v. Cleveland Browns Football Co.*, Supreme Court of the State of Ohio, August 20, 1986, viewed at oh.findacase.com.

26. William Oscar Johnson, "A Chapter Closed," *Sports Illustrated*, March 6, 1989; E. M. Swift, "Another Gusher for Jones," *Sports Illustrated*, December 12, 1994; Harris, *The League*, 597–601.

27. MacCambridge, *America's Game*, 353.

Chapter 8. Unraveling

1. Harris, *The League*, 516–21, 538–42, 644–46; Gerald Eskenazi, "The State of the NFL," *New York Times*, May 2, 1982.

2. Harris, *The League*, 589–91, 641.

3. McDonough et al., *75 Seasons,* 269–70; MacCambridge, *America's Game,* 57: Harris, *The League,* 553–55, 570, 586–88.

4. McDonough et al., *75 Seasons,* 270; MacCambridge, *America's Game,* 358–61; Harris, *The League,* 531–32, 612–13.

5. William Nack, "Give the First Round to the USFL," *Sports Illustrated,* July 7, 1986; McDonough et al., *75 Seasons,* 270; MacCambridge, *America's Game,* 360–61; Fortunato, *Commissioner,* 176–97.

6. Harris, *The League,* 646–47.

7. T. J. Quinn, "Pumped Up Pioneers: The '63 Chargers," ESPN.com, January 28, 2009.

8. Bernie Parrish, *They Call It a Game* (New York: The Dial Press, 1971), 69–74.

9. George Plimpton, *One More July: A Football Dialogue with Bill Curry* (New York: Harper and Row, Publishers, 1977), 150–51; Jack Scott, "It's Not How You Play the Game, But What Pill You Take," *New York Times,* October 17, 1971; Michael Janofsky and Peter Alfano, "Victory at Any Cost: Drug Pressure Growing," *New York Times,* November 21, 1988; Bill Gilbert, "Drugs in Sports," *Sports Illustrated,* June 23 and 30 and July 7, 1969.

10. Arnold J. Mandell, M.D., *The Nightmare Season* (New York: Random House, 1976), 173–77, 192–94, 214–15; John Underwood, "Speed Is All the Rage," *Sports Illustrated,* August 28, 1978.

11. MacCambridge, *America's Game,* 349; Don Reese and John Underwood, "I'm Not Worth a Damn," *Sports Illustrated,* June 14, 1982; "Scorecard," edited by Jerry Kirshenbaum, *Sports Illustrated,* July 5, 1982.

12. David Harris, *The Genius: How Bill Walsh Reinvented Football and Created an NFL Dynasty* (New York: Random House, 2008), 176–78.

13. Jill Lieber, "Extra Points," *Sports Illustrated,* November 3, 1986.

14. Oriard, *Brand NFL,* 121–24.

15. Michael Janovsky and Peter Alfano, "Drug Use by Athletes Runs Free Despite Tests," *New York Times,* November 17, 1988, and "Victory at Any Cost: Drug Pressure Growing," *New York Times,* November 21, 1988; Ira Berkow, "Rozelle and Fool's Gold," *New York Times,* October 28, 1988.

Chapter 9. Labor Conflict

1. Parrish, *They Call It a Game,* 158–59; Coenen, *From Sandlots,* 180.

2. Coenen, *From Sandlots,* 180–81; "The Beginning: Early Organizational Efforts," NFLPA Official History available at NFLPA Web site, https://www.nflplayers.com/.

3. Lyons, *On Any Given Sunday,* 154–55, 254–55; Coenen, *From Sandlots,* 184–86; "The Beginning: Making Ground One Inch at a Time," NFLPA Official History.

4. Parrish, *They Call It a Game,* 237–44, 249–61.

5. Michael Lomax, "The Quest for Freedom: The NFLPA's Attempt to Abolish the Reserve System," *Football Studies* 7, no. 1/2 (2004): 73–75; Oriard, *Brand NFL,* 59; Parrish, *They Call It a Game,* 262–88; "The 1960's—AFL/NFL Competition," NFLPA Official History.

6. "The 1970's; the Merger," NFLPA Official History; Lomax, "Quest for Freedom," 76–77, 84.

7. Lomax, "Quest for Freedom," 85–86; Oriard, *Brand NFL,* 55–63; Harris, *The League,* 163–64.

8. Harris, *The League,* 80–81.

9. Harris, *The League,* 165 and 183; Gwilym S. Brown, "The Battle Is Joined," *Sports Illustrated,* March 18, 1974.

10. George Plimpton, *One More July: A Football Dialogue with Bill Curry* (New York: Harper and Row 1977), 95–96.

11. Oriard, *Brand NFL,* 56.

12. Oriard, *Brand NFL,* 60–67; Harris, *The League,* 163–67; Plimpton, *One More July,* 97–98.

13. Oriard, *Brand NFL,* 67–69; Harris, *The League,* 182–83.

14. Oriard, *Brand NFL,* 69–71.

15. Oriard, *Brand NFL,* 70–79, 89; Lomax, "Quest for Freedom," 86–100; Harris, *The League,* 184.

16. Oriard, *Brand NFL,* 80–88.

17. Oriard, *Brand NFL,* 91–92, 100–102; Harris, *The League,* 184.

18. Oriard, *Brand NFL,* 62.

19. Harris, *The League,* 199–200; Lomax, "Quest for Freedom," 99.

20. *John Mackey et al., Appellees, v. National Football League et al., Appellants,* United States Court of Appeals, Eighth Circuit. -543 F.2d.606.

21. Lomax, "Quest for Freedom," 99; Harris, *The League,* 221–24, 255–57.

22. Harris, *The League,* 244–46.

23. Oriard, *Brand NFL,* 102–3.

24. Harris, *The League,* 271.

25. Oriard, *Brand NFL,* 96; Paul Zimmerman, "A Time to Light A Fire," *Sports Illustrated,* September 11, 1989.

26. Gerald Eskenazi, "State of the NFL," *New York Times,* May 2, 1982; Harris, *The League,* 498–501.

27. Oriard, *Brand NFL,* 110–11; Harris, *The League,* 500–501, 514–15, and 543; Ira Berkow, "Sports of the Times: Pro Football's Labor Scene," *New York Times,* January 23, 1982.

28. Harris, *The League,* 546; Oriard, *Brand NFL,* 110.

29. Harris, *The League,* 544–56; Oriard, *Brand NFL,* 112–13.

30. Harris, *The League,* 643–46; Oriard, *Brand NFL,* 130; "The Beginning of a Breakthrough," NFLPA Official History from NFLPA Web site, https://www.nflplayers.com/.

31. MacCambridge, *America's Game,* 366–68; Oriard, *Brand NFL,* 132–33.

32. Eskenazi, "Super Bowl XXII, NFL's Stormy Season Comes to an End," *New York Times,* January 30, 1988; Oriard, *Brand NFL,* 132, 134–36.

33. MacCambridge, *America's Game,* 371–74; Oriard, *Brand NFL,* 136; Paul Zimmerman, "Time to Light a Fire," *Sports Illustrated,* September 11, 1989.

Chapter 10. A New Era

1. Will McDonough et al., *75 Seasons,* 278–79; Karl Taro Greenfield, "The Big Man," *Sports Illustrated,* January 23, 2006.

2. Rick Telander, "The Face of Sweeping Change," *Sports Illustrated,* September 10, 1990.

3. MacCambridge, *America's Game,* 385–86; Oriard, *Brand NFL,* 142.

4. Oriard, *Brand NFL,* 145–46.

5. Yost, *Tailgating,* 3–4, 212–18.

6. Yost, *Tailgating,* 77–80; Robert V. Bellamy Jr., "The Evolving Sports Television Marketplace," in Lawrence A. Wenner, ed., *MediaSport* (London and New York: Routledge Publishers, 1998), 73–87; Mark Hyman, "How the NFL Loses Fans and Gets Richer," *Business Week,* January 26, 1998.

7. Oriard, *Brand NFL,* 169–71.

8. Ibid., 172–73, with quote from 173.

9. "Forbes: Five NFL Franchises Worth Over $1 Billion Each," Associated Press Report, available at ESPN.go.com/nfl/.

10. Frank Litsky, "On Pro Football," *New York Times,* November 21, 1993; McDonough et al., *75 Seasons,* 302; MacCambridge, *America's Game,* 390.

11. Oriard, *Brand NFL,* 152–53; MacCambridge, *America's Game,* 395–401.

12. Rick Harrow, "Model of Consistency," CBS Sportsline.com, September 4, 2002; Kurt Badenhausen, et al., "The Business of Football: The Tape on Tagliabue," Forbes.com, September 1, 2006; MacCambridge, *America's Game,* 401, 419–20; Oriard, *Brand NFL,* 152–53 and 160.

13. MacCambridge, *America's Game,* 384 and 425; Oriard, *Brand NFL, 176–78.*

14. MacCambridge, *America's Game,* 423; Rick Burton and R. Brian Crow, "A Review of the NFL's Growth in the United States: Which Games Made the Biggest Difference?" *Football Studies* 5, no. 1 (April 2002): 84.

15. MacCambridge, *America's Game,* 427–28.

16. Yost, *Tailgating,* 191–96 and 174; Quirk and Fort, *Hard Ball,* 165–67; Oriard, *Brand NFL,* 153 and 158–59.

17. Yost, *Tailgating,* 169–70 and 189.

18. E. M. Swift, "Another Gusher for Jones," *Sports Illustrated,* December 12, 1994; Richard Hoffer, "King of Texas," *Sports Illustrated,* July 16, 2007.

19. Richard Hoffer, "Cowboys For Sale," *Sports Illustrated,* September 18, 1995; Richard Sandomir, "Cowboys' Jones is Yielding No Ground," *New York Times,* September 20, 1995; Richard Sandomir, "Dollars and Dallas: League of Their Own?" *New York Times,* September 24, 1995; Timothy W. Smith, "Dallas Owner Fires Back With Suit Against N.F.L.," *New York Times,* November 7, 1995; Richard Sandomir, "Jones-N.F.L. Lawsuits May End In a Draw," *New York Times,* December 1, 1996; "N.F.L. Settles With Cowboys," *New York Times,* December 14, 1996.

20. Hoffer, "Cowboys for Sale."

21. Yost, *Tailgating,* 121–22.

22. Oriard, *Brand NFL,* 175; Gorman, Calhoun, and Rosen, *Name of the Game,* 134–35.

23. Oriard, *Brand NFL*, 179–85.

24. Yost, *Tailgating,* 133; MacCambridge, *America's Game,* 420; Gorman, Calhoun, and Rosen, *Name of the Game,* 134.

25. Yost, *Tailgating,* 106–7; Gorman, Calhoun, and Rosen, *Name of the Game,* 140.

26. Tom Lowery, "The NFL Business Machine," *Business Week,* January 27, 2003; Forbes.com.

27. Yost, *Tailgating,* 24–28, 35–39, 44–46; Oriard, *Brand NFL,* 143–46 and 250; Lowery, "NFL Business Machine."

28. Badenhausen et al., "Business of Football," available at Forbes.com.

29. Brown, *Out of Bounds,* 52.

30. William Oscar Johnson, "A Matter of Black and White," *Sports Illustrated,* August 5, 1991.

31. *The Racial and Gender Report Card* (1998, 2001, 2003, 2004, 2005, 2006, 2007, 2008, 2009), Institute for Diversity and Ethics in Sport, University of Central Florida, Orlando, available at http://web.bus.ucf.edu/sportbusiness/?page=1445; Johnnie Cochrane Jr. and Cyrus Mehri, "Black Coaches in the National Football League," available at http://www.findjustice.com/sub/b-coaches.jsp.

32. Levy, *Tackling Jim Crow,* 114–18.

33. Richard Lapchick, "Report Card: Tagliabue's Legacy Includes New Model for Racial Hiring," ESPN.com, August 17, 2006.

34. Oriard, *Brand NFL,* 250.

Chapter 11. Defending the Shield

1. Peter King, "A Man Born for the Job," *Sports Illustrated,* August 21, 2006.

2. Ibid.; Judy Battista, "And Then There Were 5 in Commissioner Search," *New York Times,* July 31, 2006; "New Commissioner Joined NFL in 1982," ESPN.com: NFL, August 8, 2006; Geoff Gloeckler and Tom Lowry, "Roger Goodell: The Most Powerful Man in Sports," *Business Week,* September 26, 2007.

3. Lee Jenkins, "The Never Ending Story: Spygate has ruled the headlines for Months. Now it's time to turn the page," *Sports Illustrated,* May 26, 2008; an excellent summary of all aspects of Spygate can be found in a series of *Boston Globe* articles at http://www.boston.com/sports/football/patriots/extras/spygate/.

4. "Goodell Strengthens NFL Personal Conduct Policy," *USA Today,* April 11, 2007.

5. Mark Maske, "Falcon's Vick Indicted in Dog Fighting Case," *Washington Post,* July 18, 2007; "Goodell tells Vick his conduct was 'cruel and reprehensible,' " *USA Today,* August 24, 2007.

6. "Vick Cleared for Preseason Participation," ESPN.com, July 28, 2009.

7. "Woman in Georgia Alleges Assault," ESPN.com, March 8, 2010; Jemele Hill, "Goodell's Slippery Roethlisberger Slope," ESPN.com, March 26, 2010.

8. Judy Battista, "N.F.L. Memo Calls on Teams to Act—The Fifth Down Blog," *New York Times,* April 15, 2010; "Goodell: Roethlisberger Violated Policy," ESPN.com, April 19, 2010; "Goodell Suspends Roethlisberger for Six Games, Orders Evaluation," NFL.com wire reports, April 21, 2010; Lester Munson, "The Justice System, Roger Goodell Style," Commentary, ESPN.com, April 21, 2010.

9. John Branch, "N.F.L. Experiment Aims to Spread Game," *New York Times,* October 23, 2007; Judy Battista, "Goodell Voices Concern Over Limbaugh—The Fifth Down Blog," *New York Times,* October 13, 2009; Selena Roberts, "The Voice From Above," *Sports Illustrated,* October 26, 2009.

10. "SI Players NFL Poll," *Sports Illustrated,* December 21, 2009; "Goodell Gets Contract Through 2015," ESPN.com, February 12, 2010.

11. Stuart Elliott, "Mending a Bruised Image," *New York Times,* August 30, 2007.

12. The Power 100, Bloomburg Business Week, September 25, 2007, http://www.businessweek.com/table/07/0926_power100.htm.

13. John Heylar, "State of the NFL? It's a Mixed Blessing," ESPN.com, January 31, 2008.

14. Richard Sandomir, "For NFL Fans, the Cable Picture Isn't Any Clearer," *New York Times,* December 27, 2006, and "A Humbling Lesson in Cable Reality," *New York Times,* December 28, 2007.

15. Richard Sandomir, "A Game of Smashmouth Cable Football," *New York Times,* November 6, 2008, and "NFL Gets a Lift from Ruling," *New York Times,* October 12, 2008, and "Comcast and NFL Network Agree to 9-Year Deal," *New York Times,* May 19, 2009; Greg Bishop and Lynn Zinser, "Senators Criticize N.F.L. for Favoring League's Cable Network, *New York Times,* October 30, 2006.

16. Michael Ozanian, "How About them Cowboys," Forbes.com, The Business of Football, September 13, 2007; Richard Sandomir, "Sports Business: DirecTV Renews N.F.L. Deal and Expands Access," *New York Times,* March 24, 2009; "Forbes: Five NFL Franchises Worth Over $1 billion Each," ESPN.com, August 31, 2006.

17. Ozanian, "How About them Cowboys."

18. Ibid.; Richard Sandomir, "A Texas-Size Stadium," *New York Times,* July 17, 2009; Mark Yost, "A Grand Corral for Cowboy Fans," *Wall Street Journal*—WSJ.com, September 8, 2009; Nicolai Ouroussoff, "Architecture Review: Supersize Stadium, With Helping of Sprawl," *New York Times,* September 18, 2009; Thayer Evans, "Cowboy's New Stadium Inspires Awe Long Before Kickoff," *New York Times,* September 21, 2009.

19. Andrew Brandt, "TV Ratings Show the Power of the NFL," *National Football Post,* February 10, 2010.

20. Kurt Badenhausen, Michael Ozanian, and Christina Smith, "Recession Tackles NFL Team Values," Forbes.com, September 2, 2009; Steven Bertoni, "Football's Billionaires," Forbes.com, September 2, 2008.

21. "Goodell Sees Merit in Expanded Season," and "Goodell on Rookie Pay: 'There's Something Wrong,' " ESPN.com, April 24, 2009 and June 27, 2009.

22. Judy Battista, "Gene Upshaw, N.F.L. Union Chief, Dies at 63," *New York Times,* August 22, 2008; "Hall of Famer Upshaw Loses Battle With Pancreatic Cancer," ESPN.com, August 21, 2008; David Zirin, "Remembering Gene Upshaw," *The Nation,* August 22, 2008; Gary Smith, "Gene Upshaw, 1945–2008," *Sports Illustrated,* September 1, 2008.

23. "Upshaw Ready for Strike if Owners Opt Out of Labor Agreement," ESPN.com, January 31, 2008; Daniel Kaplan, "NFL Owners Vote to Opt Out of Labor Deal," *The Sporting News NFL,* May 20, 2008; Battista, "Gene Upshaw"; John Clayton, "Smith Brings a Fresh Approach," ESPN.com, March 15, 2009; "Smith Elected to Head NFLPA," ESPN.com, March 15, 2009; Judy Battista, "N.F.L. Union Selects Lawyer as New Leader," *New York Times,* March 16, 2009.

24. John Clayton, "Owner's Math Simply Doesn't Add Up," ESPN.com, March 19, 2011.

25. Len Pasquerelli, "Goodell Facing Still Another Uphill Climb," ESPN.com, July 10, 2009; July Battista, "Labor Talks, the Rumblings of War, *New York Times,* August 23, 2009; "Smith: NFL to get $5B Without Playing," ESPN.com, February 4, 2010; "Goodell: NFL Needs to Invest More," ESPN.com, February 7, 2010; "Roger Goodell: NFL Union Must Concede More to get CBA Deal Done," *USA Today,* February 5, 2010; Judy Battista, "Kendall Claims N.F.L. Proposal Would Mean 18 Percent Pay Cut—The Fifth Down Blog" *New York Times,* March 4, 2010; Robert Boland, "No Carve-outs, No Cap," *National Football Post,* February 10, 2010.

26. ESPN.com News Services, "NFL Locks Out Players, Who File Suit," ESPN.com, March 12, 2011; "Roger Goodell Sends Letter to Players," ESPN.com, March 18, 2011; Andrew Brandt, "Welcome to Courtroom Football," and "Getting to Yes," *National Football Post,* March 14, 2011 and July 18, 2011; ESPN.com News Services, "Judge Rules for Players," ESPN.com, April 26, 2011; Debra Cassens Weiss, "8th Circuit Allow NFL Lockout, Overturning Lower Court Injunction," ABAJournal.com, June 11, 2011: Associated Press, "Federal Judge Rules NFL Violated Deal," ESPN.com, March 2, 2011; Lester Munson, "The NFLPA's Power Play," ESPN.com, March 3, 2011.

27. Brandt, "Getting to Yes"; Ashley Fox, "A Win for Owners, Players—and Lawyers," ESPN.com, July 27, 2011; Andrew Brandt, "Inside the Settlement Negotiations," NFP Newsletter, July 25, 2011; "Highlights of the NFL Agreement: The Fifth Down," *New York Times,* July 26, 2011.

28. Andrew Brandt, "Many Layers to NFLPA Collusion Case," ESPN.com, May 24, 2012.

29. Mark Maske, "Goodell Weighs In On Behavior, Drugs," *Washington Post,* February 3, 2007.

30. "Lawsuit Filed for Five of Six Players," ESPN.com, December 4, 2008; "NFL's Drug Suspensions of 5 Blocked by Federal Judge," ESPN.com, December 5, 2008; "Judy Battista, "N.F.L. and Union Find Some Common Ground—The Fifth Down Blog," *New York Times,* September 22, 2009; Kevin Diaz, "Williamses Loom Large in Debate on Capitol Hill," *Minneapolis Star-Tribune,* November 4, 2009; Ken Belson, "N.F.L. Seeks Congressional Help on Drug Policy," *New York Times,* November 4, 2009; "Vikings' Suspensions Remain on Hold," ESPN.com, May 21, 2010.

31. "Heavy NFL Players Twice as Likely to Die Before 50," ESPN.com: NFL, January 31, 2006. See also Mark Fainaru-Wada and Steve Fainaru, *League of Denial* (New York: Random House, 2013), 74–75.

32. John Branch and Alan Schwarz, "N.F.L. Culture Makes an Issue of Head Injuries Even Murkier," *New York Times,* February 3, 2007.

33. Fainaru and Fainaru, *League of Denial,* chapters 8–11 treat this time period in detail, and the book is indispensable to any study of this issue; Michael Oriard's essay "The Head in Football" has been published as an e-book by Now and Then Reader and is an excellent summary of these developments and the history of how head injuries have been treated in football.

34. Jesse Holland, "Congress: NFL Should Improve Benefits," *Washington Post,* June 27, 2007; "NFL and NFLPA Announce Expanded Disability Payments Program for Retired Players," RetiredPlayers.org, March 3, 2008.

35. John Clayton, "Four Safety Proposals Passed," ESPN.com, March 24, 2009.

36. Alan Schwarz, "N.F.L. Dementia Debate Could Intensify," *New York Times,* October 1, 2009.

37. Alan Schwarz, "Ex-Team Executive Sounds an Alarm on N.F.L. Head Trauma," *New York Times,* October 28, 2009; Brendan Smialowski—The Fifth Down Blog, *New York Times,* October 28, 2009; Players' Outreach Program Inc., www.playeroutreach. org; Alan Schwarz, "Commissioner Criticized Over N.F.L.'s Handling of Players' Brain Injuries," and "N.F.L. Scolded Over Injuries to its Players," October 29, 2009 *New York Times*; David Zirin, "The NFL's Concussion Conundrum," *The Nation,* November 24, 2009.

38. "Harry Carson on Concussions—The Fifth Down Blog," *New York Times,* November 3, 1980; Alan Schwarz, "Football Analysts Cast a New Eye on Injuries," *New York Times,* December 11, 2009, and "N.F.L Suspends Its Study on Concussions," *New York Times,* December 20, 2009.

39. Alan Schwarz, "N.F.L. Acknowledges Long-Term Concussion Effects," *New York Times,* December 21, 2009, and "N.F.L. Gives $1 Million to Brain Researchers," *New York Times,* April 20, 2010; Oriard, "The Head."

40. Deborah Blum, "Will Science Take the Field?" *New York Times,* February 5, 2010.

41. Reuters, "Former Super Bowl-Winning Quarterback Reports Memory Loss," NewYorkTimes.com, February 3, 2011; Melissa Isaacson, "Jim McMahon Supports Brain Studies," ESPN.com, November 10, 2010.

42. ESPNChicago.com, "Dave Duerson Had Brain Damage," ESPN.com, May 2, 2011; Katie Thomas, "N.F.L.'s Policy on Helmet-to-Helmet Hits Makes Highlights Distasteful," *New York Times,* October 21, 2010; Ashley Fox, "Would You Let Your Son Play Football?" ESPN.Com, updated May 7, 2012; David Leon Moore and Erik Brady, "Junior Seau's Final Days Plagued by Sleepless Nights," *USA Today,* June 2, 2012.

43. There have been numerous media reports on the settlement, and I relied primarily on those from the *New York Times* and ESPN.com.

44. ESPN News Services, "NFL Hammers Saints for Bounties," ESPN.com, March 21, 2012; Associated Press, "NFL Turns Over Evidence to Players," ESPN.com, June 15, 2012.

45. "Paul Tagliabue Vacates Penalties," ESPN.com news services, December 11, 2012; "Bounty Players' Ban Overturned," ESPN.com news services, September 7, 2012.

46. Sean Greg, "Why Sports Ratings Are Surging on TV," Time.com, updated 08/14/2010; Andrew Brandt, "The Busine$$ of Football: TV Ratings Show the Power of the NFL," *National Football Post,* February 10, 2010; Bill Carter, "Huge Audience for World Series Game, but N.F.L. Still Reigns"—Media Decoder Blog, http://nytimes. com, November 2, 2009.

47. Tim Layden, "The Power of the Game," *Sports Illustrated,* February 13, 2012; Associated Press, "NFL Riding Remarkable TV Ratings Into Super Bowl," *New York Times,* January 29, 2011; Richard Sandomir, "The Fifth Down: Record Ratings for the Super Bowl," *New York Times,* January 29, 2011; Associated Press, "111 Million Tuned in to Super Bowl XLV," ESPN.com. February 7, 2011; Brian Stelter, "Media

Decoder: A Super Bowl Where Viewers Let Their Fingers Do the Talking," *New York Times,* February 6, 2012.

48. Richard Sandomir, "With the Latest Network Agreements, the N.F.L. Outdoes Even Itself," *New York Times,* December 14, 2011; National Football League, "The Tradition Continues: NFL to Remain on Broadcast TV," NFL.com, December 14, 2011.

49. Steve Fainaru, "NFL Board Paid $2M to Players While League Denied Football-Concussion Link," pbs.org/wgbh/pages/frontline/sports/concussion-watch/nfl-board-paid-2m-to-players-while-league-denied-football-concussion-link.

Chapter 12. Super Sunday

1. Mary Riddell, "A Hero for Our Times," *The Observer,* October 30, 2005.

2. Gerald Eskenazi, "70,000 Football Fans Make New Orleans Throb With Super Bowl Mania," *New York Times,* January 25, 1981.

3. "Super Bowl 2007," *Advertising Age,* http://adage.com/SuperBowlBuyers/superbowl history07.html; Mike Tanier, "Excess Reigns at Super Bowl and That's No Ballyhoo," *New York Times,* January 31, 2010. Dollar figures in parentheses are 2010 dollars calculated in according with changes in the Consumer Price Index at www.measuring worth.com.

4. "CBS Costs Soar For Super Bowl," *New York Times,* January 14, 1968.

5. Super Bowl coverage, *USA Today,* January 20–22, 1989, January 27, 1995, February 3–5, 2006; "Advertising Supplement," *New York Times,* January 26, 2001.

6. Frank Litsky, "Super Bowl Is a Bonanza for Miami's Economy Lull," *New York Times,* January 14, 1968.

7. "'Good to Have People with Money,' Miami Says of New York Football Fans," *New York Times,* January 13, 1969.

8. Tad Hathaway, "Touchdown Houston: History of Roman Numerals and the Super Bowl," updated 2/1/04, www.news24houston.com; and www.visualeditions.com.

9. Richard C. Crepeau, "Sport and Society," January 30, 1994, available in the "Discussion Logs" at www.h-net.org/~arete/.

10. Gerald Eskenazi, "Money Is The Root of All Super Bowl Matters," *New York Times,* January 14, 1978.

11. "New Orleans Game Plan Offers 'Super Party' and All That Jazz," *New York Times,* January 8, 1975.

12. Crepeau, "Sport and Society," January 22, 1992.

13. William Wallace, "Super Bowl Overcome by Success," *New York Times,* January 19, 1971.

14. Lawrence W. Altman, "Heart Attacks a Peril of Super Bowl Fan," *New York Times,* January 16, 1972.

15. Dave Anderson, "Coach Nixon Sends in a Play to the Miami Dolphins," *New York Times,* January 4, 1972.

16. Tom Buckley, "Business in the Front Seat for Today's Super Bowl," *New York Times,* January 14, 1973.

17. Buckley, "Business in the Front Seat."

18. "The Super Show," *Time,* January 10, 1977.

19. Richard C. Crepeau, "Rah, Rah, The Money," *PopPolitics.com,* January 24, 2001, www.poppolitics.com archive.

20. Crepeau, "Sport and Society," January 25, 2001, January 24, 1997, and January 25, 1995.

21. Super Bowl Section, *USA Today,* January 27–29, 1995.

22. E-mail note and personal conversation with Richard Turkiewicz, June 2009; "The Super Show," *Time,* January 10, 1977.

23. John O'Connor, "TV: A Fast-Paced Super Bowl on CBS," *New York Times,* January 19, 1976.

24. Warren Farrell, "Super Bowl Ritual: Mix Masculinity with Patriotism," *New York Times,* January 15, 1978.

25. Super Bowl XXVII Section, *USA Today,* January 29–31, 1993.

26. Super Bowl XL Section, *USA Today,* February 3–5, 2006.

27. Ibid.

28. Jon Nordheimer, "Super Bowl Spectacle Today to Rivet Interest of Millions," *New York Times,* January 9, 1977.

29. Crepeau, "Sport and Society," January 24, 1996.

30. Crepeau, "Sport and Society," February 2, 2007, available at www.uta.edu/english/sla/s&sarchive.html.

31. Allen St. John, *The Billion Dollar Game: Behind the Scenes of the Greatest Day in American Sport, Super Bowl Sunday* (New York: Doubleday, 2009), 49–50.

32. Ibid., 175–76.

33. Ibid., 178–79.

34. Justin George, "Been here, loved it," *St. Petersburg Times,* January 31, 2009; Associated Press, "NBC Sells Last Super Bowl Spots on Eve of Game, Netting Record Total of $206M in Ad Revenue," *Orlando Sentinel,* January 31, 2009; Marc Topkin, "It's More Than a Game, It's Business at the Super Bowl," *St. Petersburg Times,* January 28, 2009.

35. Darren Rovell, "SportsBiz: Playboy v. Maxim Super Bowl XLIV Party Reviews," CNBC.com, February 8, 2010.

36. Mike Tanner, "Excess Reigns at the Super Bowl and That's No Ballyhoo," *New York Times,* January 31, 2010.

Bibliography

The literature on the National Football League is growing rapidly with each passing year, as more scholars are working in the field of sport history and more journalists are writing serious biography and history.

There are a number of general histories and reference works that contain summary histories. *Total Football II: The Official Encyclopedia of the National Football League,* edited by Bob Carroll, Michael Gershman, David Neft, and John Thorn (New York: Harper Collins Publishers, 1999) contains a general history, brief team histories, and short biographies of players, coaches, and executives. *The ESPN Pro Football Encyclopedia,* 2nd. ed., edited by Pete Palmer et al. (New York: Sterling Publishing, 2007) has many of the same features and is more up to date, although the quality of the historical narrative does not match that of *Total Football II.*

Among the general histories of the league, Will McDonough et al., *75 Seasons: The Complete Story of the National Football League, 1920–1995* (Atlanta: Turner Publishing, 1994) is one of the most frequently cited works. It features decade summaries, player profiles, all-decade teams, and excellent photos. There is a functional general history located at NFL.com, a labor history at NFLPA.com, and a Super Bowl history at SuperBowl.com.

Four serious historical works are required reading for anyone seeking to understand the forces that have shaped the National Football League. Michael MacCambridge's *America's Game: The Epic Story of How Pro Football Captured a Nation* (New York: Random House, 2004) picks up the history of the NFL in 1945 and takes it into the early twenty-first century. MacCambridge provides an overarching view of the growth of the NFL and the cultural appeal of the game, and explains how it has become the new national pastime. It is rich in detail within a sweeping historical context and interpretation. Craig Coenen's

From Sandlots to the Super Bowl: The National Football League, 1920–1967 (Knoxville: University of Tennessee Press, 2005) begins with the early history of the league and its struggles for survival. The author devotes considerable attention to the relationship between NFL and its host cities. It is a story of both failure and success, leading ultimately to the triumph of the NFL in the national marketplace. Coenen's analysis of labor issues, race, and drugs are significant parts of the narrative. More narrowly focused in time, David Harris's *The League: The Rise and Decline of the NFL* (Toronto: Bantam Books, 1986) examines the decentralization of the NFL in the 1970s and 1980s as Pete Rozelle's power eroded in the face of the legal struggle with Al Davis and the City of Los Angeles, and its aftermath. Harris's research is meticulous and awe-inspiring, as he has constructed this history by combing court records and the backgrounds of league officials and owners, revealing a maze of financial manipulation, shady deals, twisted ethics, and out-of-control egos. Michael Oriard in *Brand NFL: Making and Selling America's Favorite Sport* (Chapel Hill: University of North Carolina Press, 2007) laments the transformation of the NFL from a football league to a brand in a brilliantly argued and convincing narrative beginning with the 1960s and running into the early twenty-first century. Although labor issues and drugs are part of the story, in the end Oriard's major contribution is his analysis of the marketing of the league as product, image, and brand, to the detriment of the game itself.

The prehistory and early history of the NFL is the subject of several quality books and a large number of research efforts by members of the Professional Football Researchers Association. The PFRA maintains a Web site at www .professionalresearchers.org that houses all of the issues of *The Coffin Corner: The Official Magazine of the Professional Football Researchers Association*, which began publication in 1979. The site contains longer research papers dealing with the history of football from the seventeenth century to the early 1970s. The quality of the publications is uneven, but there are many that are indispensable for the study of the early years of professional football and the history of the NFL.

Two of the most informative works on the early history of professional football are Marc Maltby's *The Origins and Early Development of Professional Football, 1890–1920* (New York: Garland Publishers, 1997) and Keith McCellan's *The Sunday Game: At the Dawn of Professional Football* (Akron, Ohio: University of Akron Press, 1998). Both relate the early development of the game, primarily in Ohio and Pennsylvania, the difficulties of sustaining a franchise and a league, and the atmospherics of the semiprofessional and professional games. Maltby makes particularly good use of the FTRA materials. Robert Peterson's *Pigskin: The Early Years of Pro Football* (New York: Oxford University Press, 1997) is also useful for the early history of pro football and the first two decades of the NFL.

George Halas was clearly a major force in the history of the NFL from its beginning through the decades until his death. His autobiography, *Halas By Halas* (New York: 1979) is an indispensable first-person account of league history. Jeff Davis's *Papa Bear: The Life and Legacy of George Halas* (New York: McGraw-Hill, 2005) is an excellent companion piece to the autobiography, offering a more objective assessment of George Halas's monumental contributions to the growth and development of the NFL.

Art Rooney entered the NFL in the 1930s, and he and his family have been a force since. Andrew O'Toole's biography *Smiling Irish Eyes: Art Rooney and the Pittsburgh Steelers* (Haworth, N.J.: 2004) was the first major biography of Art Rooney and is a good starting point on the Rooney family. A more recent and scholarly work is Rob Ruck, Maggie Jones Patterson, and Michael F. Weber's *Rooney: A Sporting Life* (Lincoln: University of Nebraska Press, 2009), an indispensable interpretive work placing Art Rooney and the Rooney family within the historical context of the Pittsburgh community. Dan Rooney's *My 75 Years with the Pittsburgh Steelers and The NFL,* as told to Andrew E. Masich and David S. Halas (Philadelphia: Da Capo Press, 2007) is a first-person account of the major developments in the NFL, the on-field story of the team and its greatest players, and the contributions of the Rooney family.

John Carroll has contributed significantly to the historical record of the NFL with his two excellent biographies of significant players of the 1920s. *Fritz Pollard: Pioneer in Racial Advancement* (Urbana and Chicago: University of Illinois Press, 1992) and *Red Grange and the Rise of Modern Football* (Urbana and Chicago: University of Illinois Press, 1999) are both scholarly works of the highest quality. The Pollard biography offers insight on the issue of race in early pro football through the trials and triumphs of this great player and coach, as well as the story of the first years of pro football. The Red Grange biography assesses the life of this football icon of the 1920s and his role in the development of the National Football League.

On the issue of race in the 1920s and the coming of segregation to the NFL in the early 1930s, Alan Levy's *Tackling Jim Crow: Racial Segregation in Professional Football* (Jefferson, N.C.: McFarland, 2003) offers an excellent study of discrimination and segregation across the history of the NFL. Two other scholarly articles of importance are Thomas G. Smith, "Outside the Pale: The

Exclusion of Blacks from the National Football League, 1934–1936," *Journal of Sport History* 15, no.3 (Winter 1988): 255–81, and Michael Lomax, "The African American Experience in Professional Football," *Journal of Social History* 33, no.1 (Autumn 1999): 166–70.

Other than biographies, autobiographies, general histories, and team histories, the scholarly material on the 1930s has been limited. There is a mountain of material from the popular press. This gap is lessened by Michael Oriard's *King Football: Sport and Spectacle in the Golden Age of Radio & Newsreels, Movies & Magazines, The Weekly & The Daily Press* (Chapel Hill: University of North Carolina Press, 2001), a very good source on the game of football and its place in American culture from 1920 onward. Kevin Britz's "Of Football and Frontiers: The Meaning of Bronko Nagurski," *Journal of Sport History* 20, no.2 (Summer 1993): 101–26 is a cultural analysis of the image and popularity of the Chicago Bears running back of the '30s.

Bert Bell's NFL career began in the mid-30s, and Robert S. Lyons's biography of the highly influential NFL commissioner, *On Any Given Sunday* (Philadelphia: Temple University Press, 2010), is an excellent analysis of Bell's major contributions to the NFL's survival and its transformation into a major professional sports league. Bell was a major architect of the modern NFL and prepared it to challenge for the title of "national pastime."

The All-American Football Conference (AAFC) was formed during World War II, and in the postwar years the AAFC successfully challenged the NFL, leading to a merger of the leagues. There are several good pieces on the AAFC at the Web site of the Professional Football Researchers Association, including a short history of the league by Stan Grosshandler, a number of insightful articles by Bob Carroll, and several player profiles. The economic success of the Cleveland Browns is detailed in Mel Adelman's "Making Money (Lots of It) in Professional Football in the Late 1940s: The Case of the 1946 Cleveland Browns," *Football Studies* 7, no. 1/2 (2004): 11–36.

To some degree the history of the AAFC is the story of the success of Paul Brown and the Cleveland Browns. Andy Piascik's *The Best Show in Football: The 1946–1955 Cleveland Browns, Pro Football's Greatest Dynasty* (New York: Taylor Trade Publishing, 2007) is a solid history of the Cleveland franchise and the league. Brown's autobiography, written with Jack Clary, *PB: The Paul Brown Story* (New York: Atheneum, 1979) is a self-confident self-portrait that interprets events through Brown's eyes. Two biographies, George Cantor's *Paul Brown: The Man Who Invented Modern Football* (Chicago: Triumph Books, 2008) and Andrew O'Toole's *Paul Brown: The Rise and Fall and Rise*

Again of Football's Most Innovative Coach (Cincinnati Clerist Press, 2008) are both admiring although balanced accounts of Brown's massive contribution to professional football.

The 1950s are often described as the point at which the NFL came to the forefront of the national sporting consciousness, and the 1958 NFL Championship Game has become a marker of this development. Mark Bowden's *The Best Game Ever: Giants vs. Colts, 1958, and The Birth of the Modern NFL* (New York: Atlantic Monthly Press, 2008) offers a popular account of the game and helps to further develop the myth of its importance to the history of the league. *Sports Illustrated* grew along with the NFL during the 1950s, and their coverage of the NFL from that point on is an indispensable source of information and analysis.

Indeed the 1950s is the decade in which television became a force promoting the NFL. Three important books that examine the impact of television on sport are Ron Powers's *Supertube: The Rise of Television Sports* (New York: Coward-McCann, 1984); Benjamin Rader's *In Its Own Image: How Television Transformed Sports* (New York: 1984); and Joan Chandler's *Television and National Sport: The United States and Britain* (Urbana and Chicago: University of Illinois Press, 1988). More specialized but valuable is Robert V. Bellamy Jr., "The Evolving Sports Television Marketplace," in *MediaSport,* edited by Lawrence A. Wenner (London and New York: Routledge, 1998), 73–87. Terry O'Neil's *The Game Behind the Game: High Pressure, High Stakes in Television Sports* (New York: Harper and Row, 1989) is a first-hand account of the power of the NFL at the networks and the development of televised sport. Other relationships between the NFL and television are found in two recent histories of ESPN: James Andrew Miller and Tom Shales, *Those Guys Have All the Fun: Inside the World of ESPN* (New York: Little, Brown, 2011), and Michael Freeman's *ESPN: The Uncensored History* (New York: Taylor Trade Publishing, 2001). The battle over the NFL's blackout rule from the opposition's point of view can be found in Ellis Rubin and Dary Matera's *"Get Me Ellis Rubin!": The Life, Times, and Cases of a Maverick Lawyer* (New York: St. Martin's Press, 1989).

The desegregation of the NFL is analyzed in the works previously cited on segregation as well as in Charles K. Ross's *Outside the Lines: African Americans and the Integration of the National Football League* (New York: New York University Press, 1999). The first African American superstar in the NFL was Jim Brown of the Cleveland Browns. Brown led African American players in their challenge to segregation and racism in the league. His autobiography, written with Steve Delsohn, *Out of Bounds* (New York: Kensington Publishing, 1989), deals with this issue and with his NFL career, as does Mike Freeman's excellent biography *Jim Brown: The Fierce Life of an American Hero* (New York: Harper Collins, 2006).

Desegregation continued in the 1960s as the AFL took the lead in the recruitment of African American players. The story of the last team to desegregate is told in Thomas G. Smith's *Showdown: JFK and the Integration of The Washington Redskins* (Boston: Beacon Press, 2011). Smith relates the political story surrounding these events, with a particular stress on the role of Stewart K. Udall, the Secretary of the Interior.

The lingering effects of segregation have been apparent in a number of ways, including the phenomenon known as stacking. One of the best examinations of stacking, and there are many, can be found in Botswana Toney Blackburn's Ph.D. dissertation, "Racial Stacking in the National Football League: Reality or Relic of the Past," University of Missouri–Kansas City, 2007. Stacking and other issues of racial and sexual discrimination in the NFL have been tracked in the *Racial and Gender Report Card,* issued since 1998 by the Institute for Diversity and Ethics in Sport, University of Central Florida, Orlando. These are available on their Web site at http://web.bus.ucf.edu/sportbusiness/?page=1445.

The concept of the "American One Way," which I use to frame the 1960s, was brilliantly developed by David Zang in *SportsWars: Athletes in the Age of Aquarius* (Fayetteville: University of Arkansas Press, 2001). Two of the major figures in the NFL in the 1960s and early 1970s were Vince Lombardi and Joe Namath. There are several biographies of Lombardi, with two of the best being David Maranis's *When Pride Still Mattered: A Life of Vince Lombardi* (New York: Simon and Schuster, 1999) and Michael O'Brien's *Vince: A Personal Biography of Vince Lombardi* (New York: William Morrow, 1987). Both place Lombardi within his Catholic and football cultural milieu and have a critical element. Two items from the popular press offer insight into the Lombardi myth: Leonard Shecter's highly critical "The Toughest Man in Pro Football," *Esquire,* January 1968, and *Time* magazine's myth-enhancing cover story, "Vinni, Vidi, Vici," in the December 21, 1962, issue. A valuable interpretation of Joe Namath's place in the AFL and NFL is John D. Bloom's "Joe Namath and Super Bowl III: An Interpretation of Style," *Journal of Sport History* 15, no. 1 (Spring 1988): 66–74.

There have been several biographies of Pete Rozelle. The most recent is Jeff Davis's *Rozelle: Czar of the NFL* (New York: McGraw Hill, 2008), and it offers a fair assessment of Rozelle's contribution to the growth and development of the NFL and the many conflicts with owners and players. More laudatory in tone is John A. Fortunato's *Commissioner: The Legacy of Pete Rozelle* (Lanham, Md.: Taylor Trade Publishing, 2006).

There were a number of major innovations and developments in the Rozelle years. The AFL-NFL rivalry and merger are detailed in Larry Felser's *The Birth of the New NFL: How the 1996 NFL/AFL Merger Transformed Pro Football* (Guilford, Conn.: The Lyons Press, 2008). The merger led to the coming of the Super Bowl, which has since grown into a major national holiday. Don Weiss's *The Making of the Super Bowl: The Inside Story of the World's Greatest Sporting Event*, written with Chuck Day (Chicago: Contemporary Books, 2003), gives an insider's perspective on the origin and early development of the game, while Allen St. John's *The Billion Dollar Game: Behind the Scenes of the Greatest Day in American Sport, Super Bowl Sunday* (New York: Doubleday, 2009) details its growth to excess and decadence as a midwinter American holiday.

The Rozelle years were not without their major conflicts. David Harris's account is clearly the best in dealing with both owner and player conflicts with the commissioner. Bernie Parrish's *They Call It a Game* (New York: The Dial Press, 1971) offers an informative though biased account of early NFL labor history, as well as insight into the drug issue. Michael Lomax's "The Quest for Freedom: The NFLPA's Attempt to Abolish the Reserve System," *Football Studies* 7, no. 1/2 (2004): 70–107, is an excellent scholarly account of the central labor struggle, and Oriard's *Brand NFL* takes labor history into the settlement between Commissioner Tagliabue and Gene Upshaw.

The issue of drugs in the NFL is the subject of Arnold Mandel, M.D.'s *The Nightmare Season* (New York: Random House, 1976), in which he describes the drug culture he found while spending a season with the San Diego Chargers. Extensive cocaine use is also one subject in David Harris's biography of San Francisco's heralded coach, *The Genius: How Bill Walsh Reinvented Football and Created an NFL Dynasty* (New York: Random House, 2008).

Stadium building and the extortion of governments are described in Kenneth Shropshire's *The Sports Franchise Game: Cities in Pursuit of Sports Franchises, Events, Stadiums, and Arenas* (Philadelphia: University of Pennsylvania Press, 1995); Jay Weiner's *Stadium Games: Fifty Years of Big League Greed and Bush League Boondoggles* (Minneapolis and London: University of Minnesota Press, 2000); Mark S. Rosentraub's *Major League Lo$ers: The Real Cost of Sports and Who's Paying for It, What Governments and Taxpayers Need to Know* (New York: Basic Books, 1997); Roger G. Noll and Andrew Zimbalist's edited collection, *Sports, Jobs, and Taxes: The Economic Impact of Sports Teams and Stadiums*

(Washington, D.C.: Brookings Institution Press, 1997); and Jerry Gorman and Kirk Calhoun, with Skip Rozin, *The Name of the Game: The Business of Sports* (New York: John Wiley & Sons, 1994).

Mark Yost's *Tailgating, Sacks, and Salary Caps: How the NFL Became the Most Successful Sports League in History* (Chicago: Kaplan Publishing, 2006) cuts across labor, stadium issues, economics, and the popular appeal of the game. At a more scholarly and academic level are a collection of articles edited by Kevin Quinn, *The Economics of the National Football League: The State of the Art* (New York: Springer, 2012).

The last two chapters of this book draw heavily on the media rather than academic studies and analysis. Several writers have been particularly valuable and reliable on matters NFL. John Clayton at ESPN.com is well connected across the league and is adept at explaining the complexities of league policy and labor-management relations. Lester Munson at ESPN.com has an ability to analyze and clearly explain legal questions affecting the league. Richard Sandomir at the *New York Times* provides reliable and clear writing on the NFL and television. Judy Battista at the *New York Times* is as an extremely good analyst and reporter on the NFL. Andrew Brandt, writing for both *The National Football Post* and ESPN.com, has been a valuable source on a number of different aspects of the recent NFL. These by no means are the only quality writers covering the NFL waterfront, but they are the ones that I have relied upon most extensively, although not exclusively.

The concussion issue is now drawing considerable attention, with Mark Fainaru-Wada and Steve Fainaru's *League of Denial* (New York: Crown Archetype, 2013) the first definitive study of the NFL's response. Their bibliography provides a guide to the popular and scientific materials on the subject. In addition, PBS television's *Frontline* produced a documentary based on the book, and it is available for viewing at http://www.pbs.org/wgbh/pages/frontline/league-of-denial/. The Web site also offers numerous links to other information on the subject. Michael Oriard's essay "The Head in Football" has been published as an e-book by Now and Then Reader and offers an excellent summary of the history of concussion and head injuries in football. Gregg Easterbrook, in *King of Sports* (New York: St. Martin's Press, 2013), discusses the concussion issue, as well as a number of other controversial topics related to the NFL.

Index

Richard C. Crepeau is a professor of history at the University of Central Florida and former president of the North American Society for Sports History. He is the author of *Baseball: America's Diamond Mind, 1919–1941*.

Sport and Society

Viva Baseball! Latin Major Leaguers and Their Special
  Hunger   *Samuel O. Regalado*
Touching Base: Professional Baseball and American Culture
  in the Progressive Era (rev. ed.)   *Steven A. Riess*
Red Grange and the Rise of Modern Football   *John M. Carroll*
Golf and the American Country Club   *Richard J. Moss*
Extra Innings: Writing on Baseball   *Richard Peterson*
Global Games   *Maarten Van Bottenburg*
The Sporting World of the Modern South
  Edited by Patrick B. Miller
The End of Baseball As We Knew It: The Players Union,
  1960–81   *Charles P. Korr*
Rocky Marciano: The Rock of His Times   *Russell Sullivan*
Saying It's So: A Cultural History of the Black Sox
  Scandal   *Daniel A. Nathan*
The Nazi Olympics: Sport, Politics, and Appeasement
  in the 1930s   *Edited by Arnd Krüger and William Murray*
The Unlevel Playing Field: A Documentary History of the
  African American Experience in Sport   *David K. Wiggins
  and Patrick B. Miller*
Sports in Zion: Mormon Recreation, 1890–1940
  Richard Ian Kimball
Sweet William: The Life of Billy Conn   *Andrew O'Toole*
Sports in Chicago   *Edited by Elliot J. Gorn*
The Chicago Sports Reader   *Edited by Steven A. Riess
  and Gerald R. Gems*
College Football and American Culture
  in the Cold War Era   *Kurt Edward Kemper*
The End of Amateurism in American Track and Field
  Joseph M. Turrini
Benching Jim Crow: The Rise and Fall of the Color Line
  in Southern College Sports, 1890–1980   *Charles H. Martin*
Pay for Play: A History of Big-Time College Athletic
  Reform   *Ronald A. Smith*
Globetrotting: African American Athletes and Cold War
  Politics   *Damion L. Thomas*
Cheating the Spread: Gamblers, Point Shavers, and Game
  Fixers in College Football and Basketball   *Albert J. Figone*
The Sons of Westwood: John Wooden, UCLA, and the Dynasty
  That Changed College Basketball   *John Matthew Smith*
Qualifying Times: Points of Change in U.S. Women's
  Sport   *Jaime Schultz*
NFL Football: A History of America's New National
  Pastime   *Richard C. Crepeau*

REPRINT EDITIONS
The Nazi Olympics   *Richard D. Mandell*
Sports in the Western World (2d ed.)   *William J. Baker*
Jesse Owens: An American Life   *William J. Baker*

The University of Illinois Press
is a founding member of the
Association of American University Presses.

Composed in 9.5/14 ITC Officina Serif
with ITC Officina Sans display
by Lisa Connery
at the University of Illinois Press
Manufactured by Cushing-Malloy, Inc.

University of Illinois Press
1325 South Oak Street
Champaign, IL 61820-6903
www.press.uillinois.edu